'There are a growing number of Green Consumers nowadays who do mind about what happens and what is done to the environment generally. I think there are many more people in this country than you might think who are concerned, and many feel very strongly indeed about what is happening.'

HRH The Prince of Wales

'The public gets what it asks for: ask for the ''good stuff'' and that's what they'll have to supply. Similarly, refuse to buy the ''bad stuff'' and the market for it will collapse. The power of the public is potentially enormous — let's use it.'

Bill Oddie

'We owe it to our children to do what we can to protect the environment. This book shows how every individual can play a part.'

Richard Branson

'You as a consumer have a powerful vote. What is at stake is the quality of the world we live in. Use *The Green Consumer Guide* to cast your vote every time you go shopping.'

Paul Heiney

'The power of the exploitation lobby is enormous — but it's no match for the persuasiveness of a mass of well-informed individuals demanding more sustainable policies. What we need is facts, to strengthen our argument, and now, at last, we have them.'

Professor Chris Baines

'The Green Consumer Guide — or how to stop biting the hand that feeds us.'

Joanna Lumley

John Elkington is one of Europe's leading authorities on the role of industry in sustainable development. He runs an independent consultancy whose clients have included BP, the Design Council, Glaxo, the Nature Conservancy Council and the United Nations Environment Programme. He also sits on advisory panels at the Central Electricity Generating Board, the Merlin Ecology Fund and the Nature Conservancy Council. Having written numerous books and reports, he is also the co-author, with Tom Burke, of *The Green Capitalists*, published by Victor Gollancz in 1987.

Julia Hailes has worked in advertising and TV production. Having travelled extensively in the Americas, she joined the Earthlife Foundation in 1986 and then in 1987 helped to set up SustainAbility, 'the green growth company', with John Elkington and Tom Burke. The company aims to promote environmentally sustainable economic growth and its first publication was *Green Pages: The Business of Saving the World*, published in April 1988.

The GREEN Consumer Guide

From Shampoo to Champagne

High-street Shopping for a Better Environment

John Elkington & Julia Hailes

LONDON
VICTOR GOLLANCZ LTD
1988

First published in Great Britain September 1988
by Victor Gollancz Ltd
14 Henrietta Street, London WC2E 8QJ
Second impression September 1988
Third impression September 1988
Fourth impression September 1988
Fifth impression October 1988
Sixth impression November 1988
Seventh impression December 1988
Eighth impression January 1989

A Gollancz Paperback Original

British Library Cataloguing in Publication Data
Elkington, John, *1949–*
    The green consumer guide: from shampoo to
    champagne, high-street shopping for a better
    environment.
    1. Consumer education — Great Britain
    I. Title   II. Hailes, Julia
    648   TX335

ISBN 0-575-04177-3

Typeset in Great Britain by
Action Typesetting Limited, Gloucester
Printed and bound by Cox & Wyman Ltd, Reading

Contents

Acknowledgements

As the word went round that we were compiling the first edition of *The Green Consumer Guide*, we found ourselves being bombarded with letters and telephone calls from all over the country. Those contacting us shared one main concern — they wanted to know where to buy an astonishing range of 'green' products. Where to buy high quality recycled paper, 'clean' cars, 'cruelty-free' cosmetics and some more out-of-the-way products. Sometimes we were able to help, sometimes we couldn't.

The message was clear. A new generation of consumers has grown up at a time of increasing concern about the damage we are doing both to our local environment and to the planet. The idea that we can use our everyday consumer decisions to influence the world we live in is not new — but the power of the Green Consumer to push industry in more environmentally acceptable directions is.

At SustainAbility, the company we set up early in 1987 with Tom Burke, we are constantly looking for new ways to promote environment-friendly economic growth — what we call 'green growth'. SustainAbility's first book was *Green Pages*, subtitled the 'Business of Saving the World' (Routledge, 1988). It focuses on some of the exciting new business opportunities that are opening up across Europe in green products and services.

Throughout, we have been extraordinarily fortunate in the range of organizations and individuals who have helped us with our thinking and research. While it is impossible to list all those who have helped, certain contributions stand out.

Sheila Moorcroft and Chris and Kirk McNulty of Taylor Nelson Applied Futures helped us evaluate the potential of the Green Consumer. Jamila Maxwell and Nick Rowcliffe carried out early research for the project. Charles Secrett of Friends of the Earth helped in numerous ways, not least by ensuring that we saw early versions of *The Aerosol Connection* and *The Good Wood Guide*.

Jonathan Shopley and Tom Burke helped us keep other SustainAbility projects on the rails while we were immersed in the *Guide*. Elaine Elkington not only helped with research but supported the operation in many other ways.

Other people we should like to thank are: Julian Edwards and Stephen Locke of the Consumers' Association; Alan Gear, Jackie Gear and Pauline Pears of the Henry Doubleday Research Association; Anita Roddick and Nicola Lyon of The Body Shop International; Jane Bickerstaffe of the Industry Committee on Packaging and the Environment (INCPEN); Charlotte Mitchell of Real Foods; Marek Mayer of ENDs; and Francis Miller and Tessa Tennant of the Merlin Ecology Fund.

But the biggest single contribution has come from Victor Gollancz, where we would like to thank Liz Knights and Sarah-Jane Evans for their constant support and encouragement as the *Guide* took shape.

If you have suggestions for future editions of the *Guide*, or want to hear more about SustainAbility's other projects, contact us at SustainAbility Ltd, 1 Cambridge Road, Barnes, London SW13 0PE.

John Elkington and Julia Hailes
London, June 1988

Authors' Note

The tables and charts in this book have been researched and compiled by the authors, unless stated otherwise. Sources are given either in the column headings or as footnotes, except in the case of CFC-free aerosols. This material is taken from **Friends of the Earth**'s booklet, *The Aerosol Connection* (1988). We are very grateful for permission to quote from it.

To the best of our knowledge, the information in this book is correct at the time of going to press, but we cannot guarantee 100 per cent accuracy over such a wide range of consumer concerns. The omission of any particular brand, company or any other organization implies neither censure nor recommendation.

FOREWORD

Anita Roddick

Managing Director, The Body Shop International, plc.

As we rush towards the end of the century, we are all more concerned about how we live, what we eat, what we *consume* in all senses of the word. We are concerned about the effects our consumer lifestyle is having on our own health, of course. But we are also concerned about the knock-on effects of what we are doing on the local environment, on people in the Third World and on the planet itself.

One of the liabilities of living in a free society, where almost anything can be advertised and sold, is that false, 'plastic' needs very often force out real needs. But many consumers are no longer prepared to accept this situation: they want to buy responsible products and they want to buy them from responsible companies.

The new breed of Green Consumer is leading this groundswell. They are demanding more information about the environmental performance of products, about the use of animal testing and about the implications for the Third World. They want to know the story behind what they buy. They want to know how things are made, where and by whom. And more and more people are joining their ranks.

We have already seen the effect of concerned consumers on the food industry. People today want to know what is in what they eat and drink. *E for Additives*, the book which more than any other helped spur the move towards additive-free products, had sold more than 500,000 copies by the time its second edition was launched in 1987. Now the time has come to mobilize consumer power to tackle an even more important set of problems. This time it is not simply a question of our own personal health, but of the health of the planet itself.

Different consumers have different priorities and sensibilities, but we can see how they are increasingly focusing on certain areas of common concern. Millions of people, for example, are worried about the destruction of the ozone layer, about the accelerating loss of tropical rain forests and about the growing amount of waste generated by excessive packaging and lifestyles.

There is also concern about human rights and about the deprivation suffered in the Third World as a result of the so-called developed world's increasingly profligate lifestyle. Many of us feel strongly about animal rights and welfare, too. Where wild animals are not being trapped for their fur or hunted for their ivory, their habitat is being destroyed. The plight of the millions of animals in captivity, whether they are factory farmed or used for experiments, is a matter for deep concern.

Don't just grin and bear it. As consumers, we have real power to effect change. We can ask questions about supply and manufacture. We can request new or different products. And we can use our ultimate power, voting with our feet and wallets — either buying a product somewhere else or not buying it at all.

People's voices are being heard on these issues, and they are getting louder. We are beginning to see real changes. We are seeing changes not only in the products which appear on the supermarket shelves but also in the ways in which they are sold.

Green consumers, it must be said, are only part of the equation. *The Green Consumer Guide* shows that the growing core of green manufacturers and green retailers are also an essential part of the mix. This is where the Body Shop fits in. Our shops have always attracted customers who are well-informed and environmentally aware. They have always bought, and will continue to buy, our products because they want natural, biodegradable cosmetics, manufactured without cruelty to animals and minimally packaged. They want our refill service which saves them money — and enables them to re-use bottles.

I never set out to 'capture' Green Consumers. They didn't exist, or certainly not by that name, when I started The Body Shop in 1976. But their power is steadily growing. The new type of consumer can be found everywhere, in pin-striped suits, white coats or boiler-suits. And this trend is still in its infancy. Even so, one of the most exciting things about *The Green Consumer Guide* is the way it pulls together so many different areas in which real progress is now being made.

I'm very excited by it. I think you will be too.

THE GREEN CONSUMER

Every day of the week, whether we are shopping for simple necessities or for luxury items, for fish fingers or for fur coats, we are making choices that affect the environmental quality of the world we live in.

Take a bite out of a hamburger, we are told, and we take a bite out of the world's rain forests. Buy the wrong car and we may end up not only with a large fuel bill, but also with fewer trees and, quite possibly, less intelligent children. Spray a handful of hair gel or a mist of furniture polish from certain aerosols, and you help destroy the planet's atmosphere — increasing everybody's chances of contracting skin cancer.

Few of us can spot the links between what we do day-to-day and the environmental destruction which is happening around the world. Most fast-fooders know little — and care less — about the loss of the world's tropical forests. Yet almost two-fifths of the deforestation in Brazil from the mid-1970s to the mid-1980s was caused by the clearance of forests for cattle ranching. Much of the beef produced was destined for fast food hamburgers.

And how many of us, even if we have seen TV programmes on the newly-discovered Antarctic 'ozone hole', could say exactly what chlorofluorocarbons (CFCs) are? However, the dramatic success of the anti-CFC campaign means that millions of us do now know about the Earth's protective ozone layer. And we are also beginning to be aware of the damage that the CFC propellants used to squirt many products through the nozzle of an aerosol, that pinnacle of convenience in twentieth-century packaging, can do to the ozone layer.

But more and more of us want to do the right thing — we simply don't know how. Clearly, if the relevant information is presented in the right way, then more and more of us will become sufficiently interested to take action through our day-to-day decisions.

Part of the solution, in fact, is in your hands. Whether you are in the supermarket, the garage, the garden centre or the travel agent's, this first edition of *The Green Consumer Guide* tells you which products to avoid and which to buy.

The *Guide* does not promote a 'hair-shirt' lifestyle. It is designed to appeal to a 'sandals-to-Saabs' spectrum of consumers. The information provided is intended to ensure that, whatever your lifestyle, you will know where to find attractive, cost-competitive products and services which are environmentally acceptable and — as far as possible — a pleasure to use.

The *Guide* does not aim to be totally comprehensive. Instead, it looks at the environmental implications of a wide range of consumer decisions and pinpoints what ordinary consumers can do to cut down their contribution to priority environmental problems. Nor can we aspire to be totally up-to-date. The speed with which this whole area is moving means that new issues are constantly emerging, leading to new business initiatives and to the launch of new environment-friendly products.

The real message of the *Guide* is that the Green Consumer is here and is already having a tremendous impact. Remember the changes that have already taken place: the replacement of 'hard' detergents with 'soft', more biodegradable products; the gradual shift from leaded to unleaded petrol; and the growth in demand for health foods and organically grown produce.

Many environmental organizations and some consumer groups are now working to accelerate this trend. We set out on the preparation of the *Guide* by sending a questionnaire to Britain's leading environmental organizations. We asked them whether they thought that the consumer could play a significant role in tackling the problems that most concerned them. An overwhelming 88 per cent said that the consumer could have a major impact.

When asked what consumers could do, most of the organizations mentioned product boycotts. If consumer power is to be used in support of environmental objectives, however, boycotts alone are unlikely to be sufficient. Indeed, groups like Friends of the Earth are now developing more sophisticated

initiatives, like *The Good Wood Guide*, designed to help consumers switch from products made from hardwoods stripped
from tropical forests to those made from wood grown in forests
managed with the future very much in mind.

It is the consumer's ability to change from Brand X to Brand Y
— or, even more worryingly for manufacturers and retailers, to
stop buying a particular product altogether — that makes producers sit up and take notice. In Britain, three days before
Friends of the Earth was to follow up its listing of 'ozone-
friendly' aerosols with a listing of those brands which do contain
CFCs, the eight largest aerosol manufacturers (**Beecham**, **Carter-
Wallace**, **Colgate-Palmolive**, **Cussons**, **Elida Gibbs**, **Gillette**,
L'Oreal and **Reckitt and Colman**) announced that they would
phase out CFC propellants by the end of 1989. Those companies
alone accounted for 65 per cent of the UK toiletries market. **Boots**
and **Schwarzkopf** said they would follow suit. Several
companies, including **Johnson Wax** and **Osmond Aerosols**, had
helped force the industry's hand by agreeing to label their
products as CFC-free.

So don't feel that your decision to buy or not to buy scarcely
registers on the scale. Market researchers, and the companies
they serve, sit up and take notice when thousands of people start
to behave in the same way. Make sure manufacturers or retailers
notice you by writing to tell them why you are avoiding their
products or why you have switched to their brands. Remember,
unless you ask for organic food, CFC-free aerosols or
environment-friendly holiday packages, they are unlikely to be
offered.

Demand green products and you help develop new market
opportunities for manufacturers and retailers — encouraging
them to invest in new products and services specifically aimed at
the Green Consumer.

Persuade one major company to change its tack and others are
likely to follow. **McDonald**'s decision to abandon the use of CFCs
in fast-food cartons in the States was one of the environmental
milestones of 1987. And the threat that consumers might boycott
Big Macs was a deciding factor in the company's decision.
Competitors like **Wimpy** promptly started talking to their carton
suppliers, explaining: 'We don't want to be left behind.' In 1988,

McDonald's is in the process of removing CFCs from their cartons in the UK.

One of the trends which is giving the Green Consumer much greater commercial clout is the ageing of the 'Baby Boom' generation, which can also be described as the first 'environmental generation', now aged between 25 and 45. This is also the sector of society enjoying the most rapid growth in disposable income and so it is their spending power that many manufacturers are particularly concerned to capture.

Twenty years on from the heady days of the late sixties, many baby boomers still subscribe to the idea of the 'low impact lifestyle'. Some of them may, for instance, decide to eat more raw food in a bid to save energy, or use vinegar instead of bleach as a toilet cleaner in order to cut pollution. But for many more of their contemporaries shopping has become a leisure activity in itself. For these consumers the choice is between different brands of commercially produced goods, not between consumerism and non-consumerism. It would be wrong to underestimate the importance of either group. The Lifestyle movement is absolutely right when it calls on people to 'Live Simply That Others May Simply Live'. But in today's consumer-orientated society the high-spending Green Consumer can pack more environmental punch than almost anyone else.

Wherever you fall on the spectrum of Green Consumer Lifestyles, *The Green Consumer Guide* is designed to help you make informed choices and to leave manufacturers and retailers in no doubt that a growing number of their customers are now looking for products that are not going, quite literally, to cost the earth.

Don't forget how important it is to let other people know about the issues. Write to your local newspapers and to the national press. Contact your MP. And if local issues are your target, get in touch with your local councillors and with the relevant local government department, water authority or central government department. Above all, join relevant campaigning or lobbying organizations. Your subscription counts — and your membership stands as a 'vote' for the agenda promoted by the organization — or organizations — you are backing. Wherever possible, buy goods through the catalogues offered by such organizations. A guide to the various groups is given on pages 324–31.

A final point: it is inevitable in producing the first edition of a guide like this that we will have overlooked some products and manufacturers. If you think there is something missing, please let us know. Write to us at: SustainAbility Ltd, 1 Cambridge Road, Barnes, London SW13 0PE. This feedback will help us in compiling future editions of *The Green Consumer Guide*.

KEY ISSUES FOR THE GREEN CONSUMER

In general, the Green Consumer avoids products which are likely to

- endanger the health of the consumer or of others

- cause significant damage to the environment during manufacture, use or disposal

- consume a disproportionate amount of energy during manufacture, use or disposal

- cause unnecessary waste, either because of over-packaging or because of an unduly short useful life

- use materials derived from threatened species or from threatened environments

- involve the unnecessary use — or cruelty to — animals, whether this be for toxicity testing or for other purposes

- adversely affect other countries, particularly in the Third World

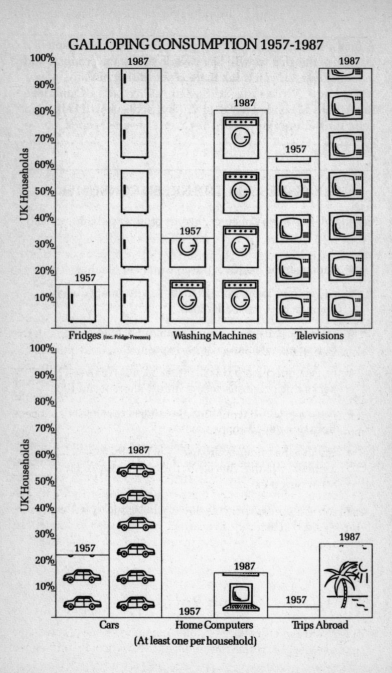

GALLOPING CONSUMPTION 1957-1987

GALLOPING CONSUMPTION

When the Consumers' Association launched its magazine *Which?* in 1957, it printed 10,000 copies. Now, thirty years on, it goes to over one million subscribers and is read by very many more.

In 1957 Britons knew nothing of Access cards or acid rain, of cordless phones or conservation areas, of digital watches or disposable razors. Britain had no microchips, no Minis, no motorways and no plastic refuse sacks. There was no Minister of Consumer Affairs and no Environmental Minister. The Consumer Revolution has swept through the country at high speed. The resulting pollution and waste have been key factors in the equally rapid development of the environmental revolution.

If the basic trend in consumerism continues, as is predicted, then total annual consumer spending in the UK could reach over £200 billion (at 1980 prices) by New Year's Eve 1999. This would imply that each of us would be spending on *average* 40 per cent more than in the mid-1980s.

One area where we are spending increasing amounts of money is on consumer durables. They accounted for less than 4 per cent of our expenditure in the early 1950s, compared with more than 11 per cent in the 1980s and it is predicted that the figure will be as much as 15 per cent by the end of the century. New consumer durables are constantly appearing: by 1985, for example, the video recorder could be found in one in three British homes.

Global Revolution

Television and other forms of telecommunication have created a 'global village' in which the model lifestyle is heavily influenced by the American way of life. As companies push for larger markets they promote this often inappropriate way of life to the Third World, putting increasing pressure on already overtaxed environments. Should American patterns of consumption and waste be imitated around the world, the environmental effect would be enormous.

The American Way of Life

The average consumer in the USA

- drinks more soft drinks than tapwater

- eats one teaspoon of artificial colours, flavours and preservatives a day

- produces 4 kg (9 lb) of hazardous waste every day

- uses energy equivalent to the detonation of more than 7.7 kg (17 lb) of TNT explosive every hour of each day

- and, as a motorist, drives an average of 48 km (30 miles) every day of the week.

Multiply these figures by the number of Americans (over 244 million in 1987) and they represent staggeringly large amounts of energy, raw materials and waste. Every day, for example, Americans use around 60 billion kilowatt-hours of energy and produce some 620 million kg (1.5 billion lb) of hazardous waste.

What the West Consumes

The average person in the developed world is likely to be consuming, directly or indirectly:

- more than 120 kg (264 lb) of paper a year, compared to an average per capita consumption of just 8 kg (17.6 lb) in the Third World

- over 450 kg (990 lb) of steel, compared with 43 kg (94.6 lb), and 26 kg (57.2 lb) of other metals, compared with 2 kg (4.4 lb)

- and purchased energy equivalent to almost 6 tonnes
  of coal a year, compared with 0.5 tonnes

The global population is growing by 80 million a year — or by
more than the population of Southampton every day. As a result,
it is expected to reach 6 billion by the year 2000 and to exceed 10
billion by the middle of the twenty-first century.

The world already manufactures seven times more goods than
it did in 1950 and, if Third World consumption levels *were* to be
raised to those of the industrialized world then, by the time
population growth levelled off some time in the twenty-first
century, a further five- to ten-fold increase in manufacturing
would be necessary. In the 1960s and 1970s we thought we
would run out of energy and raw materials. Now the real threat
seems to be the problems caused by the rapid destruction of the
planet's plant and animal life and the destabilization of the
atmosphere and climate.

The Conscious Consumer

Fortunately, we are all becoming more aware of the threats to the
environment. There are a number of reasons for this. For
example:

- Between 1957 and 1987 the proportion of
  households owning at least one television rocketed
  from 66 per cent to near-saturation (98 per cent).
  Documentaries on the environment have made an
  enormous impact and the media have brought the
  horrors of a string of environmental disasters into
  our living rooms. Together they make up an
  alphabet of catastrophes: A for the 220,000 tonnes of
  oil that belched from the *Amoco Cadiz*, B for the
  2,500 people gassed in Bhopal, C for the radioactive
  cloud which blanketed much of Europe following
  the reactor fire at Chernobyl, and so on.

- 350 films from 28 countries were entered for the fourth Environmental Film Festival, Ecovision '87. There has been a noticeable shift from straight-forward nature and wildlife films to in-depth coverage of complex issues.

- The number of new book titles on the environment published every year has grown dramatically — and continues to climb. Some of this tidal wave of new books have sold spectacularly well: David Attenborough's *Life on Earth*, which was linked to a major TV series, sold over 4 million copies.

Thirty years ago the environmental lobby was relatively weak. The World Wildlife Fund, now the World Wide Fund for Nature, was not launched until 1961 and environmental groups like Friends of the Earth and Greenpeace were products of the late 1960s and early 1970s. But by the early 1980s the total membership of Britain's environmental and conservation organizations had grown to around 3 million. Greenpeace's worldwide membership jumped by about 400,000 after the sinking of the *Rainbow Warrior*.

More members mean more political muscle. Although environmentalists often despair at how long it takes to bring new laws into force once a problem has been identified, they have achieved major advances, particularly following Britain's entry into the EEC.

Indeed, many products are 'greened' without the average consumer ever being aware of the fact. EEC legislation, for example, imposes new standards which all new models or product generations have to meet if they are to be sold in Europe.

But people can still be persuaded to buy the most extraordinary products. Tokyo's top department stores have been selling cans of compressed oxygen as an antidote to the exhaust fumes which pervade the city. The real challenge, however, will not be to develop new markets for expensive gimmicks like these, but to encourage consumers to use *The Green Consumer Guide* and to consciously seek out and buy green products and services. Don't buy oxygen, in short — buy a cleaner car or switch to public transport.

As far as the emergence of the Green Consumer is concerned, continental Europe — and particularly West Germany — has been the pioneer.

But Britain is now catching up. Rising standards of living have often led to increasing public concern about environmental issues. When *Which?* surveyed its subscribers late in 1986, for example, *nine out of ten* reported that they were worried by pollution and other environmental problems. This was a fairly dramatic finding, given that when *Which?* first appeared environmental issues were not even on the agenda.

Which? followed up the report of its findings with a review of some of the major environmental issues of the day. It pointed out that 'cleaning up pollution isn't cheap. And the costs will ultimately be borne by consumers — in the form of more expensive electricity, cars, water or higher taxes. Yet trying to save money now by failing to control pollution', it warned, 'could mean that we (or future generations) could end up paying more later on.'

Which? also made some initial suggestions on ways that the consumer could help even up the environmental balance sheet. 'Whatever you decide to do,' it concluded, 'you may have to be content with tackling just the tip of the iceberg. You can't clean up industrial emissions, or rivers, or reduce radiation levels singlehanded. On the other hand, governments need pressure to act. By writing to your MP, to manufacturers or water authorities, you could help create this pressure. What's more, there are a lot of consumers — and each individual action (saving energy, going easy on household chemicals, and so on) adds up.'

The range of issues which can be addressed by consumer power is very considerable. Equally, as later chapters show, the range of actions that the ordinary consumer can take is very much greater than the initial *Which?* survey seemed to suggest.

COSTING THE EARTH

Many of us assume that when it comes to complicated environmental problems — destruction of the ozone layer, tropical deforestation, pollution of the seas — then the Government will handle them. That's what we vote them in for, isn't it? But the unfortunate fact is that in the 1980s the British Government has dragged its heels on many environmental issues, from acid rain to lead in petrol.

Putting together a simple picture of the many different types of damage we are inflicting on the world is not easy. But we must attempt it, before looking at what the individual consumer can do to help prevent such damage. Let's approach the task from the outside in.

Destruction of the Ozone Layer

The sun burns 5 million tonnes of hydrogen a second and its core reaches temperatures of some 15 million °C. It radiates a phenomenal amount of energy into space: more than would be produced by 200,000 million million of our largest existing commercial nuclear reactors.

Earth intercepts only a billionth of the sun's total output, but this is enough to do everything from driving the climate, including the winds and water cycle, and fuelling the growth of the world's crops, right through to burning incautious sun-bathers.

Indeed, the solar energy entering our atmosphere every year is roughly equivalent to 500,000 billion barrels of oil or 800,000 billion tonnes of coal. This is about a million times more oil than we think there may be left in the planet's proven oil reserves.

Only a small proportion of this energy ever reaches the ground where we jog, walk and sunbathe, which is just as well. If the sun's raw energy were ever to break through to ground level, life as we know it would be sizzled off the face of the earth. Luckily, much of it is reflected back into space by cloud cover. And the sunshine that does reach the ground is made much less hazardous by something that happens in the upper reaches of the atmosphere.

Located between 20 and 50 km (12 – 30 miles) above the earth's surface, the ozone layer screens out around 99 per cent of the potentially deadly ultra-violet (UV) radiation in the incoming sunshine.

Yet the ozone layer is so rarified that if you could compress it to the density of air at sea level, it would be little more than the thickness of the sole of your shoe. Any thinning of this fragile shield inevitably increases the amount of UV radiation reaching the ground.

Just how harmful is ultra-violet radiation?

UV radiation increases the number of skin cancers — it has been estimated that even a 1 per cent reduction in atmospheric ozone could cause 15,000 new cases of skin cancer each year in the United States alone.

It increases the number of people suffering from cataracts and other eye diseases and causes extensive damage to crops and other vegetation. It also threatens ocean food chains, because many plankton are highly sensitive to UV radiation. Plankton are the essential food source for many fish and are also important in oxygen production.

CFCs (chlorofluorocarbons)

The first real evidence that the ozone layer might be threatened was produced by two American scientists in 1974. They warned that man-made chemicals known as chlorofluorocarbons (CFCs) could also thin the ozone layer. CFCs are often used as propellants in aerosols, in fridges and air-conditioning plants (where they serve as coolants), in dry-cleaning solvents, in the plastic foam used to make hamburger and other fast-food cartons, in materials used for furniture stuffing and in insulation products.

When they were discovered in 1928, CFCs seemed to be perfect chemicals. They were odourless, non-toxic, non-flammable and chemically inert. Unfortunately, however, they are so stable that they can hang around in the atmosphere for more than 100 years, slowly drifting up into the stratosphere. Ironically, too, the most useful types of CFC (particularly CFCs 11 and 12) turn out to be the most damaging. Once in the stratosphere, their chemical structure means that they begin to destroy the ozone molecules that protect Earth from UV radiation.

The scientific debate about the extent to which such chemicals destroy ozone raged for years, but eventually a new scientific consensus began to emerge. CFCs, it was concluded by the late 1970s, certainly could damage the ozone layer, but the effects were likely to be less serious than had originally been thought — and would be a long time coming. But the chemical industry, which produced nearly 800,000 tonnes of CFCs in 1985 alone, was sitting on a time-bomb. That year, British scientists discovered an 'ozone hole' opening up over Antarctica.

The evidence had been in American hands for ten years, in the form of data collected by orbiting space satellites, but the computers which processed the data ignored the ozone hole because they had been programmed to treat such things as impossible. Once these data were processed into images, it became clear that the computers had been turning a blind eye to an extraordinary phenomenon. The size of the hole varies through the year, but can cover an area as large as the United States. Soon other scientists were finding evidence of at least one more ozone hole, this time over the Arctic.

Scientists agreed that the peculiar conditions found at the Poles, particularly the extreme cold and low sunlight for months on end, may have been aggravating the situation. However, the implication was that CFCs could well lead to a global thinning of the ozone layer.

A mass of new research results and growing public concern led to the signing of the Montreal Protocol by the USA, the EEC and 23 other countries late in 1987. The aim was to cut world CFC consumption 20 per cent by 1994 and another 30 per cent by 1999. But, for the foreseeable future, this agreement will simply slow down the rate of ozone depletion because of the longevity of CFCs. Consequently, the destruction of the ozone layer is likely to be in the headlines for many years to come.

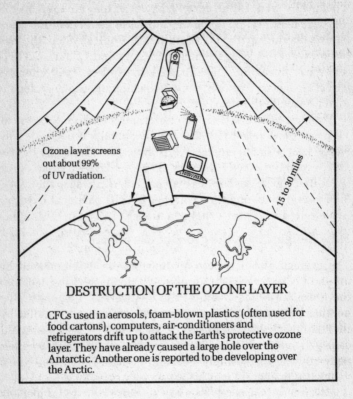

Ozone layer screens out about 99% of UV radiation.

15 to 30 miles

DESTRUCTION OF THE OZONE LAYER

CFCs used in aerosols, foam-blown plastics (often used for food cartons), computers, air-conditioners and refrigerators drift up to attack the Earth's protective ozone layer. They have already caused a large hole over the Antarctic. Another one is reported to be developing over the Arctic.

The Greenhouse Effect

CFCs also contribute to another global environment problem, whose longer term impact could be even greater.

Although between a third and a half of the earth's incoming solar energy is immediately reflected back into space by cloud, the atmosphere as a whole works very much like a greenhouse, trapping heat. If things go wrong and too much heat is retained, the implications for our future on this planet could be grave indeed.

What causes the greenhouse effect?

Carbon dioxide (CO_2) is the most important 'greenhouse gas'. It acts rather like a blanket around the planet, holding in much of the solar radiation which would otherwise escape into space.

The level of CO_2 in the atmosphere has been growing inexorably since the Industrial Revolution. Between the 1850s and the 1970s, carbon dioxide levels grew by as much as 25 per cent.

The main reason for this worrying trend is the ever-growing quantity of fossil fuels (coal, oil and gas) burned for heat or power, although the burning of firewood — and of forests — also aggravates the problem. Startlingly, however, each CFC molecule turns out to be 10,000 times worse than each carbon dioxide molecule in terms of its contribution to the greenhouse effect.

How dangerous is the greenhouse effect?

The average global surface air temperature has increased by around 1°C over the last 150 years. Within the next few decades, the greenhouse effect could raise the average temperature by another degree, with a rise of several more degrees possible by the second half of the 21st century. Such temperature rises would cause dramatic changes in the earth's climate and weather patterns. The increasingly severe droughts in the River Nile's water catchment area may be just an early symptom.

A warmer atmosphere would also cause melting of glaciers and ice-caps, with the result that sea levels could rise by a metre or more. In the longer term, low-lying cities like London, Bangkok, New York and Tokyo could be swamped by the ever-rising tides. Rainfall and monsoon patterns would shift, possibly turning areas like the rice-growing regions of Asia and the Great Plains of America into dust bowls. Kansas could become the Ethiopia of the twenty-first century.

These changes in global temperature may not sound enormous, but the Earth has not been 1°C warmer than it is today since before the dawn of civilization. In short, we are conducting an unprecedented experiment with our planet.

Dying forests

The rapid destruction of forests in many parts of the world is removing one of the natural reservoirs which would otherwise 'sponge up' excess carbon dioxide. We tend to think of tropical forests when we think of disappearing forests, forgetting that Britain once was cloaked in trees so that it might have been possible for a squirrel to travel from what is now Sherwood Forest to Land's End without touching the ground. And, as we shall explain, Europe's forests are also severely threatened by acid rain.

Despite the scale of forest damage in Europe, Scandinavia and North America, however, the loss of the World's tropical forests is the No. 1 natural resource problem. As many as half of Earth's species live in these forests, which cover less than 2 per cent of the globe. The role of this planetary green belt in maintaining the regional — and even global — climate can hardly be over-estimated. Yet some scientists claim that the world's rainforests are now producing more carbon dioxide than they absorb, as large areas are burned down.

- Of an estimated total area of 2 billion hectares (7 – 8 million sq miles) of tropical forests, some 11 – 15 million hectares (up to 58,000 sq miles) are lost each year — an area the size of Austria. An area equal to 20 football pitches is lost every minute.

- In 1982, in what was described as the worst ecological disaster of the century, some 3.24 million hectares (12,500 sq miles) of forest were destroyed in a fire which swept across Kalimantan, Indonesia. The risk of such catastrophic fires increases as deforestation reduces rainfall in nearby areas.

- As the forests disappear, the pace of soil erosion accelerates. In Guatemala, an average of around 1,200 tonnes of soil are lost every year from each square kilometre of land. As a result, it becomes harder to feed the population and, in countries like India and Bangladesh, the silt shortens the life of dams and can cause widespread flooding in lowland areas.

- As we wrote this chapter, the news came through that at least 300 people had died and over 60,000 had been left homeless during 'freak' floods in Rio de Janeiro. Brazilian geologists say the floods were no freak. They were caused by the relentless felling of the country's forests — and there is worse to come.

- Because of such environmental destruction, 20 per cent of the 5 – 10 million species now known are likely to be extinct by the year 2000 — and in 50 years more than half will be gone if present rates of extinction continue.

The effects of these environmental changes can be seen even in non-tropical countries. 'Blood rain', stained red by Saharan dust, fell over Britain several times in 1987. As the deserts spread in Africa and soils are whipped away by the wind, there have been more episodes of 'blood rain' in the 1980s than there were in all the previous decades of the twentieth century.

Acid rain

In many parts of North America, Scandinavia and Europe, bleached tree skeletons give mute testimony to the unseen poisons carried on the wind.

When sulphur dioxide and other gases produced by the burning of fossil fuels are washed out of the sky as acids, they have a devastating effect on wildlife, buildings and human health. Ironically, acid rain problems are partly the result of previous pollution control efforts. The sequence of events in Britain, repeated in other parts of the world, went something like this:

Following the deaths of over 4,000 people during London's Great Smog of 1952, still the world's worst single pollution disaster, the Government brought new smoke control laws into force. Smokeless zones were introduced and power stations were built with much taller chimneys, to disperse the smoke and gas formed when fossil fuels are burned. As a result, the air in many major cities became much cleaner, but at the expense of distant areas — where much of the pollution fell back to earth as acid rain, mist or snow. Motor vehicles, as we shall see later, also make a major contribution to acid rain problems in some countries.

Some facts about acid rain

- Each year, about 300,000 tonnes of sulphur from Britain, West Germany and other countries rain down on Sweden.

- In 1986, Britain emitted some 3.7 million tonnes of sulphur dioxide, mainly from its power stations, and 'exported' around two-thirds to other countries.

- The UK is also suffering increasing acid rain damage. In 1984, for example, black snow which fell at Aviemore, Scotland, was as acid as vinegar.

- Sweden was the first to recognize the acid rain problem. Hundreds of Scandinavian lakes are now too acid to support fish and other aquatic life. And other countries are now waking up to the threat. Over half of West Germany's forests are dead, dying or in decline. In Switzerland, a third of the forests are dying. Forty per cent of Dutch forests show signs of damage.

- By 1993, if present trends continue, Britain should have achieved a 30 per cent reduction in sulphur dioxide emissions. But it could still be producing as much sulphur dioxide as France, West Germany, Sweden, Denmark, Norway, Austria, Switzerland, Luxembourg and the Netherlands put together.

Finding the energy

Our future contribution to such pollution problems as the greenhouse effect and acid rain will very much depend on what mix of energy supply technologies we end up using. The options include: *fossil fuels*, such as oil, gas and coal; *nuclear power*, using today's fission reactors or (possibly) tomorrow's fast breeder or fusion reactors; *renewable energy*, harnessing the sun, winds, waves, tides, geothermal heat or plants and animals; and *energy efficiency*, which cuts across all of these — and is the key to *The Green Consumer Guide*'s recommendations on energy.

Fossil fuels — Oil and Gas

Oil is the most popular fuel at present, but it is a finite resource. World supplies are likely to be severely depleted within 35 years. The production of oil from the North Sea oilfields has already peaked — and gas production will follow suit. Oil pollution also remains a considerable problem. The supertanker disasters of the 1970s may have ensured that tanker operations are better managed and policed, but the Ohio disaster of early 1988 underlined the continuing risks.

- An estimated 4.5 million litres (1 million gallons) of diesel oil escaped from a ruptured storage tank into Ohio's Monongahela River, causing considerable environmental damage and polluting drinking water used by tens of thousands of people. At the same time, thousands of people in Moscow were finding their tapwater undrinkable because it had been contaminated with petrol.

- Every year, over 10 million tonnes of man-made, oil-related compounds are released into the European atmosphere. The two major sources are solvents and cars, each contributing about 40 per cent of the emissions. These help cause widespread pollution, including smogs in large cities like Berlin, London, Los Angeles, Mexico City and Tokyo, and acid rain damage in the wider countryside.

- Emissions of nitrogen oxides, which can also cause smogs and acid rain, rose rapidly to reach 1.9 million tonnes in 1986. The two major contributors to nitrogen oxide pollution are power stations (783,000 tonnes in 1986) and vehicles (784,000 tonnes). Indeed, vehicle exhaust fumes are implicated in the death of many German forests.

Fossil fuels — Coal

A hundred years from now, we shall still be using liquid fuels although they will be very much more expensive. Some of them may well be made from coal, the old fossil fuel standby. There may be enough coal in Britain for two or three hundred years, but its extraction causes considerable environmental problems and, when burned, it is the worst contributor to acid rain (via the production of sulphur dioxide and nitrogen oxides) and to the greenhouse effect (via carbon dioxide). The challenge for the future is to develop clean coal technologies and the electricity supply industry is already moving in this direction. But they are unlikely to be cheap.

Nuclear power

However much damage the burning of fossil fuels may cause, nuclear power remains the least popular energy technology with environmentalists — and with the public. The shadow of the Chernobyl nuclear disaster in the Ukraine still hangs over Europe.

- A study by the European Consumer Bureau, which links EEC consumer organizations, concluded that the radioactive cloud which spread out from the damaged reactor at Chernobyl carried radiation equivalent to that which would be produced by 2,000 atomic bombs of the size that obliterated Hiroshima in 1945.

- The cost of the disaster for the Soviet Union alone had reached an estimated £8 billion by early 1988.

Some 135,000 people had to be evacuated and the
immediate death toll of over 30 lives is likely to
grow considerably as radiation-related diseases
surface.

● The relevant Soviet ministries have been instructed
to ensure 'the 100 per cent safety of nuclear power
plants'. Given the experience of Chernobyl, of Three
Mile Island in the United States and of Sellafield in
Britain, it would take an ultra-optimist to believe
that this is a reasonable target for any country
possessing nuclear power.

And even ardent supporters of nuclear power tend to draw the
line at having the resulting wastes dumped in *their* locality. This
is an area where the NIMBY syndrome, short for 'not-in-my-
backyard', applies with a vengeance.

Renewable energy sources

Renewable energy sources may be less polluting and are
certainly less likely to blow up or melt down, but because
renewable energy is more diffuse than that found in fossil fuels or
the uranium burned in nuclear reactors, the facilities needed to
capture it tend to be more extensive.

Some problems with renewable energy

● A solar energy installation able to produce as much
energy as a nuclear reactor might take up to 20 sq km
(5,000 acres), compared to about half a sq km (150
acres) needed for the reactor plant.

● It would take perhaps 200 – 300 large windmills to
produce the same amount of power as a nuclear
reactor, with each group of 25 machines needing an
area of around 16 sq km (4,000 acres). Large
windmills, as their neighbours know, can be noisy
and may interfere with TV reception.

● And if you decide to grow crops to convert into oil,

fuel alcohol or gas, you would need to plant up to
500 sq km (125,000 acres) to achieve the same
energy output as a nuclear reactor.

In itself this is no argument against renewable energy, whose
role is bound to grow in the future. But it is clear that there are
going to be some very difficult trade-offs to be made.

There is no such thing as a totally 'green' source of energy. Some
energy supply technologies, including nuclear power, may pose
less of a problem as far as acid rain or carbon dioxide build-up are
concerned, but any form of energy supply, even renewable
sources like wind or tidal power, can damage the environment.

Given all the complications of the energy question, the most
effective choice for the Green Consumer is to go for energy
efficiency, whatever product or piece of equipment is on the
shopping list and whichever source of energy is being used. To
give just one example of how this can help, British Coal ruefully
estimated in 1987 that energy efficiency and new technologies
were cutting demand for coal by some 200,000 tonnes a year.

The Waste Age

Waste is another inevitable by-product of a Consumer Society.
Whether we are punching round washers from rectangular
sheets of metal, unwrapping a chocolate bar or removing the
packaging from a new washing machine, each of us produces an
ever-increasing volume of waste every year. If there were only a
few million of us that might be acceptable, but with over 50
million Britons and around 100 times as many people now living
on the planet as a whole, it simply cannot go on.

The problems of what to do with waste are becoming ever more
pressing. Wastes in the wrong place cause pollution. Finding
enough holes in which to dump our refuse is also becoming
increasingly difficult. And, inevitably, the amount of non-
renewable mineral resources available to us is constantly falling
as we consume the more accessible deposits.

WHAT WE THROW AWAY EVERY YEAR

Waste from total UK population	Waste per head in UK

Collected Rubbish

20 million tonnes

2 dustbins per week
(per household)

Paper & Board

equivalent to
130 million trees

equivalent to more than
2 trees per person

Drink Cans

5 billion

90

Food Cans

3.9 billion

70

Pet Food Cans

2 billion

35

Bottles & Jars

6 billion

107

Plastics

2.5 million tonnes

45 kg

(All figures are approximate. 1 billion = 1,000,000,000)

Throwaway lines

- The average Briton throws away about ten times his or her own body weight in household refuse every year. The national total is about 20 million tonnes.

- Over 130 million trees are cut down every year to satisfy our paper and board needs. The average British family of four threw away six trees' worth in 1987. The days when Britain was self-sufficient in most wood products have long gone. Today around 90 per cent of the pulp Britain needs has to be imported.

- Nearly 4.5 billion drink cans were thrown away in Britain during 1986. Placed end to end, they would have reached the Moon. This figure more than doubles when aerosols and other cans are included.

- Every year, around 6 billion bottles and jars are used in Britain, amounting to over 1.5 million tonnes of glass. And we also get through over 2.5 million tonnes of plastic each year.

The problems of over-packaging and waste are pressing — and can only grow more difficult. These issues surface everywhere you go in the High Street, even if they are not explicitly covered in every section of the Guide.

River and sea pollution

Our inability — or unwillingness — to handle waste properly is everywhere apparent. After 25 years of steady improvement, the average quality of Britain's rivers has started to fall again. Reported pollution incidents rose from 12,500 between 1980 and 1985 to 21,095 between 1986 and 1987. Water pollution incidents caused by farms rose from less than 1,500 in 1979 to 3,800 in 1987.

There are many reasons for this worsening trend, but the

farming industry must take a good deal of the responsibility. Although industry contributes most of the heavy metals and chemical effluents found in rivers and estuaries, major sources of agricultural pollution include artificial fertilizers, silage effluents, manures and slurries.

An indication of the scale of the farming industry's contribution to water pollution is the fact that 56 per cent of the prosecutions made in 1986 were the result of agricultural practices or accidents, compared to 42 per cent following industrial pollution.

- Britain's 8 million pigs produce around 4 kg (8.8 lb) of slurry per head per day. Overall, farm animals produce up to 200 million tonnes of excreta a year. Because it is both stronger and more concentrated, this material is typically three times as polluting as the sewage produced by people. The attempt to industrialize pig farming, using intensive livestock units, has made a bad problem infinitely worse.

- Nitrates from fertilizers pollute both surface and underground water, and are implicated in stomach cancer in adults and the so-called 'blue baby syndrome' in the newborn. As many as 5 million Britons may be drinking water that periodically contains more nitrate than EEC standards now permit.

And if you thought that oil pollution was a thing of the past, it is worth noting that around 60 per cent of all industrial pollution incidents involved oil leaks or spills.

Sea pollution has also been causing considerable concern. An inter-governmental conference in 1987 focused public attention on the amount of pollution going into the North Sea. One of the most worrying indications that the North Sea is under increasing stress, particularly around river estuaries, comes from surveys of fish disease.

- Forty per cent of a sample of 20,000 flatfish taken off the Dutch coast were found to have cancerous

tumours or bacterial skin diseases. The Dutch
government institute which carried out the research
blamed effluents from industry and agriculture.

● Similar surveys carried out by the British
Government around the Thames estuary found that
11 per cent of fish were affected, although surveys
by Greenpeace suggested that up to a third (34 per
cent) were affected in some areas.

● Following widespread seal deaths in the North Sea
in 1988, scientists said that pollutants had
weakened the animals' resistance to disease. They
were becoming more susceptible to a herpes-like
virus.

● At the same time, massive fish-kills were caused by
a giant bloom of yellow algae along 1,000 miles of
coastal Denmark, Sweden and Norway. Artificial
fertilizers, washed into the North Sea, may be to
blame.

Most consumers may feel that they can spot diseased fish
before they eat them, but other problems may be harder to avoid.
Some 20 million cubic metres of sewage and other wastes produced by 145 million Europeans are discharged every day into
the North Sea. Indeed, according to the Coastal Anti-Pollution
League, nearly 200 of 690 British beaches it studied are likely to
be affected by discharges of totally untreated sewage.

Sewage pollution affects even Britain's most popular beaches,
including the Blackpool Pleasure Beach which attracted 6.5
million people in 1986. Holidaymakers are not going to put up
with such conditions indefinitely. (See *The Travel Agent*, pages
274–6, for a survey of clean beaches.)

Apart from sewage, a wide range of agricultural, industrial and
urban waste products and effluents reach our coastal waters and
seas — through rivers, sewers, pipe discharges and the operations of dumping vessels. Toxic metals and pesticides are of
particular concern, and it is now recognized that industrial and
urban air pollution swept out to sea is also a major contributor to

some forms of marine pollution. For too long, our approach has been one of 'out of sight, out of mind'. But change is now very much in the wind.

The Disappearing Countryside

As we move into the Leisure Age, most people have more time to spend out in the environment, whether it be by the sea or in the open countryside. Many are becoming concerned about what they see there — and particularly about the rate at which rural Britain is disappearing.

- By the mid-1980s, 95 per cent of Britain's lowland grasslands and herb-rich meadows lacked any significant wildlife interest, with only 3 per cent unaffected by agricultural improvement.

- Something like 40 per cent of lowland heath had been destroyed, mostly by agricultural conversion, afforestation or buildings.

- And somewhere between a third and half of all Britain's ancient woodlands had been lost since the end of the Second World War, generally replaced by conifer plantations.

- Nearly 200 sq km (50,000 acres) of land have been lost under Britain's motorways (see also pp. 113 – 14).

- As a result, when the occasional unspoiled, 'time-warp' farm comes on the market, like Dorset's Lower Kingcombe Farm did during 1987, the interest is so intense that the bidding threatens to go off the scale as developers compete with conservationists.

Many farmers and foresters argue that the loss of such farmscapes, and of the wildlife they harbour, is unavoidable. It is the price-tag, they say, on a world where our supermarket shelves are packed with a great diversity of affordable food and other goods. But growing numbers of people are sceptical.

A less obvious way in which our consumer lifestyles put pressure on the countryside is through the construction of reservoirs to supply our increasing demand for water. This pressure, combined with the growing interest of the water industry in charging for water according to the amount you consume, will help promote awareness of the water-efficiency of such appliances as washing machines and dishwashers.

Endangered Species

Extinction is a natural process. Well over 90 per cent of species that have ever lived on the Earth have disappeared. Many were replaced by others which were better adapted to changing environments, although some disappeared as the result of massive natural disasters.

The appearance of the human species began a significant acceleration in the average extinction rate, however, as we hunted for food, commerce and sport and converted entire landscapes into increasingly controlled farmscapes.

By the early years of the 20th century, roughly one species a year was being lost to extinction, but the pace of environmental degradation and species destruction has since taken off at an alarming rate. By the mid-1980s, we were losing perhaps one species *a day* from the 5 – 10 million species thought to exist. We may lose another million species by the end of the century.

Each species we push into extinction is like a thread pulled from the tapestry of life. You can pull a fair number of threads out of a tapestry without appearing to affect it, but then whole sections fall to pieces.

As consumers, we may be encouraged to buy a range of products made from animal or plant products derived from endangered species. Without our realizing it, our consumer choices can sometimes tighten the screw on endangered animals and plants.

While most of us may now be aware of the threat to species like the tiger, gorilla, elephant or rhinoceros, the threat to many other species is not yet widely recognized. Following consumer boy-cotts during the 1970s, whale products are no longer used in cosmetics, although oil from the endangered basking shark is. Endangered reptiles may turn up in the form of handbags, wallets, purses, belts or suitcases. Sea turtles are turned into stuffed specimens, shells, soup, oil, combs or jewellery.

Many of us know of the threat to cacti and orchids, but few of us realize that even plants like cyclamen, widely sold in garden centres, are now endangered in the wild. As long as it is cheaper to uproot wild plants than to artificially propagate the species, some people will continue to raid the threatened wild resources of countries like Portugal, Spain or Turkey. Guidance on some products to avoid is given in later chapters.

Animal welfare

Animal welfare is a key issue for the Green Consumer. This, it hardly needs saying, is a highly charged subject, with different campaigning organizations taking very different policy stances. Some, like the Animal Liberation Front (ALF), are willing to break the law to bring animal abuse to an end. Others, like the Fund for the Replacement of Animals in Medical Experiments (FRAME), work with major manufacturing companies to develop alternatives to animal testing.

Whatever views you may hold on animal rights and welfare, certain basic facts are indisputable.

- Factory farming methods are now part and parcel of meat, poultry and egg production. Around Britain, up to 500,000 breeding sows are kept in tiny stalls, lying on concrete floors in the dark. 45 million chickens are kept in crowded battery cages.

- In order to keep animals alive and growing in such unnatural conditions they have to be dosed with antibiotics and growth hormones.

- Laboratory animals endure convulsions, vomiting

and choking. During 1985, almost 10,000 animals, including guinea pigs, dogs and monkeys, were killed or died in experiments on household products. Millions more were involved in tests, but survived. The fact that in 1986 168,000 fewer animals were used in tests reflects the growing pressure to reduce their use in experiments.

The use of animals for safety research, 1986*

- 55,301 animals were used in the testing of pesticides and fungicides

- 23,565 were used to test herbicides and other substances designed to boost or retard plant growth

- 72,150 in tests of industrial chemicals

- 9,309 in tests of household chemicals

- 15,652 in tests of cosmetics and toiletries

- 8,988 in tests of food additives

- 752 in tests of tobacco and tobacco substitutes

- 1,809 in tests of plant and animal toxins

- 35,512 in tests of environmental pollutants

*Figures are according to the RSPCA.

If the information on cruelty-free products in the following chapters whets your appetite for more, order a copy of the RSPCA's new Green Consumer brochure and buy a copy of *The Cruelty Free Shopper*, published by the Vegan Society in 1987. This small book covers food and drink, toiletries and cosmetics, remedies, footwear and clothing, household goods and gifts — all produced without animal products or animal testing.

ANIMAL WELFARE ORGANIZATIONS IN BRITAIN

Organization	Main aim	No of members (approx)	Membership fee	What you get
RSPCA (Royal Society for the Prevention of Cruelty to Animals) The Causeway Horsham West Sussex RH12 1HG Tel: 0403 64181	The prevention of cruelty and the promotion of kindness to animals	23,000	£8	Postal vote for council Quarterly magazine Campaign literature
FRAME (Fund for the Replacement of Animals in Medical Experiments) 5b The Poultry Bank Place St Peter's Gate Nottingham NG1 2JR Tel: 0602 584740	To promote the development of alternatives to the use of live animals in research. Also to hasten better protection of laboratory animals via legislation and testing regulations	2,000	£5	FRAME News, quarterly Educational packs Regional organizations meetings
BUAV (British Union for the Abolition of Vivisection) 16a Crane Grove London N7 8LB Tel: 01-700 4888	To abolish by law all vivisection (experiments on living animals) and to campaign for the rights of animals in the UK and internationally. Advocates vegetarianism and veganism.	13,000	£6	The Liberator, bi-monthly Introduction pack Events Contacts list

Organization	Main aim	No of members (approx)	Member-ship fee	What you get
Animal Aid 7 Castle Street Tonbridge Kent TN9 1BH Tel: 0732 364546	To increase public awareness of the abuse of animals, particularly in vivisection and factory farming. Promotes vegetarianism, preventative and alternative medicine and cruelty-free cosmetics	12,000	£5	Outrage, bi-monthly Introductory pack Events and demonstrations Leaflets
National Anti-Vivisection Society 51 Harley Street London W1N 1DD Tel: 01-580 4034 Subsidiary: **Lord Dowding Fund for Humane Research**	To seek total abolition of animal experiments through public and political campaigning	90 local groups, branches or contacts	£4	The Campaigner, bi-monthly Campaigns
World Society for the Protection of Animals (WSPA) 106 Jermyn Street London SW1Y 6EE Tel: 01-839 3026	To promote effective means for the protection and conservation of animals in any part of the world and for the prevention of cruelty	10,000[1]	£5	Animals International, tri-annual Bi-annual meeting

1. The WSPA is an international organization. It has c. 14,000 members or donors in the USA.

We now begin our progress down the Green High Street. The following eight chapters look at the environmental acceptability of products which you will find on offer at the DIY store, the garden centre, the garage, the chemist's, the electrical shop, the supermarket, the travel agent and the gift shop.

For the sake of convenience, some stores have been wrapped into others: the alcoholic drinks you might buy in the off-licence, for example, are covered in the 'Beers, Wines and Spirits' section of the Supermarket chapter.

Clearly, time and space constraints have meant that we have had to curtail our coverage of some High Street activities — and exclude others altogether. Many of these will be covered in future editions of The Green Consumer Guide.

THE HARDWARE
AND DIY STORE

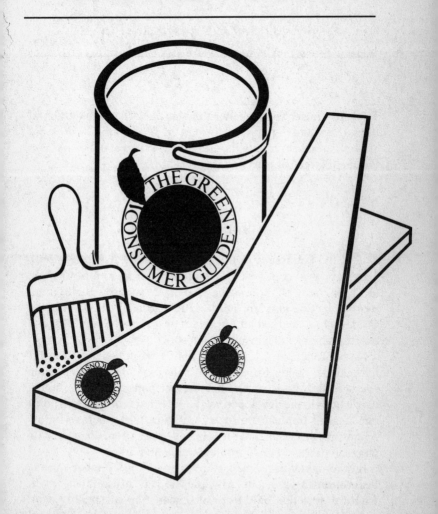

There has never been a better time for the DIY enthusiast. And things are looking up for the Green DIY-er, too. There are environmentally acceptable alternatives to just about every item you are likely to buy, as this chapter shows.

Good Woods

One of the key issues in this section is tropical deforestation. Tropical hardwoods (which mainly come from rain forests) are used for many DIY purposes. This fact has been highlighted recently by Friends of the Earth's publication of *The Good Wood Guide*, which marked an important new stage in the linking of environmental and consumer concerns.

Ninety-five per cent of Britain's supplies of tropical hardwoods come from badly managed and unsustainable sources. Britain is one of the largest consumers of tropical hardwoods in the developed world. As Friends of the Earth point out, uses of tropical timber include furniture, doors, window frames, construction, boat-making — even coffins. Britain is the largest importer of sawn tropical timber in Europe.

Environmentalists managed to get the **Timber Trade Federation** to agree, in principle, a Code of Conduct which would ensure that only tropical timber from sustainably managed sources would be allowed into Britain. The **National**

Association of Retail Furnishers endorsed the code and helped Friends of the Earth to produce the *Guide*. And a number of companies involved in this industry subsequently formed the **Association of Woodusers Against Rainforest Exploitation (AWARE)**.

When choosing tropical wood products (from **Bedroom furniture** to **Veneers**), watch out for the *Good Wood Guide* Seal of Approval displayed in your local shops. The Seal is awarded on a yearly basis. Department and furniture stores, DIY outlets and timber yards are all eligible. For a detailed listing of suppliers of sustainably produced tropical timber and wood products — and of alternative materials and products — buy a copy of the relevant regional edition of the *Guide*, published by Friends of the Earth and the National Federation of Retail Furnishers.

Each regional *Guide* is broken down into three main parts:

- The **Green pages** list the retailers, manufacturers, importers, shippers, architects, local authorities and other institutional users of tropical woods who are actively helping to save rain forests by obtaining timber from an ecologically benign source.
  Companies listed in this section have been awarded the Seal of Approval. An interesting entry is

Traidcraft, the mail-order retailer, who have withdrawn mahogany products of uncertain origin — and now stock tropical timber products from locally or communally managed forests.

● The **Yellow pages** list companies or institutions which are helping the campaign to save rain forests but may still be using some non-sustainably produced tropical timber. **Courts**, which sells general furniture through outlets around the country, is an example of a major company falling into this category.

● The **Pink pages** name retailers and suppliers who are selling tropical hardwood products that are contributing to the destruction of rain forests. Examples here include furniture retailers such as: **Habitat**, **House of Fraser**, **Peter Jones**, **Harrods**, **Liberty & Co**, **Maples**, **Army & Navy**, **British Home Stores**, **John Lewis**, **D.H. Evans**, **Debenhams**, **Selfridges**, **Marks & Spencer**. Timber and DIY merchants such as: **Magnet & Southerns**, **Jewsons**, **Sainsbury's Homebase**, **Payless DIY**, **Do It All**, **B & Q DIY Superstores**, **Sandell Perkins**, **James Latham**, and **Texas Homecare**. This section also lists, wherever possible, suitable alternatives to these products.

The aim of the *Good Wood Guide* is to assist the consumer and to encourage the tropical timber industry — including suppliers, importers, manufacturers and retailers — to switch to tropical hardwoods that have been grown sustainably, for example in plantations established on already degraded land.

Remember that softwoods can be used instead of hardwoods in many applications. Where durability is a priority, however, the timber industry tends to treat softwoods with pentachlorophenol (PCP), Lindane, tributyl tin oxide (TBTO) and dieldrin (see under Wood treatment chemicals entry for possible problems and alternatives). Briefing papers on these pesticides can be obtained free of charge from Friends of the Earth.

CHOOSING ACCEPTABLE WOOD PRODUCTS

SUSTAINABLY MANAGED TROPICAL TIMBER

Name of timber	Area of origin	End-uses and characteristics
Teak [1] *Tectona grandis*	Plantations in Java, Thailand and Burma	Furniture, boat-building, high-class joinery, wooden floors. Used in both solid and veneer form
Greenheart [1] *Ocotea rodiaei*	Selectively felled on very low intensity basis from traditional exporters' concessions in Guyana	Marine construction, street furniture, applications where extreme durability is required
Rubberwood *Hevea braziliensis*	Previously disregarded waste-product of Malaysian rubber production. Plantation grown, on one-for-one replacement basis	Furniture components, general joinery, suitable as replacement for ramin

TEMPERATE HARDWOODS:
ALTERNATIVES TO TROPICAL TIMBER

Alder *Alnus species*	Europe, Eastern North America	Light red to orange-brown, flecked with short dark lines. Straight, fine grain and even texture. Seasons well, very water-resistant
Apple *Malus sylvestris*	Europe, North America	Dense, with fine texture. Turns and finishes well
Ash *Fraxinus species*	Europe	Furniture, joinery, tools and sports equipment. Exceptionally strong; very pale with attractive grain
Aspen *Populus tremuloides*	North America	Interior joinery

Name of Timber	Area of origin	End-uses and characteristics
Beech *Fagus* and *Nothofagus* species	Europe, North America	Furniture, joinery, veneers and flooring. Hard and strong but can be bent and turned very easily. Knot-free with flecked grain pattern giving a uniform and attractive finish
Birch *Betula* species	Europe, North America	Plywood, furniture, flooring
Cherry *Prunus* species	Europe	High quality wood used in very fine joinery, particularly for decorative veneers
Elm *Ulmus* species	Europe, Eastern North America, Japan	Mainly used in construction. Very resistant to splitting due to cross grain. 'Partridge breast' finish. White elm has great bending properties. Highly water-resistant
Hickory *Carya* species	North America	Shock-resistant, so used for tool handles, sports goods
Lime *Tilia* species	Europe	Carving, turnery
Maple, Sycamore *Acer* species	Europe, North America	Furniture, joinery. Maple has attractive finish eg 'Bird's Eye Maple'. Sycamore is lighter and easier to work
Oak *Quercus* species	Europe, North America, Japan	Construction, joinery, furniture, boat-building. Strong, durable; white oak stronger than red
Pear *Pyrus communis*	Europe	Used for musical instruments, carving, turning and veneers. Pale and pink-brown; easily stained and polished
Plane *Platanus hybrida*	Europe	Decorative work, inlay
Poplar *Populus* species	Europe	Pallet blocks, turnery

Name of timber	Area of origin	End-uses and characteristics
Black Walnut *Juglans* species	Europe, North America	Major use is for gun-stocks. Previously used in cabinet-making. Chocolate to purple-brown. Seasons well

SOFTWOODS:
ALTERNATIVES TO TROPICAL HARDWOODS

Yew *Taxus baccata*	Europe	Furniture, interior joinery
Whitewood *Liriodendron, Abies* and *Picea* species	North America	Carpentry, furniture and boat-building. Good quality, soft and easily worked. Often used for kitchen furniture
Pine *Pinus* species	Europe, North America	Joinery, construction, furniture, packaging
Larch *Larix* species	Europe	Planking, construction, poles
Hemlock *Tsuga heterophylla*	North America	Construction, joinery
Spruce *Picea* species	UK, North America	Construction, joinery

1. These timbers may come from either sustainable or non-sustainable sources. There is, as yet, no means of identifying the precise origin of commercially available supplies. It is only through the establishment of a clear labelling system that timber consumers will be able to ensure that supplies are not from forest destructive sources.

Source: *The Good Wood Guide* (Friends of the Earth, 1988)

ALONG THE SHELVES

Anti-fouling paints

Widespread evidence that the anti-fouling paints based on tributyl tin (TBT) damage marine wildlife and oyster farms has caused considerable concern. The industry has switched to alternative formulations (often based on copper) which are less toxic to organisms like oysters and dogwhelks. **Geedon Marine** offers anti-fouling paints based on teflon, a non-stick polymer, but its paint is the most expensive on the market. There is also some concern that its anti-fouling properties are too low for British waters. For the latest information, contact the Nature Conservancy Council.

Asbestos and asbestos substitutes

Asbestos had many uses in its heyday, but turned out to be a health time-bomb. There is no known safe exposure limit. Despite the asbestos scares, some DIY home decorators are still at risk. *Wondertex*, produced by **Ready Mixed Concrete**, is a type of ceiling plaster which contains 4 per cent white asbestos. It is meant to be available only to professional contractors, who would use protective clothing, but unscrupulous hardware outlets have been selling it to members of the general public. The pack merely sports a logo saying 'Take care with asbestos'. Householders are vulnerable if they use the product or if they sand down ceilings which have been constructed or filled with the material.

There is also now some evidence that a number of the materials used as asbestos substitutes may cause cancer and other health problems. Workers producing mineral wool, for example, have shown higher-than-normal levels of lung cancer, as have those producing glass fibre. The best advice for the moment is to avoid all asbestos products and to treat similar fibrous material, like the mineral wool used to insulate lofts, with extreme caution.

Bathroom fittings

Mahogany is the most popular wood, aside from pine. Unfortunately, it comes from tropical forests, so the Green Consumer will try to avoid mahogany products such as mirror frames, toilet seats, tooth-brush holders or shelving, unless supplied by companies given a clean bill of health by *The Good Wood Guide* (see pages 39 – 40).

Baths

Bathing was a major step forward in the history of hygiene, but baths use a great deal of water — much of it expensively heated. If you decide to use a bath rather than a shower, you are likely to use over 250 per cent more water. Clearly, the smaller the bath you use, the more water-efficient you will be. Avoid corner baths. They use much more water and the water you lie in tends to cool down faster. If at all possible, use a shower rather than a bath.

Batteries

According to the British Batteries Manufacturers' Association, some 400 million batteries are sold in Britain each year and the range of equipment requiring them increases all the time. Many batteries contain hazardous materials, including cadmium and mercury. About a third of world cadmium consumption, for example, goes into batteries and over 80 per cent of the mercury emitted into the environment by French households is in the form of ba tteries. The incineration of wastes including batteries can lead to air pollution problems. Indeed, the Danes have banned mercury oxide batteries, to ensure that they are not incinerated.

It is not economic to recycle batteries, the industry says, although Sweden and Switzerland have developed battery collection schemes. Unfortunately, as the Swedes have found, this simply concentrates the pollution problem, with the batteries needing to be disposed of in ultra-secure landfills. The Swiss, pragmatic as ever, send their waste batteries out of the country for disposal elsewhere.

The British industry plans to cut the mercury content of batteries by 70 per cent over five years. In the meantime, batteries may not be the No. 1 environmental problem, but they are environmentally undesirable. The various battery types are identified on the pack, although rarely in the case of zinc carbon batteries. They contain different levels of hazardous materials:

- **Zinc carbon batteries**, such as **Ever Ready**'s *Blue Seal* and *Red Seal*, are the most common small batteries and contain very small amounts of mercury in the form of mercuric chloride, and smaller amounts of cadmium. They are used in radios, cycle lamps, torches, shavers, clocks, calculators and TV remote control units.

- **Alkaline manganese batteries**, made by manufacturers like **Duracell**, **Ever Ready**, and **Kodak**, offer a far superior performance in most applications. But they contain more mercury than zinc carbon batteries. Remember, too, that when manufacturers claim that their alkaline batteries 'last up to six times longer', they are comparing them to zinc carbon batteries. When used in less demanding applications, where zinc-based batteries tend to perform better, alkaline batteries last up to three times as long. Alkaline batteries are used in personal stereos, cameras, camera flashguns and portable hi-fis.

- **Button cells** require materials of the highest energy

density because they are so small. Mercuric oxide and silver oxide are preferred materials. Silver oxide is more expensive, however, and can have a shorter shelf life, so mercury oxide wins out. Button cells are not recycled: the silver contained in a silver oxide watch battery is worth no more than 1p. Mercury cells are used in hearing aids and some cameras, and should be properly disposed of. Health authorities take back hearing aid batteries for disposal and **Duracell** say they also take mercury cells back. But camera shops do not.

- **Nickel-cadmium rechargeable batteries**, including **Ever Ready**'s *RX* brand, obviously contain toxic cadmium. Rechargeable batteries can be recharged as often as 500 times. Although more expensive initially, rechargeable batteries can work out cheaper in the long run. They have to be recharged several times during the normal life of an equivalent alkaline battery, however. And they must also be used very carefully, or their life is shortened. As a result, they have so far won only a small share of the consumer market.

- **Lithium** batteries, such as **Kodak**'s *Ultralife* and *Photolife* lithium products, are more expensive, but hold great longer-term promise. Lithium offers higher voltages in small batteries than do such materials as silver and mercury. Kodak also claim that their lithium batteries last 'up to ten times' longer than general zinc carbon batteries and 'twice as long' as current high performance 9-volt alkaline batteries.

So which battery should you buy? Difficult. The best advice is probably as follows:

1. See whether you can't use mains power rather than batteries. If you can, do. Manufacturing batteries can take 50 times more energy than they produce.

2. If 'green' (mercury-free) batteries come onto the market, give them a try. At the time of writing, however, they are on sale in France but not in Britain.

3. Pick the battery most suitable to the appliance you are using. Remember, whichever batteries you use, don't use new batteries with old ones. The new batteries try to recharge the old and their life is cut significantly as a result. If you are using mercury- or cadmium-containing batteries, make sure they go into your dustbin, rather than throwing them away in the open environment. Mercury hearing-aid batteries should be returned to the manufacturer or to your local surgery.

4. If you have a piece of equipment that is a heavy user of batteries, consider using a rechargeable battery.

Bedroom furniture

Beds, bedheads, chests, wardrobes or book-cases may be made from tropical hardwoods. Check before you buy. Acceptable alternative materials include cherry and yew (see pages 41 – 3).

Blockboard, chipboard and plywood

Over 40 per cent of Britain's plywood comes from tropical countries. *The Good Wood Guide* includes a list of suppliers of blockboard, chipboard and plywood products made from sustainable tropical woods, or from acceptable alternatives such as temperate hardwoods or softwoods.

Carpet and upholstery cleaners

There are many serviceable non-aerosol products but if you must use an aerosol, try **Domestic Fillers**' *Big D Carpet Cleaners* or **Johnson Wax**'s *Glory* rug shampoo. Both are 'ozone-friendly'.

Cavity wall insulation   See Home Insulation.

Dining room furniture

Don't buy furniture made from woods like mahogany or teak, which will have come from tropical forests. If you check around the major stores, you will discover that some furniture made by **G Plan** and sold by **John Lewis** falls into this category. Some own-brand storage units offered by **Heal's** are made from teak, instead of acceptable alternative materials like oak. Some of **Marks & Spencer**'s own brand furniture, trollies and video units are made from mahogany.

Doors

We import something like 1.5 million doors from tropical countries each year. DIY stores like **Magnet & Southerns**, **Sainsbury's Homebase**, **Payless DIY**, **Do It All**, **B & Q DIY Superstores** and **Texas Homecare** sell doors made from tropical hardwoods. Ask for softwood or non-tropical hardwood doors.

Double-glazing   See Home Insulation.

Draught-proofing   See Home Insulation.

Dustbins

Before you rush out and buy more dustbins to contain your increasing waste-stream, think about whether you can recycle materials like glass, paper or plastics. You may find you still need more dustbins, but you will be using them to hold the different separated materials. As a minimum, you should be able to track down glass and paper recycling schemes. On the Continent, particularly in Switzerland, you can already buy purpose-designed, multi-compartment dustbins.

Electrical equipment

For information on how to save money on your electricity bills by using energy-efficient equipment, see *The Electrical Shop*.

Fabric and leather treatments

Avoid products that come in aerosols. Where you can't avoid them, check through the list for an ozone-friendly brand.

CFC-FREE AEROSOLS

Cleaners

Amway	Drifab (fabric cleaner)
Amway	Pre-Wash Laundry Spray
Domestic Fillers	Big D Collars 'N' Cuffs (pre-wash stain remover)
Johnson Wax	Dry Clean (grease spot remover)
Johnson Wax	Shout (laundry soil and stain remover)
Safeway	Safeway Pre-Wash Stain Remover

Shoe and Leather Polishes

Punch	Leather Care (cleans and polishes all leathers)
Punch	White-on-White (recolours white leather)
Punch	Scotchguard Protector for Leather and Suede
Punch	Patent Glow (spray-on shine)
Punch	Quickshine (cleans and protects all smooth and delicate leathers)
Punch	Saddle Soap (cleans and preserves leather)
Punch	Suede & Fabric Shampoo (cleans footwear and accessories)

Water Repellents

Punch	Scotchguard Protector for Leather & Suede
Punch	Scotchguard Fabric Protector
Servisol	Super 40

Miscellaneous

Sargom	Fire Barrier (fire-proofing treatment for natural and synthetic fibres)
Scholl	Sneaker Treater (keeps shoes fresh and odour free)

Fire extinguishers

When you buy fire extinguishers, beware those with CFCs. **Kleeneze**'s *Fire Extinguisher*, for example, is CFC-free.

Garden furniture

Avoid furniture made from teak and other tropical hardwoods. Alternatives include cane, wickerwork, and wood and canvas.

Gloves

Try not to buy endless packs of disposable gloves, whether for painting and decorating or for use in the kitchen or the garden. Buy a sturdy, long-lasting pair, even if they're more expensive initially.

Glues

Most glues release solvents, which are an increasing pollution problem. In a small way they help create the photochemical smogs that cause respiratory problems and kill trees. Don't buy larger quantities of glue than you need — and use it sparingly. Keep the lid on the can, or the cap on the tube, whenever you are not using the glue. This stops solvents escaping and extends the life of the glue. For the sake of your own health make sure that your home is well-ventilated when you are using glues or solvents.

Home insulation

Saving energy makes excellent sense, both financially and environmentally. A range of fact-filled brochures on insulation are available from the **Energy Efficiency Office**. Probably the best simple guide for the consumer is *Energy Savings with Home Improvements*, produced by *Which?* and Hodder & Stoughton.

The top energy conservation priority is generally to ensure that your **hot water tank** is insulated. Fit a really thick insulating jacket around the tank and you can cut heat loss by as much as 75 per cent. Check that your preferred brand conforms to British Standard B.S.5615:1978, which includes energy efficiency criteria. One way of guaranteeing this is to to look for the Kitemark (see page 144).

As much as 20 per cent of your energy bill could be saved by installing **loft insulation**. Even if there's some insulation there already, topping it up to the correct depth will usually pay for itself in less than three years.

As much as a quarter of the heat lost from your home is lost through draughts. Although they find their way through gaps in floorboards, under skirting boards and around electrical fittings and loft hatches, up to half the draughts come through undraught-proofed windows and doors. **Draught-proofing** will save you up to 10 per cent of your heating bills, depending on how draughty your home is.

Single glazed windows lose up to 25 per cent of your heat. If you install **double glazing**, you can halve the heat loss through your windows. The key to double glazing's effect is not the thickness of the glass but the thickness of the air space between the inner and outer panes of glass. The first few millimetres are by far the most important, and about 20 mm of air space is the best.

Try to avoid double glazing units which are framed with tropical hardwoods. Many units, including those offered by market leaders like **Everest**, use such hardwoods. If you are buying aluminium frames, specify those with what is known in the trade as a 'thermal barrier'.

Generally a task for the professional rather than for the DIY enthusiast, it is often worth investing in **solid wall insulation**. More heat is lost through the walls of the average house than through any other part — and houses with solid walls lose more than those with cavity walls. Nonetheless, proper wall insulation can stop up to two-thirds of this heat loss.

For **external insulation**, the options include rendering, resin coating, cladding boards, tiles, slates, pebble dash and other commercially available finishes. (But remember that if you want to change the outside appearance of your house you may need planning permission.) Internal insulation is often achieved by using 'thermal boards', which are usually only available by order from builders' merchants.

Cavity wall insulation involves filling the cavity within your walls with an insulating material. You can tell whether or not your house has cavity walls by checking the length of the bricks: if they are all nine inches long, the chances are that you have cavity walls. Generally, cavity wall insulation is done by a contractor, who will use one of three types of material:

- **Foam (urea formaldehyde or UF foam)**. But remember that UF foam can cause indoor pollution problems if improperly installed. Contact approved professional installers through the Cavity Foam Bureau.

- **Mineral wool (glass or rock)**. But handle any such materials with particular care. There is concern that they may be implicated in long-term health problems. Contact Eurisol UK Mineral Wools Association.

- **Polystyrene beads (or granules)**. Contact the Expanded Polystyrene Cavity Insulation Association.

Note: Over-insulating your home can cause indoor air pollution problems. See Ventilation.

Hot water tank   See pages 51 and 143 – 6.

Insecticides

See overleaf for a listing of CFC-free insecticidal aerosols. Remember that many of these insecticides are almost as bad for you as they are for the insects. There are chemical-free options — try using a fly-swat or fly papers, or open a window and shoo the insect outside.

CFC-FREE AEROSOLS

For Flying Pests

Bayer	Autan (insect repellent)
Bayer	Mafu Fly Spray
Betterware	Fly Killer
Boots	Fly Spray
British Products	Sanmex Fly and Wasp Killer
Cooper	Flykiller
Domestic Fillers	Big D Fly and Wasp Killer
Domestic Fillers	Big D Fly Killer
Fisons Horticulture	Fisons Insect Spray for Houseplants
Haventrail	Provence Fly and Wasp Killer
E. R. Holloway	Gnome Fly Killer
ICI PPD	Dragon (general purpose)
ICI	Waspend
Jeyes	Di-Fly
Johnson Wax	Raid Dry Fly and Wasp Killer
Kalium	Buzzoff (domestic fly killer)
Keen	Flying Insect Killer
Keen	Tox (fly spray)
Kleeneze	Exterminator (fly spray)
Napa	Doom — Moth Proofer
Napa	Doom — Tropical Strength Fly and Wasp Killer
Permaflex	Perma (insectox)
Phillips Yeast Products	Pest Kill (household insecticidal spray)
Rentokil	Fly & Wasp Killer
Temana	Vapona Flykiller
Wellcome	Cooper Regular Flykiller

For Crawling and Plant Pests

Ashe	Cooper Garden Pest Killer
Ashe	Vapona Green Arrow
Bayer	Mafu Creepy Crawly
Boots	Garden Insect Killer
BP Detergents	BP 'BOP' Insect Killer
Fisons Horticulture	Fisons Insecticide for Houseplants
Gerhardt	Dethlac (kills cockroaches, ants and other crawling insects)
ICI	Rapid (kills greenfly and blackfly)
ICI	Sybol 2 (insecticide plant care)
ICI	Karispray (houseplant insecticide)
Johnson Wax	Raid Triple Action Ant & Crawling Insect Killer

Keen	Keen Superkill Ant & Roach Exterminator
Napa	Doom — Ant and Crawling Insect Killer
Napa	Doom — Flea Killer
Rentokil	Ant & Crawling Insect Killer
Rentokil	Blackfly & Greenfly Killer
Rentokil	Carpet Beetle Killer & Moth Proofer
Rentokil	Cut 'n' Spray (houseplant insecticide)
Rentokil	Flea Killer
Rentokil	Greenhouse & Garden Insect Killer
Rentokil	Houseplant Insect Killer

Kitchen furniture and equipment

Mahogany and other tropical hardwoods often turn up in saucepan handles, carving boards, cabinets and shelving. There are many alternatives.

Loft insulation   See Home Insulation.

Paints

We rarely think of our health or the environment when buying paint, but we should. First, avoid **asbestos-based paints** (only sold for professional use and will be labelled). The next thing to watch for is the **lead content** of paints. Glosses, undercoats, primers and varnishes have traditionally used lead as a drying agent, although lead has now been phased out by the paint industry.

If you have surfaces which you have reason to suspect were painted with leaded paint, the official advice is:

● don't burn off the paint with a blowlamp (this causes fumes)

● don't rub down with dry sandpaper, especially with

> a power sander (this will produce lead-rich dust in the air)

- don't burn paint debris, put it in the dustbin

- keep decorating clothes separate from other clothes

- wash your hands before eating

- re-paint with low-lead paint.

Presumably, one has to use chemical paint-stripper, one of the most hazardous of household products. If you want to check whether you have a problem, ask your local Environmental Health Department. *Note:* emulsion paint does not contain lead. If you are using spray paints, look out for CFC-free aerosols.

CFC-FREE AEROSOLS

Briggs	Gryphon Paint Sprays (decorative paints)
Certified Laboratories	Certi Line (line marking paint)
Chemsearch	Hy Zinc (protective zinc coating)
Chemsearch	Chem Line (line marking paint)
English Abrasives	HomeStyle (spray paints)
RS Components	Hammer Blue (corrosion protection)
RS Components	Hammer Silver (corrosion protection)
RS Components	Hammer Bronze (corrosion protection)

Showers

Use a shower rather than a bath and you save not only water but also energy.

Solid fuel heating

Over half the heat from a traditional open fire goes straight up the chimney. But if you use smokeless fuel in a modern appliance, you can achieve relatively high energy efficiencies, without causing too much pollution. Remember, though, that smokeless fuels take a fair amount of energy to produce — and some smokeless fuel plants have been a chronic source of local air pollution!

'Natural' smokeless fuels are anthracite and Welsh Dry Steam Coal, while 'manufactured' smokeless fuels include *Coalite*, *Homefire*, *Phurnacite*, *Rexco*, *Royal* and *Sunbrite*. It is important to check that your solid fuel heater has been approved under the Domestic Solid Fuel Appliances Approval Scheme (DSFAAS). This scheme sets certain standards for energy efficiency and environmental performance.

Solar energy

Unfortunately, installing equipment to collect solar energy is still too expensive for most of us. The exceptions are when you are having a new house built or a roof replaced which happens to point in the right direction. If you want to find out more about solar heating, contact: the **Building Research Establishment**; the **Solar Energy Unit**; the **International Solar Energy Association**, UK Section; or the **National Centre for Alternative Technology**.

Solid wall insulation   See Home Insulation.

Veneers

Since around 95 per cent of the tropical timber imported into Britain comes from forests which are being 'quarried', rather than managed on a sustainable basis, you can assume that most tropical hardwood veneers come from unacceptable sources. African walnut, agba, bubinga, ebony, Honduras cedar, Indian laurel, kingwood, mahogany, obeche, sapele, teak, tulipwood, wenge and zebrano are some of the woods to be wary of.

Instead, ask for veneers based on apple, ash, aspen, beech, box, cherry, chestnut, elm, lacewood, larch, maple, myrtle, oak, olive, pear, pine, poplar, sycamore, European walnut or yew.

Ventilation

Many of the products we use can cause a build-up of noxious substances inside our homes. For example, gas cookers, flueless water heaters, open fires, and gas or paraffin heaters all need a supply of fresh air to work safely. If there is too little oxygen, they may produce higher quantities of pollutants like carbon monoxide.

Solvents (found in glues and other adhesives, cleaning fluids, *Dab-it-off* and other dry cleaners, *Tippex*, paints, paint thinners, paint strippers and brush storers) can lead to irritation of the throat and lungs. Some medical experts believe they can also lead to memory loss.

Another indoor pollution problem is formaldehyde, found in such products as cavity wall insulation foams, disinfectants, detergents and some cosmetics. Less commonly, invisible radon gas can accumulate in some houses.

If your home has inadequate ventilation, such pollutants can build up to dangerous levels. Check that there is adequate ventilation, particularly if you are using solid fuel, gas or oil heating — even more so if you use paraffin or bottled-gas heaters.

Don't block air bricks or ventilating grilles, which are necessary for all fuel-burning appliances, including boilers — except those with balanced flues. Inadequate ventilation can lead to the build-up of condensation and to mould problems.

It is also worth pointing out that many houses in the West of England (particularly in Devon and Cornwall) and in Scotland are built on, and in many cases of, granite. This can release radon, an invisible and inert gas thought to be responsible for 1,000 – 1,500 cases of lung cancer each year. If you live in such a house, you may need to have an impermeable floor installed to keep the radon out. If you want to check whether your house is in a high-risk area, contact the Environmental Health Officer at your Local Authority.

Water efficiency

The average Briton uses around 130 litres (28 gallons) of water a day, while the average family of four uses about 3,500 litres (770 gallons) a week. Our national thirst for water grew by 54 per cent between 1961 and 1985 – 86. Each year, every one of us, on average, uses an extraordinary 45,500 litres (10,000 gallons).

Except during droughts, we hardly give water a thought: we are not 'water conscious' in the way that we have been increasingly 'energy conscious' since the oil crises of the 1970s. But the more water we use, the more likely it is that delightful valleys will need to be flooded for reservoirs, that rivers will be heavily managed as aqueducts (reducing the variety of wildlife along their course) and that the treatment capacity of sewage works will be exceeded, leading to sewage pollution of local rivers.

MAJOR USES OF WATER IN THE HOME

Use	Average water consumption	% of total water used
WC flush	10 litres a flush (2.2 gallons)	32
Baths	80 litres (17.6 gallons)	
Showers	30 litres (6.6 gallons)	17
Washing machines	100 litres for a wash (22 gallons)	
Dishwashers	50 litres a wash (11 gallons)	12
Outside use: Garden sprinklers	10 litres every minute (2.2 gallons)	3

There is currently little incentive to repair a dripping tap or to conserve water, but the use of metering to determine water charges could help change attitudes significantly. It was interesting, for example, that when we were doing our survey of washing machines and dishwashers (see *The Electrical Shop*), manufacturers generally had the energy use figures to hand, but many were surprised to be asked for their appliance's water consumption.

They will be less surprised when more of us have water meters. A water meter is a simple, small device, about the size of a grapefruit. It is worth thinking about installing a meter if you currently pay a lot for water services or if you don't use much water. A useful survey of the costs and benefits associated with metering appeared in *Which?* in November 1986. Experience in the United States suggests that metering can cut water use by between 10 and 40 per cent.

The cost of cleaning up Britain's rivers and waterways to EEC standards, estimated at an additional £6 billion over the next few years, is likely to push up water charges by about 50 per cent, in real terms. The Water Authorities Association estimated that the average domestic water bill would double (from £99 a year to £180) between 1987 and 1992. As water prices rise, water efficiency is likely to become a much more pressing priority.

WCs

The WC is the biggest water user in your home. Each flush consumes some 10 litres (2.2 gallons). It also indirectly consumes electricity, as your local water station switches on its pumps to maintain the pressure in the system. You can buy 'dual-flush' WCs which use either 5 litres (1.1 gallons) or the normal amount, the choice being yours. Recently introduced are WCs which use 7 litres for a standard flush — and the manufacturers claim they are just as efficient.

Wood treatment chemicals

To make softwoods last longer, a wide range of chemicals are used. The dangers involved have been underscored by the controversy over the use of *Lindane* (which contains organochlorine pesticides) by **Rentokil**, with the families of a number of the company's workers claiming that the chemical had led to deaths from cancer, leukaemia or aplastic anaemia.

It is not easy to find out what is in many wood treatment formulations, but it is suspected that Rentokil's main dry rot and wet rot treatment fluid contains pentachlorophenol (PCP), Lindane and tributyl tin oxide (TBTO). Some of these products are available in DIY stores.

If you are buying wood preservatives for your loft, remember to buy a brand that is not deadly to bats (see table). There are no significant health risks associated with these flying mammals. Unfortunately, the use of organochlorine woodworm killers and fungicides has caused devastation in many of Britain's bat populations. The situation is now improving since the introduction of the synthetic pyrethroid insecticides, such as permethrin and cypermethrin, which are much less toxic to mammals than Lindane. One company which has gone to considerable lengths to develop bat-friendly wood treatment chemicals for professional use is **Stanhope Chemical Products**.

BAT-FRIENDLY REMEDIAL TREATMENT FLUIDS FOR WOOD

For Do-it-yourself Use

Brands	Type	Active Ingredients
Cuprinol woodworm killer (S)	solvent	permethrin
Cuprinol 5 Star (S)	solvent	permethrin, acypetacs zinc
Cuprinol Clear (S)	solvent	acypetacs zinc
Solignum Clear	solvent	permethrin
Triton	emulsion	permethrin

For Professional Use

Ambersil Ecology insecticide	emulsion	permethrin
Ambersil Ecology fungicidal insecticide	emulsion	permethrin, borester
Antel woodworm killer	emulsion	permethrin
Catomance Brunol PY	solvent	permethrin
Catomance Brunol PC	emulsion	permethrin
Cube woodworm killer concentrate/P	emulsion	permethrin
Cube fungicide/insecticide concentrate/PB	emulsion	permethrin, borester 7
Cube woodworm fluid/P	solvent	permethrin
Cube fungicide/insecticide fluid/PB	solvent	permethrin, borester 7
Cuprinol insecticidal emulsion concentrate	emulsion	permethrin
Fosroc Protim woodworm killer P	solvent	permethrin
Fosroc Protim WB10	aqueous	boron compound
Ness Presotim water mix concentrate	emulsion	permethrin
Remtox AQ Standard II	emulsion	permethrin
Remtox AQ Standard V de luxe	emulsion	permethrin

Brands	Type	Active Ingredients
Remtox dual purpose II de luxe	emulsion	permethrin, borester 7
Remtox dual purpose Formulation 2	solvent	permethrin, borester 7
Rextox woodworm killer II	solvent	permethrin
Rentokil woodworm fluid	solvent	permethrin
Safeguard Permethrin woodworm killer (PWK)	emulsion	permethrin
Safeguard dual purpose (BP)	emulsion	permethrin, borester 7
Solignum Clear	solvent	permethrin, organoboron ester, zinc
Solignum woodworm killer concentrate/P	emulsion	permethrin
Solignum remedial fluid/PB	solvent	permethrin, organoboron ester
Sovereign fungicide/insecticide II	solvent	permethrin, borester 7
Sovereign insecticide II	solvent	permethrin
Sovereign aqueous fungicide/II	emulsion	permethrin, borester 7
Sovereign aqueous insecticide II	emulsion	permethrin
Sovex permethrin insecticide/fungicide	emulsion	permethrin, borester 7
Sovex permethrin insecticide	emulsion	permethrin
Stanhope Brunol PY	solvent	permethrin
Stanhope Brunol PC	emulsion	permethrin
Tenneco Organics Nubex emulsion P	emulsion	permethrin
Tenneco Organics Nubex all-purpose woodworm killer P	solvent	permethrin
Triton Trimethrin	emulsion	permethrin
Wykamol woodworm killer	solvent	permethrin
Wykamol dual purpose AQ concentrate	emulsion	permethrin, organoboron ester

Source: Nature Conservancy Council

USEFUL ADDRESSES

Association of Woodusers Against Rainforest Exploitation (AWARE), PO Box 92, London N5 2JJ

Building Research Establishment, Garston, Watford, Herts WD2 7JR. Tel: 0923 676612

Cavity Foam Bureau, PO Box 79, Oldbury, Warley, West Midlands B69 4BW. Tel: 021 544 4949

Energy Efficiency Office, Thames House South, Millbank, London SW1P 4QJ. Tel: 01-211 3000

Eurisol UK Mineral Wools Association, 39 High Street, Redbourn, Herts AL3 7LW. Tel: 058 285 4624

Expanded Polystyrene Cavity Insulation Association, 5 Belgrave Square, London SW1X 8PH. Tel: 01-235 9483

International Solar Energy Association, UK Section, 19 Albemarle Street, London W1X 3HA

National Association of Retail Furnishers, 17–21 George Street, Croydon CR9 1TQ

National Centre for Alternative Technology, Llwyngwerm Quarry, Machynlleth, Powys SY20 9AZ. Tel: 0654 2400

Nature Conservancy Council (NCC), Northminster House, Peterborough PE1 1UA. Tel: 0733 40345

Solar Energy Unit, University College, Newport Road, Cardiff CF2 1TA.

Timber Trade Federation, Clareville House, 26–27 Oxenden Street, London SW17 4EL. Tel: 01-839 1891

THE GARDEN
CENTRE

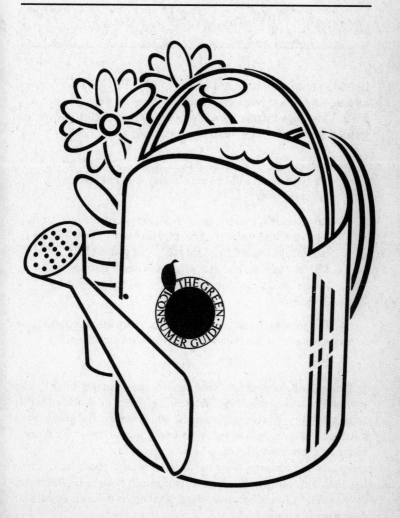

> Pesticides and herbicides: the killers in your garden shed
>
> Organic fertilizers and soil improvers
>
> Lawn care without chemicals
>
> Planting a drought garden

In 1985 alone Britons spent nearly £600 million on gardening, buying 45 million houseplants, 40 million packets of seeds and 35 million rose bushes. We also spent around £30 million on **garden pesticides**. The main product types are:

- **herbicides**, or weed killers, which can be either total (eg path weed killers) or selective (eg lawn weed killers)

- **insecticides**, including products for controlling pests such as greenfly, blackfly and whitefly, and insects which attack plant roots. Slug and snail killers make up another relatively small market sector, as do the chemicals designed to kill spiders and ants

- **fungicides**, which attack fungi responsible for plant diseases such as black spot, mildew, botrytis and root diseases.

Worldwide, pesticides continue to cause major health and environmental problems. According to the World Health Organisation (WHO), at least 10,000 people die every year because of pesticide poisoning, most of them in the Third World. Some die because they accidentally swallow or inhale pesticides, some because they eat contaminated foods and some because they absorb the chemicals through their skin. Research at Imperial College, London, suggests that these figures could be considerably higher.

There are many reasons why these problems have become so serious in the Third World. Perhaps most important, products banned here are sold there. Pesticides are frequently misused, often because the label is in the wrong language or because the user can't read. Safety equipment is either not available, or is unsuitable for tropical conditions.

By contrast, the garden chemicals we are allowed to use in Britain are carefully tested, but the active ingredients in many of the brands we can buy at the garden centre are dangerous substances in anyone's terms. Some of the chemicals that are permitted in Britain are banned in other countries.

One of these chemicals, **2,4-dichlorophenoxyacetic acid (2,4-D)**, has been used as a herbicide for decades. Recent American research, however, suggests that farmers exposed to 2,4-D for more than 20 days a year are six times more likely to develop a cancer known as non-Hodgkin's lymphoma. Frequent users, who mixed or applied the chemicals, were eight times more likely to develop the disease than people who had not been exposed to the herbicide.

Another class of pesticides whose use in Britain causes continuing concern are the 'drins' (**aldrin**, **dieldrin**, **endrin** and **isodrin**). All of these chemicals can be concentrated in a mother's milk, so that babies — who are more vulnerable because of their low body weight — receive a disproportionate dose. Although their use is strictly controlled, they can still be used for treating bulbs, seed-potatoes and timber.

A great deal of effort goes into making sure that today's garden chemicals are relatively safe to use. A single new pesticide can cost £10 million to test and bring to market. For every 10,000 chemicals tested, only one is likely to be marketed. But pesticides are designed to kill and, while they may be more specific than they were, their use has been associated with damage to wildlife, such as birds and hedgehogs, and to other plants; and with human health problems, including 'sensitization' to chemical sprays.

Ironically, at a time when many of us have more leisure time because of the shrinking working week or unemployment, we are often prepared to spend considerable sums of money to buy convenience. We nurture our plants with hissing hoses and

THE RISKS IN GARDEN CHEMICALS

Chemical	Typical usage	Banned or restricted outside UK?	Dangerous to animals or birds?	Dangerous to fish?
Alloxydim sodium	Garden weedkiller			
Amintriazole (Amitrole)	Path weedkiller			
Atrazine	Path weedkiller		✓	✓
Bupirimate	Fungicide Aphid and caterpillar killer			✓
Carbaryl	Worm killer			✓
Carbendazim	Fungicide			
Chlordane	Worm killer	✓	✓	✓
Chloroxuron	Lawn weedkiller Moss killer			
Copper	Fungicide		✓	✓
2,4-D	Lawn weedkiller Path weedkiller	✓		✓
Dalapon	Garden weedkiller			
Dicamba	Lawn weedkiller			✓
Dichlobenil	Garden weedkiller			✓
Dichlorophen	Fungicide Lawn weedkiller Moss killer			✓
Dichlorprop	Lawn weedkiller			✓
Dimethoate	General insecticide Aphid and caterpillar killer	✓	✓	✓
Dinocap	Fungicide			✓
Diquat	Path weedkiller Garden weedkiller		✓	

Dangerous to bees and other insects?	Spray drift problem and/or harmful to plants?	Persistence: long or medium	Resistance developed in some pests?	Irritant to eyes, skin and/or respiration?	Possible carcinogen (C) teratogen (T) mutagen (M)[1]
			✓	✓	T?
	✓		✓	✓	CTM
✓	✓	L	✓		M
			✓	✓	T?
✓		M	✓	✓	CTM
		M	✓		CM
✓		L		✓	CTM
				✓	T?
	✓	L			T?
	✓			✓	CT
	✓			✓	T?
	✓			✓	M
	✓		✓		T? M?
					T?
	✓			✓	T?
✓		M	✓	✓	M
✓	✓	M	✓	✓	M
		L		✓	T

THE RISKS IN GARDEN CHEMICALS (continued)

Chemical	Typical usage	Banned or restricted outside UK?	Dangerous to animals or birds?	Dangerous to fish?
Fenarimol	Fungicide			✓
Fenitrothion	Aphid and caterpillar killer		✓	✓
Ferrous sulphate	Moss killer			
Gamma HCH	General insecticide Ant killer	✓	✓	✓
Lindane	Aphid and caterpillar killer			
Malathion	General insecticide Aphid and caterpillar killer			✓
Mancozeb	Fungicide			
MCPA	Path weedkiller Lawn weedkiller			✓
Mecoprop	Lawn weedkiller			
Mercurous chloride	Fungicide		✓	✓
Metaldehyde	Slug and snail control		✓	✓
Methiocarb	Slug control		✓	✓
Paraquat	Path weedkiller Garden weedkiller	✓	✓	
Permethrin	General insecticide Aphid and caterpillar killer Ant killer Fungicide			✓
Piperonyl butoxide	General insecticide			

Dangerous to bees and other insects?	Spray drift problem and/or harmful to plants?	Persistence: long or medium	Resistance developed in some pests?	Irritant to eyes, skin and/or respiration?	Possible carcinogen (C) teratogen (T) mutagen (M)[1]
			✓		T? M?
✓		M		✓	M
	✓				M
✓	✓	M–L			C T
					C T
✓	✓	M	✓	✓	T
		L		✓	T? M
	✓			✓	T
	✓			✓	T?
✓		L			T? M?
✓					T?
✓					T?
	✓			✓	T M
✓	✓			✓	C
					C

THE RISKS IN GARDEN CHEMICALS (continued)

Chemical	Typical usage	Banned or restricted outside UK?	Dangerous to animals or birds?	Dangerous to fish?
Pirimicarb	Aphid and caterpillar killer		✓	
Pirimiphos methyl	General insecticide Aphid and caterpillar killer Ant killer			✓
Propin-canazole	Fungicide			✓
Pyrethrum	General insecticide Ant killer			
Resmethrin	General insecticide			✓
Simazine	Path weedkiller Garden weedkiller			
Sodium chlorate	Path weedkiller			
Sulphur	Fungicide			
Tecnazene	General insecticide	✓		✓
Thiophanate methyl	Fungicide	✓		✓

Source: Soil Association.

1. Source: London Food Commission.

Dangerous to bees and other insects?	Spray drift problem and/or harmful to plants?	Persis-tence: long or medium	Resistance developed in some pests?	Irritant to eyes, skin and/or respir-ation?	Possible carcinogen (C) teratogen (T) mutagen (M)[1]
✓					T?
✓		M		✓	M
				✓	T?
		M		✓	T?
✓		M			T? M?
✓	✓	L	✓	✓	M
	✓	L		✓	M
	✓	M		✓	T?
	✓	M	✓	✓	C T?
	✓	M	✓	✓	C T?

synthetic fertilizers and pesticides. Instead of hoeing and tugging at weeds, we turn to 'chemical hoes'.

Much of this convenience is bought at the expense of the wildlife which would otherwise share our gardens with us. Happily, more and more gardeners are becoming concerned about the effects of the chemicals they use and are looking for alternatives. Those who have used organic gardening techniques for years know that they are not only effective, but also safer and cheaper than using garden chemicals. The chart on pages 68 – 73 tells you the hazards associated with some commonly used chemicals. Under the individual sections of *The Organic Gardener's Guide* (pages 75 – 102) we list the hazards associated with proprietary brands.

The first step is to get rid of the chemicals you already have. Be extremely careful about how you dispose of them. Check whether your local council has a hazardous waste collection service. Most haven't. If this is the case, ask your local councillors and your MP to look into the possibility of setting up such a service. In the meantime, follow our guidelines on page 101.

It can still prove difficult to track down a reliable supplier of organic products. Most garden centres have well-established relationships with chemical firms and are not enthusiastic about switching to organic or low-chemical suppliers. A directory of key suppliers mentioned in this section will be found on pages 103 – 6.

Going organic

'Converting a garden from "chemical" to organic methods is not just a question of exchanging one spray for another,' says Pauline Pears of the **Henry Doubleday Research Association**, the organization that founded the National Centre for Organic Gardening. 'The main aim must be to create a healthy balanced environment in which plants can grow and thrive. Going organic may also require converting yourself, the gardener; it is essential to get away from the way of thinking that sees every insect as a pest, every plant out of place as a weed and every solution to a problem in a spray.'

There is no particular mystery about organic gardening. There are three ground-rules.

1. Stop using chemicals. The organic gardener starts off by ensuring that the soil has a good structure. The keys to soil fertility are animal manures (best composted before use), garden compost and leaf mould.

2. Make sure that your soil is properly looked after.

3. Encourage natural life — not just the obvious birds and bees, but also the millions of insects and other organisms which help make a healthy garden.

THE ORGANIC GARDENER'S GUIDE

Ant killers

If ants are a particular nuisance in the home, or are helping to infest roses with the aphids they 'farm', try pouring boiling water into their nest. Alternatively, there is borax. This may not be an 'organic' product, but it is generally safe in the sort of quantities needed to kill ants. They eat each other's droppings, effectively sharing their digestive systems. So the borax is transported back to the nest, destroying it completely. Derris and pyrethrum are two safe plant-based pesticides for use against ants — but do check the pack to make sure that the product does not contain other, more dangerous, chemicals (see table overleaf).

Aphids and caterpillars

If you are plagued by aphids, try Derris Dust or Liquid Derris. This is a Malayan fish poison, usually sold as a 5 per cent solution with soft soap. Although harmless to mammals and birds, remember that it is poisonous to insects, fish and tortoises. Suppliers and brands are: **Battle, Hayward & Bower** (*Liquid Derris Greenfly Spray*), **Cumulus Organics** (*Liquid Derris*), **Fisons**

ANT KILLERS

The chemical hazards in proprietary brands

Trade name and supplier[1]	Description and suppliers' recommendations for use[1]	Chemicals they contain[1]	Problems and hazards (see key)[2]
Anti-Ant Duster (**PBI**)	Control of ants indoors and outdoors	pyrethrum	6M, 8
Fisons Ant Killer (**Fisons**)	Control of ants, earwigs, woodlice and other crawling pests outdoors	phoxim	no data
ICI Ant Killer	Dust for the control of ants, earwigs, woodlice and wasps	pirimiphos-methyl	3, 4, 6M, 8, 11
Murphy Ant Killer Powder (**Fisons**)	Powder for the control of ants	gamma-HCH	1, 2, 3, 4, 5, 6M – L, 9, 10
Nippon Ant Killer (**Synchemicals**)	For the control of ants in nests	borax	no data
Nippon Ant and Crawling Insect Killer (**Synchemicals**)	Aerosol spray for the control of ants and other crawling insects	permethrin tetramethrin formulated	3, 4, 5, 8, 9 no data

Key: 1 Banned/restricted outside the UK; 2 Dangerous to animals/birds; 3 Dangerous to fish; 4 Dangerous to bees/other insects; 5 Spraydrift problem and/or harmful to plants; 6 Persistence, Long or Medium; 7 Resistance developed in some pests; 8 Irritant to eyes, skin and/or respiratory system; 9 Possible carcinogen; 10 Possible teratogen; 11 Possible mutagen

1. Source: British Agrochemicals Association Ltd booklet, *Directory of Garden Chemicals*.
2. Source: Soil Association.

(*Murphy Derris Dust*), **ICI** (*Derris Dust*), **PBI** (*Liquid Derris*), and **Synchemicals** (*Derris Dust*).

Soft soap is made with caustic potash. All aphids have a delicate wax layer on the surface of their bodies, which soft soap destroys. Beneficial insects, including ladybirds and hoverflies, have tougher skins and waxes which protect them. Leading soft soap brands and suppliers are: *Savona* (**Chase Organics**, **Henry**

APHID AND CATERPILLAR CONTROLS
The chemical hazards in proprietary brands

Trade name and supplier[1]	Description and suppliers' recommendations for use[1]	Chemicals they contain[1]	Problems and hazards (see key)[2]
Bio Flydown (**PBI**)	For control of household pests, including whitefly, scale and mealy bug	permethrin	3, 4, 5, 8, 9
Bio Sprayday (**PBI**)	For control of whitefly, greenfly, blackfly, caterpillars, leaf hoppers and thrips	permethrin	3, 4, 5, 8, 9
Boots Caterpillar and Whitefly Killer	Liquid control for caterpillars, pea maggot, and whitefly	permethrin	3, 4, 5, 8, 9
Boots Greenfly and Blackfly Killer	Control of blackfly and greenfly on flowers, fruit and vegetables	dimethoate	1, 2, 3, 4, 6M, 7, 8, 11
Fenitrothion (**PBI**)	For control of greenfly, blackfly, capsid and caterpillars in fruit and vegetables; codling moth and sawfly (maggots in fruit) in apples and pears; raspberry beetle	fenitrothion	2, 3, 4, 6M, 8, 11
Fisons Greenfly and Blackfly Killer	For systemic and contact control of greenfly and blackfly	dimethoate	1, 2, 3, 4, 6M, 7, 8, 11
		malathion	3, 4, 5, 6M, 7, 8, 10
		lindane	9, 10
Malathion Greenfly Killer (**PBI**)	For control of greenfly, blackfly, whitefly, red spider mite, thrips, leaf miner, woolly aphid, mealy bug, and scale insect	malathion	3, 4, 5, 6M, 7, 8, 10

APHID AND CATERPILLAR CONTROLS (continued)

Trade name and supplier[1]	Description and suppliers' recommendations for use[1]	Chemicals they contain[1]	Problems and hazards (see key)[2]
Murphy Fentro (**Fisons**)	For control of greenfly, caterpillars, sawfly, capsids, beetles, etc	fenitrothion	2, 3, 4, 6M
Murphy Liquid Malathion (**Fisons**)	For the control of greenfly, whitefly, red spider, mite, mealy bug, scale insects etc	malathion	3, 4, 5, 6M, 7, 8, 10
Murphy Systemic Insecticide (**Fisons**)	For the systemic control of greenfly, whitefly, red spider mite, mealy bug, scale insects etc	dimethoate	1, 2, 3, 4, 6M, 7, 8, 11
Rapid Greenfly Killer (**ICI**)	An aerosol spray for the quick control of greenfly and blackfly	pirimicarb	2, 4
Roseclear (**ICI**)	For complete control of mildew, blackspot and greenfly	bupirimate pirimicarb triforine	3, 7, 8 2, 4 no data
Sybol (**ICI**)	For control of most garden and greenhouse pests, including whitefly and red spider mite	pirimiphos-methyl	3, 4, 6M, 8, 11
Sybol Aerosol (**ICI**)	For control of most garden and greenhouse pests, including whitefly and red spider mite	pirimiphos-methyl synergized pyrethrins	3, 4, 6M, 8, 11 no data

Key: 1 Banned/restricted outside the UK; 2 Dangerous to animals/birds; 3 Dangerous to fish; 4 Dangerous to bees/other insects; 5 Spraydrift problem and/or harmful to plants; 6 Persistence, Long or Medium; 7 Resistance developed in some pests; 8 Irritant to eyes, skin and/or respiratory system; 9 Possible carcinogen; 10 Possible teratogen; 11 Possible mutagen

1. Source: British Agrochemicals Association Ltd booklet, *Directory of Garden Chemicals*.
2. Source: Soil Association.

Doubleday Research Association (HDRA) and **Koppert**) and *Soft soap*(**HDRA**).

Some organic gardeners also recommend an application of 'do-it-yourself' nicotine insecticide for aphids. But now that people are giving up smoking, the idea of boiling up old cigarettes seems less appealing. An alternative is to cut up and boil rhubarb leaves, mixing the resulting solution with soft soap. Avoid killing the larvae of ladybirds, hoverflies and lacewings, all of which prey on greenfly.

If an infestation of caterpillars has got beyond the stage where you can pick individual caterpillars off the plant, try derris, pyrethrum or *Bacillus thuringiensis* (Bt). Bt is a natural virus which kills many caterpillars. Leading suppliers of *Bactospeine* are: **Chase Organics**, **Cumulus Organics**, **HDRA**, **S. E. Marshall** and **Seagold-Silvaperl**.

Biological controls

Instead of using chemicals, encourage a particular pest's natural enemies, be they insects, viruses or fungi. Buy a parasitic wasp to control whitefly in greenhouses, for example, or a predatory mite to control red spider mite. Caterpillars can be sprayed with *Bacillus thuringiensis*, which causes a natural bacterial disease in caterpillars. (But make sure you spray pest caterpillars, not those of butterfly species which make summer gardens such a pleasure.) See Aphids and caterpillars.

Bird repellents

Birds are one of the great attractions of British gardens — and they help keep garden pests under control. Sometimes, however, they can cause problems in orchards or vegetable plots. Walk-in fruit cages are expensive but effective; make sure, though, that the cage is properly constructed so birds are not caught and strangled by the netting. Other methods for scaring birds include *Humming Line*, which is stretched between canes and hums in the wind; the *Tisara Goshawk*, a black plastic outline of a hawk available from **Tisara Bird Control Systems**; *Glitterbangs*, aluminium foil strips that flutter and crackle in the wind; the

Scaraweb, a fine, biodegradable webbing that is stretched over fruit trees to protect them from bird attack; and cotton, threaded between sticks over seedlings. A leading supplier is **Chase Organics**.

Bonfires

Most gardeners who light bonfires to get rid of their garden waste would be astounded both at the hazards they run by breathing bonfire fumes — and at the amount of money they send up in smoke.

Cigarette smoke contains perhaps 0.2 parts per million (ppm) of cancer-causing benzopyrenes, whereas ordinary garden bonfire smoke contains around 70 ppm (or 350 times as much). And, at the same time as it poisons both you and your neighbours, your bonfire is also turning valuable humus into ashes. The solution: turn your garden wastes into compost.

Compost

The compost heap has been described as the 'heart of organic gardening'. Whether your soil is cold, damp clay or dry and sandy, compost will help boost its fertility. There are two types of composting: *aerobic* and *anaerobic*. The first, which involves storing biodegradable materials in a drum-like container or brick-built construction, needs a constant flow of air from below, whereas the second works best when starved of oxygen.

By providing an adequate supply of air through aerobic compost, through holes in the drum or between the bricks, you effectively create a slow biological 'bonfire' in which millions of bacteria break down the wastes into humus. An aerobic compost can reach temperatures of 150–170°F, hot enough to destroy weed seeds, pests and disease-promoting organisms.

An anaerobic compost heap takes longer to break down the wastes, but is generally even simpler to operate. A hole in the ground into which waste is tossed will eventually produce usable compost. For a really effective compost you should include fibrous materials and all the ingredients should be well mixed.

You may need an 'activator' to get the compost going, like the yeast needed to start beer fermenting. You can buy powdered seaweed for the purpose, and proprietary products such as **QR**'s *Herbal Compost Maker* or **Fertosan**'s *Compost Accelerator*. Many organic gardeners believe that animal or human urine is just as effective — and it is certainly much cheaper! (See also Grobags, Mushroom Compost, Organic Manures, Peat and Worms.)

Composters

If you have a small town garden, the best option may be to buy a commercial composter. You can buy aerobic composters, like the *Tumbler* ('Rich Compost in 21 Days', from **Blackwell Products**). The barrel in which the compost is produced holds up to 0.22 cubic metres (8 cu ft) of waste and is made from recycled plastic. The system can be delivered to your door for around £35. A modified system, the *Liquid Feed Kit*, can produce organic 'liquinure' for use on your plants.

Endangered plants

A useful source of information on how to grow endangered plants in your garden is the National Council for the Conservation of Plants and Gardens. The organic gardener is typically enthusiastic about trying out some of these rarer varieties, recognizing not only that diversity is the key to a healthy garden but also that conservation can be fun!

Fencing

If you are about to put up a garden fence, consider using *Durapost*. Manufactured by **Duraplast**, Durapost fencing posts and rails are made from recycled plastics. They look like wood, you can use them like wood (you can nail, staple, drill and screw into them), but they are much less likely to splinter, rot or crack than ordinary wood. Your fence could last much longer as a result.

Fertilizers

Artificial fertilizers do not benefit the soil as much as organic manures. They can make the soil acid, drive worms away and may also trigger rapid sappy growth in plants by releasing a burst of free nitrate. Ironically, too, over-use of fertilizers can damage overall soil fertility by 'locking up' essential elements like calcium and magnesium — and by suppressing the activity of natural soil organisms that normally fix nitrogen from the air or make phosphate available to plants.

The Soil Association points out that mineral fertilizers should be used as a supplement to, rather than as a replacement for, natural nutrient recycling in the soil. The aim must be a slow, balanced uptake of nutrients by plants. As a rough guide, the Soil Association:

- PERMITS rock phosphate, feldspar, magnesium limestone, calcium sulphate, ground chalk, limestone, seaweed, unadulterated seaweed foliar sprays, calcified seaweed, basic slag, rock potash, bonemeal, fish meal, hoof and horn meals, and wood ash.

- RESTRICTS THE USE OF dried blood, wood shoddy, hop waste, leather meal, sulphate of potash, kieserite, borax, Epsom salts and aluminium phosphates.

- PROHIBITS all other mineral fertilizers, including nitrochalk, Chilean nitrate, urea, muriate of potash, slaked lime, quicklime and unrecognized organic fertilizers.

Liquid fertilizers: Try *Farmura* liquid organic fertilizer or *Super Natural* organic liquid plant food, both made from farmyard manures. There are also a number of seaweed-based products, such as **Maxicrop**'s *Natura Seaweed Extract*. For houseplants, try *Pure Goodness*, *Biolan Extra* houseplant food sticks or *Super Natural* house plant compost. Write to the National Organic Gardening Centre for a copy of their catalogue, which contains all these products — and hundreds more. (See also under Composters.)

Fungicides

Bordeaux Mixture, the standard copper sulphate fungicide, is widely accepted as an alternative to synthetic chemical fungicides — although organic gardeners would only use it as a last resort. So, wherever possible use cultural methods as your first line of defence against pests. Bordeaux Mixture prevents disease on fruit trees, potatoes and tomatoes, including leaf mould, potato blight and peach leaf curl. Leading suppliers are: **Chase Organics**, the **Henry Doubleday Research Association** and **Synchemicals**.

FUNGICIDES

The chemical hazards in proprietary brands

Trade name and supplier[1]	Description and suppliers' recommendations for use[1]	Chemicals they contain[1]	Problems and hazards (see key)[2]
Bio Multirose (**PBI**)	For the control of major rose pests and diseases and as a foliar feed	triforine dinocap sulphur permethrin	no data 3, 4, 5, 6M, 7, 8, 11 5, 6M, 8 3, 4, 5, 8, 9
Bio Multiveg (**PBI**)	To control major diseases and pests and as a foliar feed	carbendazim copper oxychloride sulphur permethrin	6M, 7, 9, 11 2, 3, 5, 6L 5, 6M, 8 3, 4, 5, 8, 9
Boots Garden Fungicide	To control diseases of fruit, vegetables, roses and bulbs	carbendazim	6M, 7, 9, 11
Calomel Dust (**PBI**)	To control club root in brassicas and white rot in onions	mercurous chloride	no data
Dithane 945 (**PBI**)	For the control of potato blight, rose blackspot, leaf mould, rust, downy mildew, leaf spot, apple and pear scab, peach leaf curl etc	mancozeb	6L, 8, 11

FUNGICIDES (continued)

Fisons Mildew and Blackspot Killer	Systemic control of powdery mildew and blackspot on roses and of mildew on ornamentals	fenarimol	no data
Fungus Fighter (**May & Baker**)	For use on a range of garden and greenhouse diseases	thiophanate-methyl	1, 3, 5, 6M, 7, 8, 9
Murphy Tumblebite (**Fisons**)	For the control of mildew and blackspot on roses, rust on roses and antirrhinums, and mildew on all ornamentals	propiconazole	3, 8
Nimrod T (**ICI**)	For systemic control of powdery mildew, blackspot, scab and leaf spot. For use on roses, other ornamentals, apples, blackcurrent and gooseberries	bupirimate triforine	3, 7, 8 no data
Supercarb (**PBI**)	Wettable powder for control of garden fungal diseases	carbendazim	6M, 7, 9, 11
Bio Roota (**PBI**)	A rooting liquid and fungicide	1-naphthyl-acetic acid dichlorophen	no data 3

Key: 1 Banned/restricted outside the UK; 2 Dangerous to animals/birds; 3 Dangerous to fish; 4 Dangerous to bees/other insects; 5 Spraydrift problem and/or harmful to plants; 6 Persistence, Long or Medium; 7 Resistance developed in some pests; 8 Irritant to eyes, skin and/or respiratory system; 9 Possible carcinogen; 10 Possible teratogen; 11 Possible mutagen

1. Source: British Agrochemicals Association Ltd booklet, *Directory of Garden Chemicals*.
2. Source: Soil Association.

Grobags

There has been a massive increase in demand for 'grobags', introduced by **Fisons** in the mid-1970s. Other suppliers include

PBI, **Arthur Bower**, **Godwins** and **ICI**. None of these products are organic, however; the only organic product which is widely available is produced by **Stimgro**. To cut the pressure on Britain's wetlands, avoid peat-based grobags and switch to compost. (*Note*: many 'compost' products sold in garden centres are based on peat. Check before you buy.)

Herbs

There are few sources of organically grown herbs. Leading suppliers are **Hambleden Herbs**, the **National Centre for Organic Gardening** and **Suffolk Herbs**.

Insecticides

There is no organic equivalent to the general insecticide. Even so, you should avoid using general insecticides. They certainly kill pests, but also destroy beneficial insects and other wildlife which are important to your garden's health. Many of the insects you would kill are harmless natural predators which control potentially destructive pests. Other pest predators, such as birds and frogs, may also be affected. If you must use an aerosol spray, check pages 54 – 5 for CFC-free aerosols.

Lawns

There are estimated to be 90,000 hectares (222,300 acres) of lawn in Britain, an area of land almost three times the size of the Isle of Wight! Enormous quantities of chemical fertilizers, herbicides and insecticides are used to keep the nation's lawns green — yet you can save yourself a great deal of money by cutting down on the chemicals you use.

First ask yourself, are you trying to develop a lawn in the wrong place? If you try to produce a fine, velvety sward on poorly drained land, or under trees, you are likely to hit problems however many chemicals you use. Choose your lawn plants carefully: use meadow grass under trees, clover on poor soils and yarrow where the soils are likely to be very dry.

Wild and wild flower lawns: You may be better off with a wild lawn. Plants like plantain and yarrow will thrive, attracting butterflies, bees and other insects into your garden. Or you may choose to sow a wild flower lawn. If you do, remember that you will need to use an area with poor soil — otherwise grasses and weeds will soon swamp your carefully chosen wild flowers. Never feed a wild flower lawn and make sure you cut it after the flowers have set seed. You will find excellent advice on how to proceed in Chris Baines's book, *How to Make a Wildlife Garden* (Elm Tree Books, 1987).

Rake and aerate: If you opt for a conventional lawn, rake it vigorously once a month during the growing season. Aerate the soil with a fork, particularly if it is likely to be heavily used. If you allow the soil to become compacted, the root zone will be starved of air — and you will be faced with waterlogging, browning and bare patches.

Fertilizers: Every time you mow a lawn, you are removing nutrients. Don't dump the first mowing of the year back on the lawn, because the grass will be long and an unhealthy 'thatch' may develop. But do recycle mowings later in the year. This will not totally eliminate the need for some additional feeding, however.

Remember that artificial fertilizers do not benefit the soil as much as organic manures. For non-vegetarians, blood, fish and bonemeal offer useful sources of nitrogen and phosphates. Seaweed meal is an excellent source of potash.

Moss killers: An organic lawn, with its worm population intact and the soil naturally aerated, should be less likely to produce moss. Moss is encouraged by acid soil, summer drought and too much shade. The first step if your lawn is mossy is to check whether it is properly drained. If a lawn has been over-rolled or trampled, use a spiked roller or fork to help aerate it. Vigorous raking can also help discourage moss.

Sometimes, where the lawn is run-down or has been poorly laid, it may be necessary to relay the turf on proper drainage. If you have rushes or horsetail on your lawn, then you have really got problems.

If poor drainage does not seem to be the problem, moss can also be a protest against mowing without feeding. Try feeding the

HERBICIDES AND FERTILIZER MIXTURES FOR LAWNS
The chemical hazards in proprietary brands

Trade name and supplier[1]	Description and suppliers' recommendations for use[1]	Chemicals they contain[1]	Problems and hazards (see key)[2]
Boots Lawn Weed and Feed Soluble Powder	Weedkiller with fertilizer	dichlorprop MCPA	3, 5, 8 3, 5, 8, 10
Boots Total Lawn Treatment	To kill moss, difficult weeds and worms, and to boost grass	dichlorophen urea formulated with mecoprop dichlorprop 2,4-D dicamba benazolin	3 5, 8 3, 5, 8 1, 3, 5, 8, 9, 10 3, 5, 8, 11 no data
Fisons Lawncare Liquid Lawn Fertilizer and Weedkiller	To kill lawn weeds and feed the grass	MCPA mecoprop dicamba	3, 5, 8, 10 5, 8 3, 5, 8, 11
Green Up Lawn Feed and Weed **(Synchemicals)**	To kill lawn weeds and feed the grass	2,4-D dicamba	1, 3, 5, 8, 9, 10 3, 5, 8, 11
Lawnsman Mosskiller **(ICI)**	For the control of moss, liverworts, lichen, algae on lawns and to 'green up' the grass	chloroxuron dichlorophen ferrous sulphate	8 3 5, 11
Murphy Lawn Weedkiller and Lawn Tonic **(Fisons)**	To kill lawn weeds and stimulate the grass	2,4-D dichlorprop urea	1, 3, 5, 8, 9, 10 3, 5, 8 no data
Supergreen and Weed **(May & Baker)**	To give combined feed and weed for lawns	2,4-D mecoprop NPK fertilizer	1, 3, 5, 8, 9, 10 5, 8 no data

Key: 1 Banned/restricted outside the UK; 2 Dangerous to animals/birds; 3 Dangerous to fish; 4 Dangerous to bees/other insects; 5 Spraydrift problem and/or harmful to plants; 6 Persistence, Long or Medium; 7 Resistance developed in some pests; 8 Irritant to eyes, skin and/or respiratory system; 9 Possible carcinogen; 10 Possible teratogen; 11 Possible mutagen

1. Source: British Agrochemicals Association Ltd booklet, *Directory of Garden Chemicals*.
2. Source: Soil Association.

MOSS KILLERS

The chemical hazards in proprietary brands

Trade name and supplier[1]	Description and suppliers' recommendations for use[1]	Chemicals they contain[1]	Problems and hazards (see key)[2]
Bio Moss Killer (**PBI**)	For control of moss, algae, lichen, on turf, paths, walls, and roofs	dichlorophen	3
Green Up Mossfree (**Synchemicals**)	Fast kill of moss on lawns	ferrous sulphate heptahydrate	5, 11 no data
Moss Gun (**ICI**)	Control of moss, algae, lichen on lawns, paths, drives and other hard surfaces	dichlorophen	3
Murphy Tumblemoss (**Fisons**)	To kill and prevent lawn moss and green up grass	chloroxuron ferric sulphate urea	8 no data no data

Key: 1 Banned/restricted outside the UK; 2 Dangerous to animals/birds; 3 Dangerous to fish; 4 Dangerous to bees/other insects; 5 Spraydrift problem and/or harmful to plants; 6 Persistence, Long or Medium; 7 Resistance developed in some pests; 8 Irritant to eyes, skin and/or respiratory system; 9 Possible carcinogen; 10 Possible teratogen; 11 Possible mutagen

1. Source: British Agrochemicals Association Ltd booklet, *Directory of Garden Chemicals.*
2. Source: Soil Association.

lawn with poultry manure (from your nearest chicken farm) or dried sewage sludge (often available from your local sewage works). Alternatives are concentrated animal manures and dried blood, fishmeal or bonemeal.

Pest control: First, 'weeds'. Don't let the chemical companies persuade you that an all-grass lawn is essential. If you are prepared to accept a certain amount of diversity in the plants which live in your lawn, you can cut your garden chemical bill substantially. This diversity will also support more wildlife, which can help cut pest problems in the rest of your garden.

Common lawn pests include 'leather jackets' (crane fly larvae) and chafer grubs. The best way to control leather jackets, which feed on grass roots and cause yellowing or browning of your

LAWN WEEDKILLERS

The chemical hazards in proprietary brands

Trade name and supplier[1]	Description and suppliers' recommendations for use[1]	Chemicals they contain[1]	Problems and hazards (see key)[2]
Bio Lawn Weedkiller (**PBI**)	Liquid lawn weed control	2,4-D	1, 3, 5, 8, 9, 10
		dicamba	3, 5, 8, 11
Boots Lawn Weedkiller	Liquid control for a broad spectrum of lawn weeds	2,4-D	1, 3, 5, 8, 9, 10
		dichlorprop	3, 5, 8
		mecoprop	5, 8
Fisons Lawn Spot Weeder	Foaming aerosol for spot treatment of most lawn weeds	2,4-D	1, 3, 5, 8, 9, 10
		dicamba	3, 5, 8, 11
Green Up Weedfree Lawn Weedkiller (**Synchemicals**)	Most common lawn weeds	2,4-D	1, 3, 5, 8, 9, 10
		dicamba	3, 5, 8, 11
Verdone 2 Spot Weeder (**ICI**)	Aerosol, isolated weeds of small weedy patches in lawns	2,4-D	1, 3, 5, 8, 9, 10
		mecoprop	5, 8
Supertox Lawn Weed Spray (**May & Baker**)	Liquid for control of broad spectrum of weeds in lawns	2,4-D	1, 3, 5, 8, 9, 10
		mecoprop	5, 8

Key: 1 Banned/restricted outside the UK; 2 Dangerous to animals/birds; 3 Dangerous to fish; 4 Dangerous to bees/other insects; 5 Spraydrift problem and/or harmful to plants; 6 Persistence, Long or Medium; 7 Resistance developed in some pests; 8 Irritant to eyes, skin and/or respiratory system; 9 Possible carcinogen; 10 Possible teratogen; 11 Possible mutagen

1. Source: British Agrochemicals Association Ltd booklet, *Directory of Garden Chemicals*.
2. Source: Soil Association.

lawn, is to ensure that the lawn is properly drained. Rolling the ground in the spring helps to discourage chafer grubs, which otherwise cause small patches of grass to die.

If you find you have moles, and you are not prepared to put up with them, we don't know of a cruelty-free cure. Smoke, or placing slates across their tunnels usually only diverts them elsewhere in the garden. We would like to hear of any tried and tested methods.

Worms: Many gardeners consider worms to be pests in lawns, because of the surface 'casts' they produce. These can simply be raked away — no organic gardener would countenance any approach designed to kill or discourage worms.

Manures

You can buy a range of pre-packed, bulky organic manures, although to get truly organic ones you are probably going to have to travel far afield. The National Centre for Organic Gardening offers *Cowpact* (compressed cow pats, with one bag sufficient to cover 160 square yards) and *Super Natural*. Alternatively, make an arrangement with your nearest farm or stables. But remember that the manure may contain chemical residues from the animals' diet, in which case it will not be 'organic'. These residues will diminish the longer you leave it standing.

Mulching

Weeds can be kept down by covering the earth around plants with compost or other 'mulching' materials. Avoid plastic mulches: use biodegradable mulching materials like straw, forest bark or even newspaper. One commercial mulching product widely sold in garden centres is *Hortopaper*, made from compressed peat (see Peat) and cellulose. The product certainly helps to keep weeds down, but it has its drawbacks: it is unsightly. It is also unsuitable for exposed sites and spring-planted crops. Another alternative is to grow 'green manure' plants (dug in later to fertilize the soil) on beds that will be empty for a time. The crop you choose will depend partly on the length of time the ground is going to be fallow, but examples are alfalfa (lucerne), broad bean (both nitrogen-fixing) and mustard (which is not nitrogen-fixing).

Mushroom compost

Mushroom farms used to be a tremendous source of used compost, but as the industry has taken off it has become much harder to find mushroom composts which do not contain high levels of chalk and insecticide residues. If you can track down an organic mushroom grower, it may be worth paying over the odds for his (or her) spent compost.

Paths

Be wary of path weedkillers. The organic alternatives are hand weeding and hoeing. *In extremis*, use a flame gun.

WEED CONTROLS FOR PATHS, DRIVES AND UNCULTIVATED AREAS

The chemical hazards in proprietary brands

Trade name and supplier[1]	Description and suppliers' recommendations for use[1]	Chemicals they contain[1]	Problems and hazards (see key)[2]
Atlacide Extra Dusting Powder (**Chipman**)	Non-selective weed control on garden paths, drives and patios	sodium chlorate	5, 6L, 8, 11
		atrazine	2, 3, 4, 5, 6L, 7, 8, 11
Boots Long-Lasting Weedkiller	Long-term weed control in paths and drives	aminotriazole	5, 7, 8, 9, 10, 11
		atrazine	2, 3, 4, 5, 6L, 7, 8, 11
Boots Sodium Chlorate Weedkiller	For total weed control on paths, drives and wasteland	sodium chlorate fire depressant	5, 6L, 8, 11
Fisons Path Weedkiller	Control of all weeds on paths for a full season	aminotriazole	5, 7, 8, 9, 10, 11
		MCPA (sodium salt)	3, 5, 8, 10
		simazine	4, 5, 6L, 7, 8, 11
Hytrol (**Agrichem**)	Total weed control on paths, drives and non-cultivated areas for two seasons	aminotriazole	5, 7, 8, 9, 10, 11
		2,4-D (sodium salt)	1, 3, 5, 8, 9, 10
		diuron	no data
		simazine	4, 5, 6L, 7, 8, 11

WEED CONTROLS FOR PATHS AND DRIVES (continued)

ICI Sodium Chlorate	Weed control on paths, drives and wasteland	sodium chlorate	5, 6L, 8, 11
Murphy Path Weedkiller (**Fisons**)	Liquid for control of weeds on paths and drives	aminotriazole	5, 7, 8, 9, 10, 11
		atrazine	2, 3, 4, 5, 6L, 7, 8, 11
Pathclear (**ICI**)	Soluble grains for weed control on paths and drives	aminotriazole	5, 7, 8, 9, 10, 11
		diquat	2, 6L, 8, 10
		paraquat	1, 2, 5, 8, 10, 11
		simazine	4, 5, 6L, 7, 8, 11
Super Weedex (**Fisons**)	Weeds in paths and drives	aminotriazole	5, 7, 8, 9, 10, 11
		simazine	4, 5, 6L, 7, 8, 11
Total Weed (**May & Baker**)	Weeds in paths, drives and hard surfaces	simazine	4, 5, 6L, 7, 8, 11
		aminotriazole	5, 7, 8, 9, 10, 11
		ammonium thiocyanate	no data

Key: 1 Banned/restricted outside the UK; 2 Dangerous to animals/birds; 3 Dangerous to fish; 4 Dangerous to bees/other insects; 5 Spraydrift problem and/or harmful to plants; 6 Persistence, Long or Medium; 7 Resistance developed in some pests; 8 Irritant to eyes, skin and/or respiratory system; 9 Possible carcinogen; 10 Possible teratogen; 11 Possible mutagen

1. Source: British Agrochemicals Association Ltd booklet, *Directory of Garden Chemicals*.
2. Source: Soil Association.

Peat

Peat helps the soil's structure, but it comes from wetlands which are generally best left as they are. The raised bogs from which much peat is extracted have taken thousands of years to develop, growing by as little as one millimetre a year. They are important wildlife habitats and their destruction tends to be irreparable.

Widely used as a soil conditioner and 'fertilizer', peat is actually very poor in plant nutrients. It breaks down rapidly in the soil, disappearing within a year or two. Acceptable alternatives include **ICI**'s composted *Forest Bark*. **Camland Products** also do a good range of composted bark, including fine grades which can be used to replace some of the peat used in potting compost. Alternatively, use compost (see Compost and Grobags).

Pest and disease control

Once you have decided to abandon synthetic garden chemicals, the next step is to learn how to control pests and disease the organic way. Here are some guidelines:

- Don't try to force plants to grow in situations that don't suit them. A rose grown against a house, where it will be short of water, will inevitably suffer from mildew.

- If you know you have a particular pest or disease in your garden, try to find plants which are naturally resistant. Buy certified virus-free stock when planting soft fruit or potatoes. Be wary of accepting plants from other gardeners — they may be the horticultural equivalent of the Trojan Horse.

- Don't plant large 'monocultures' — mix your plants. Gardeners have long believed, for example, that if you plant marigolds alongside carrots or potatoes, you can control pests like carrot fly or eel worm

- Make sure you sow seed or plant seedlings at the right time. Vigorous growth is often a plant's best defence. Plant too early and your plants will be unnecessarily vulnerable.

- Identify your problem. The more you know about the pest or disease which is damaging your plants, the less likely it is that you will use the wrong garden chemical. Often you will find that the problem will solve itself. The bean weevil, for example, eats notches out of broad bean leaves, but beans normally grow so fast that there is no danger to the crop.

- Pests such as caterpillars and sawfly larvae can often simply be picked off by hand. Diseased leaves, fruit and other plant material should be cleared away. In this case, you may need to resort to a bonfire, to ensure sterilization of material you may wish to return to the garden. The ash can be added to the compost heap.

- Whatever you grow, encourage natural pest and disease controls. The best way to do this is to provide habitats and food plants for some of the insects and other creatures which prey on pests. A small pond could provide a home for toads and frogs, whose diet includes slugs (see Slugs and Snails). Attract birds by providing nesting sites (bird boxes, hedges and space behind climbers) and winter food (leave ornamental plants to go to seed and provide food dispensers). Grow hardy annuals like *Limnanthes douglassi* (the 'poached egg' plant) and *Convolvulus tricolor*, which provide food for the hoverflies whose larvae consume large numbers of greenfly, blackfly and other aphids.

- Introduce biological controls (See Biological Controls).

- Protect crops with a physical barrier. The Green Consumer will probably not buy plastic 'pop' bottles, but one idea is to collect everyone else's plastic lemonade bottles and saw them in half. The ends can then be used as mini-cloches for seedlings. Use old carpet underlay around the base of your brassicas, which will help confuse the cabbage root fly.

- If, after all this, a particular pest gets out of hand and you feel you have to use a chemical spray, the National Centre for Organic Gardening recommends a small number of chemicals, including pyrethrum and borax.

GENERAL INSECTICIDES

The chemical hazards in proprietary brands

Trade name and supplier[1]	Description and suppliers' recommendations for use[1]	Chemicals they contain[1]	Problems and hazards (see key)[2]
Bio Long-last (**PBI**)	For the control of all foliar pests in the garden	dimethoate permethrin	1, 2, 3, 4, 6M, 7, 8, 11 3, 4, 5, 8, 9
Boots Garden Insect Spray	As an aerosol general insecticide	gamma-HCH piperonyl butoxide pyrethrins	1, 2, 3, 4, 5, 6M – L, 9, 10 9 no data
Crop Saver (**PBI**)	Control of insects on vegetables	permethrin malathion	3, 4, 5, 8, 9 3, 4, 5, 6M, 7, 8, 10
House Plant Pest Killer (**Synchemicals**)	General purpose insecticide on houseplants	pyrethrum resmethrin	6M, 8 3, 4, 6M
Murphy Pest and Disease Smoke (**Fisons**)	For control of greenhouse pests and disease	gamma-HCH tecnazene	1, 2, 3, 4, 5, 6M – L, 9, 10 1, 3, 5, 6M, 7, 8, 9
Py Powder (**Synchemicals**)	An insecticide in the home and garden	pyrethrum piperonyl butoxide	6M, 8 9
Waspend (**ICI**)	An aerosol spray for the control of flying and crawling insects in the home	pirimiphos-methyl synergised pyrethrins	3, 4, 6M, 8, 11 no data

Key: 1 Banned/restricted outside the UK; 2 Dangerous to animals/birds; 3 Dangerous to fish; 4 Dangerous to bees/other insects; 5 Spraydrift problem and/or harmful to plants; 6 Persistence, Long or Medium; 7 Resistance developed in some pests; 8 Irritant to eyes, skin and/or respiratory system; 9 Possible carcinogen; 10 Possible teratogen; 11 Possible mutagen

1. Source: British Agrochemicals Association Ltd booklet, *Directory of Garden Chemicals*.
2. Source: Soil Association.

Potting compost

Among the brands to look for are *Turning Worms*, *Super Natural* house plant compost and *Cowpost* — all of which are available from the National Centre for Organic Gardening. (See Manures and Worms)

Seeds

Picking the right seeds and plants is half the battle in organic gardening. There are a growing range of organically grown seeds. The National Centre for Organic Gardening shop sells *Atlas* organic seeds. (See also Wildflower Seeds.)

Slugs and snails

Organic products aimed at slugs and snails are: *Fertosan Slug Powder* (from **Chase Organics**, **Fertosan** and **Henry Doubleday Research Association**), *Septico Slug Killer* (**Cumulus Organics**), **Pelco Products'** *Slug Beer Trap* and *Slug Pub*, and **Langdon**'s *Slug Jug Trap* and **Impregnated Tape's** *Slug Tape*.

One well-proven cure which you can try at no cost involves burying an empty half grapefruit skin in the ground, to make a small pond which is then partly filled with beer. Expect to find a skin-full of inebriated and/or drowned slugs and snails in the morning.

Natural predators which help control slugs — and to a lesser extent snails — include birds, frogs, toads, hedgehogs, centipedes, the carnivorous slug (*Testacella haliotidea*) and slow-worms (*Anguis fragilis*).

SLUG, SNAILS AND WORM CONTROLS

The chemical hazards in proprietary brands

Trade name and supplier[1]	Description and suppliers' recommendations for use[1]	Chemicals they contain[1]	Problems and hazards (see key)
Autumn Toplawn (**PBI**)	For control of worms and leatherjackets in lawns	carbaryl and fertilizer	3, 4, 6M, 7, 8, 9, 10, 11
Boots Slug Destroyer Pellets	For the control of slugs and snails	metaldehyde	2, 3, 4
Chlordane 25 (**Synchemicals**)	Worm killer for lawns	chlordane	no data
Fisons Slug and Snail Killer	To control slugs and snails	metaldehyde	2, 3, 4
ICI Mini Slug Pellets	To control slugs and snails	metaldehyde	2, 3, 4
Murphy Slugit Liquid (**Fisons**)	To control slugs and snails	metaldehyde	2, 3, 4
Slug Guard (**PBI**)	To control slugs, snails, leatherjackets, millipedes and woodlice	methiocarb	2, 3, 4
Slug Mini Pellets (**PBI**)	To control slugs and snails	metaldehyde	2, 3, 4

Key: 1 Banned/restricted outside the UK; 2 Dangerous to animals/birds; 3 Dangerous to fish; 4 Dangerous to bees/other insects; 5 Spraydrift problem and/or harmful to plants; 6 Persistence, Long or Medium; 7 Resistance developed in some pests; 8 Irritant to eyes, skin and/or respiratory system; 9 Possible carcinogen; 10 Possible teratogen; 11 Possible mutagen

1. Source: British Agrochemicals Association Ltd booklet, *Directory of Garden Chemicals*.
2. Source: Soil Association.

Trees

Dutch Elm Disease, modern farming methods, and the hurricane of October 1987 have helped denude many parts of Britain of trees. Plant trees wherever you can, and stick to native species (which are preferred by wildlife) wherever possible.

One exception, however, must be the elm. Following the loss of more than 15 million elms in Britain, **Pitney Bowes** (a firm supplying mailing, business and retail systems) launched its 'Elms across Europe' initiative in 1979. This was designed to promote the planting of new elm species which are resistant to Dutch Elm Disease. Young trees of the *Sapporo Autumn Gold* disease-resistant elm can be ordered from Pitney Bowes. Check current prices, but as a rough guide a single elm cost £2.04 in late 1987, with 50 or more priced at £1.80 per tree. Postage and packaging was extra.

Watering

The average garden sprinkler uses 200 gallons (910 litres) of water an hour. The more water you use, the more likely it is that unspoiled valleys will have to be flooded for reservoirs. Consider planting a 'drought garden', or at least choose plants which are not unduly thirsty.

To show what the gardener can do to cut down on the average garden's thirst, Anglian Water has planted a 'drought garden' near Rutland Water, the largest man-made lake in Europe. This project was partly undertaken to defuse local concern about the flooding of the valley — and to show that we are all to blame for such environmental losses. 'If only a percentage of our customers vary their gardening techniques,' Anglian Water's Kate Godley explained, 'this will go a long way towards relieving the extra demand on water supplies, especially in dry periods.'

The drought garden contains over 150 species of attractive trees, shrubs and other plants that need very little water. They range from acid loving plants, such as rhododendrons and heather, to alpine plants like anemone, antenaria and semper-vivum. Thyme, camomile and fennel are amongst a wide variety of herbs which have been flourishing in the garden.

Weeds

Hand weeding, hoeing and mulching are the organic answers to weeds. Use natural mulching materials, which will bio-degrade readily when their useful life is over. A small number

CONTROLLING WEEDS
AMONGST FLOWERS AND VEGETABLES
The chemical hazards in proprietary brands

Trade name and supplier[1]	Description and suppliers' recommendations for use[1]	Chemicals they contain[1]	Problems and hazards (see key)[2]
Casoron G4 (**Synchemicals**)	For use in rosebeds and shrubberies, as well as for total weed control on paths, drives etc	dichlobenil	3, 5, 7
Couch and Grass Killer (**Synchemicals**)	Control of couch grass and other annual perennial grasses in ornamentals, fruit and vegetables	dalapon	5, 8
Herbon Dalapon (**Atlas**)	Weed control in fruit, flowers and shrubs	dalapon	5, 8
Herbon Garden Herbicide (**Atlas**)	Control annual weeds and grasses in garden vegetables, bulbs, herbaceous corms, shrubs and trees	propham chlorpropham diuron residual	no data no data no data
Weed Out (**May & Baker**)	Control of couch and other perennial grasses amongst growing plants	alloxydim sodium	7, 8
Weedex (**Fisons**)	Weed control in paths, drives, roses and certain fruit trees, shrubs and vegetables	simazine	4, 5, 6L, 7, 8, 11
Weedol (**ICI**)	Control of weeds amongst flowers, shrubs, fruit and vegetables	diquat paraquat	2, 6L, 8, 10 1, 2, 5, 8, 10, 11

Key: 1 Banned/restricted outside the UK; 2 Dangerous to animals/birds; 3 Dangerous to fish; 4 Dangerous to bees/other insects; 5 Spraydrift problem and/or harmful to plants; 6 Persistence, Long or Medium; 7 Resistance developed in some pests; 8 Irritant to eyes, skin and/or respiratory system; 9 Possible carcinogen; 10 Possible teratogen; 11 Possible mutagen

1. Source: British Agrochemicals Association Ltd booklet, *Directory of Garden Chemicals*.
2. Source: Soil Association.

of commercial mulching materials are also now available. Wherever possible, however, use your own compost. Ground cover plants can also help eliminate the need for weeding. (See also under Mulching.)

Wild flower seeds

Once wild flowers would have been hoed or sprayed to the ground. Remember, though, that wild plants are not only beautiful to the eye but can also attract wildlife into your garden — helping to keep many pest species at bay.

Suffolk Herbs include a wide range of wild flowers in their catalogue. John Stevens, who runs the firm with his wife Caroline, recommends the following wild flowers to gardeners making their first steps in wild flower gardening: the corncockle (*Agrostemma githago*), cowslip (*Primula veris*), the crane's-bill family (*Geraniaceae*), greater knapweed (*Centaurea scabiosa*), greater stitchwort (*Stellaria holostea*), harebell (*Campanula rotundifolia*), musk mallow (*Malva moschata*), primrose (*Primula vulgaris*), red campion (*Silene dioica*) and wood vetch (*Vicia sylvatica*). Other suppliers of wild flower seeds include: **Lynn Houseplants**, the **Rural Protection Association**, and **Kevan Chambers**.

Worms

The humble worm is one of the organic gardener's most important allies. Worms aerate the soil, so expect problems if you succeed in killing them, as some people try to do, to keep their lawns free from worm casts.

To boost your garden's worm population, and fertility, you can now buy worms, worm eggs and worm-worked composts from a number of firms. Worm-worked materials boost plant growth by

If You Must Spray . . .

- Read the label on the product before you buy it. Check for particularly hazardous ingredients. If you are using an aerosol, track down CFC-free brands. Remember, too, that most accidents with chemicals in the garden involve the under-5s: store garden chemicals safely.

- Use only recommended dosage rates. Higher rates are wasteful, rarely improve pest control and can often lead to plant damage.

- Never mix two chemicals, unless the labels specifically tell you to do so. Wash out the mixer and sprayer before and after each spraying, to avoid accidental mixing of different chemicals. Be especially careful when changing from herbicides to insecticides or fungicides.

- If you spray from too close a range, you can damage plants. Visible wetting of plant foliage with aerosol sprays is neither necessary nor desirable.

- Do not spray in bright sunshine: this can lead to plant damage, even if you are only spraying water.

- If you are picking vegetables or fruit, check the pesticide application instructions to ensure that you leave a long enough interval between spraying and harvesting. If the instructions on the can or pack tell you to avoid touching or eating the plant or fruit for a period, the chances are that the chemical will be harmful to birds and other wildlife.

- NEVER dispose of surplus pesticides in or near ponds, watercourses, marshy areas or ditches. Don't discharge pesticides through garden drainage systems. If you must put them down the drain, use your internal drains, which are connected to the sewage treatment system. The government's current pesticides approval scheme means that they must be formulated so that they can be safely discharged in this way.

making nutrients more available to plants and improving the soil's water-holding capacity. The materials offered by **Turning Worms** are endorsed by the Soil Association. On a larger scale, **British Earthworm Technology** offers the *Lo-Tech Worm Bed* to enable enterprising farmers or smallholders to produce compost and worms.

USEFUL ADDRESSES

Blackwell Products, Unit 4, Riverside Industrial Estate, 150 River Way, London SE10 0BE. Tel: 01-854 1844

British Earthworm Technology, Harding Way, St Ives, Cambridge PE17 4WR. Tel: 0480 300144

Duraplast, Stone House, Old Woods, nr Bomere Heath, Shrewsbury SY4 3AX. Tel: 0939 290298

Hambleden Herbs, Henley-on-Thames, Oxfordshire. Tel: 0491 571598

Kevan Chambers, NPK, 542 Parrs Wood Road, East Didsbury, Manchester M20 0QA

Lynn Houseplants, Station Road, Terrington St Clement, King's Lynn, Norfolk PE34 4PL

National Council for the Conservation of Plants and Gardens, c/o RHS, Wisley Gardens, Woking, Surrey GU23 6QB

Pitney Bowes, The Pinnacles, Harlow, Essex CM19 5BD. Tel: 0279 37756

Rural Protection Association, The Old Police Station, Lark Lane, Liverpool 17

Soil Association, 86-88 Colston Street, Bristol BS1 5BB. Tel: 0272 290661

Tisara Bird Control Systems, 29 Bloomfield Road, Bath BA2 2AD

Turning Worms, Unit 42, Glan-yr-Afon Industrial Estate, Llandbadarn, Aberystwyth, Dyfed SY23 3JQ. Tel: 0970 617574

ORGANIC SUPPLIERS

Suppliers	Selected products and brands on offer	Availability
Battle, Haywood and Bower Victoria Chemical Works Crofton Drive Allenby Road Industrial Estate Lincoln Tel: 0522 29206	**Crop Protection** *Amcide; Bordeaux Mixture; Derris* dust; liquid Derris green-fly spray; **Other** A wide range of veterinary products and non-organic range.	**Mail Order** No **Other Remarks** Organic products available through HDRA and some other catalogues
Chase Organics (GB) Ltd Coombelands House Coombelands Lane Addlestone Weybridge KT15 1HY Tel: 0932 858511	**Seeds** Green manure seeds; grass mixtures; undressed seeds for plants and vegetables. **Compost and Composting** *QR* organic compost activator; worm products; seed and potting composts; spent mushroom compost; comfrey plants. **Fertilizers** *SM3* seaweed extract; *Biolan Extra* plant food sticks; bone meal; hoof and horn fertilizer; cofuna and others. **Crop Protection** *Bactospeine, Bordeaux Mixture, Derris* dust and liquid Derris, *Fertosan* slug powder, pyrethrum, *Savona* aphid soap, *Amcide* (safest weedkiller).	**Mail Order** Yes **Other Remarks** Catalogue is comprehensive and gives explanations about the products and uses. Some products are available through a limited number of shops, including HDRA.
Cumulus Organics & Conservation Ltd Two Mile Lane Highnam Gloucester GL2 8DW Tel: 0452 305814	**Organic Produce** A wide range of organic products. **Seeds** Non-treated vegetable and herb seeds. **Composts and Composting** *Stimgro* range; rose food; mushroom compost. **Fertilizers** Blood; calcified seaweed; hoof and horn; pure blood; fish and bone; foliar feed. **Crop Protection** Derris dust and spray, *Septico* slug killer, *Bactospeine, Bordeaux Mixture, Amcide* weed killer. **Other Products** Some equipment.	**Mail Order** Yes **Other Remarks** Also available through other organic suppliers.

ORGANIC SUPPLIERS (continued)

Suppliers	Selected products and brands on offer	Availability
Fertosan Products Ltd 2 Holborn Square Lower Transmere Birkenhead Merseyside L41 9HQ	**Crop Protection** Fertosan slug and snail killer (not organic, but used by some organic gardeners). **Compost and Composting** Compost makers.	**Mail Order** No **Other Remarks** Available from Chase Organics and HDRA
Henry Doubleday Research Association (HDRA Ltd) National Centre for Organic Gardening Ryton-on-Dunsmore Coventry CV8 3LG Tel: 0203 303517	**Organic Produce** Most organic produce that is on the market is available through HDRA. **Seeds** A wide range of seeds, including some undressed ones. **Compost and Composting** Cowpact, Super Natural organic compost, Turning Worms products, seed compost and potting compost. **Fertilizers** Maxicrop liquid seaweed; blood, fish and bonemeal; bonemeal; calcified seaweed; gypsum; hoof and horn fertilizer; organic complete fertilizer; rock phosphate; rock potash; seaweed meal. **Crop Protection** Bactospeine, Bordeaux Mixture; Derris; pyrethrum; Fertosan slug killer and Savona soap. **Other Products** A wide range of vegetables including rare species. Also a large selection of books on gardening and a range of booklets with specific information on organic alternatives.	**Mail Order** Yes **Other Remarks** There is a shop on the premises which sells a wide range of organic produce, including wines and vegetables. There is a canteen which serves organically grown food (including meat) and wines. **Membership** HDRA membership includes: magazines with organic gardening advice and developments; details of local groups; a newsletter; advice if you write in; free admission to Ryton Gardens; access to rare vegetable varieties; and the use of HDRA reference library.

E.W. King & Co. Ltd
Monks Farm
Pantlings Lane
Coggeshall Road
Kelvedon
Essex CO5 9PG
Tel: 0376 70000

Seeds Large supplier of undressed seed.

Mail Order Yes
Other Remarks Available from them directly and: HDRA, Chase Organics, Suffolk Herbs.
Main Garden Centres also sell the seed, but the packets do not indicate whether they are dressed or not. Dressed and undressed seeds are not identified in their catalogue.

Koppert (UK) Ltd
PO Box 43
Tunbridge Wells
Kent TN2 5BY
Tel: 0892 36607

Crop Protection *Savona* (aphid control); *Anstrip* (white-fly control); *Spidex* (parasitic predators to spiders).

Mail Order Not direct
Other Remarks Chief outlets are HDRA (Savona only) and by mail order: Chase Organics, Unwin Seeds, Cumulus Organics, Kent Garden Centre, Arable Bulb and Seed Company. Not generally available through garden centres.

Stimgro Ltd
Bridge House
High Street
Tonbridge
Kent TN9 1DR
Tel: 0732 364322

Fertilizers *Maxicrop* range, including two organic products: Maxicrop seaweed extract and Maxicrop calcified seaweed. Others do not meet organic standards because they have added nutrients: Maxicrop tomato fertilizer; Maxicrop complete garden feed; Maxicrop houseplant food; Maxicrop moss killer and lawn tonic.
Compost and Composting *Stimgro* range, including: Stimgro organic cow manure; Stimgro organic rose food; Stimgro organic multi-purpose compost; and Stimgro organic lawn food and dressing.

Mail Order No
Other Remarks Widely available

ORGANIC SUPPLIERS (continued)

Suppliers	Selected products and brands on offer	Availability
Suffolk Herbs Sawyers Farm Little Cornard Sudbury Suffolk CO10 0NY Tel: 078722 7247	**Herbs** Organic herbs. **Seeds** For herb lawns; wild flower seeds (native and naturalized wild flowers and mixtures for conservation); useful plants 'to attract predators and repel pests'. **Composts and Composting** Herbal compost activator;concentrated organic dung; blood fish and bone; bone meal; Dolomite lime; SM3 liquid seaweed extract and others. **Fertilizers** *Farmura; Marinure;* seaweed meal; QR. **Crop Protection** Bordeaux Mixture; *Derris; Fertosan; Py* powder and spray; *Savona; Septico* slug killer.	**Mail Order** Yes **Other Remarks** Many products available from other organic suppliers.

THE GARAGE

Traffic jams and pollution have been around since horse-drawn days when tonnes of ripe dung lay about in the streets, giving off clouds of methane gas. But with an estimated 500 *million* motor vehicles now in use world-wide, some 350 million of them cars, the stresses on the environment are growing rapidly. Not long ago it seemed that only distant cities like Los Angeles and Tokyo suffered from traffic smog. Now this yellowy haze can also sometimes be seen in Britain and even in West Germany, where they have done much to curb car pollution.

Not surprisingly, some cities have begun to lose patience with the car. Rome declared large areas of the historic centre of the city off-limits to the car for a whole day — albeit with little success. Meanwhile, across the border in Switzerland, Lucerne's city council voted to buy five bicycles for civil servants, to replace their chauffeur-driven cars.

Cycles, in fact, are the most energy-efficient form of locomotion yet invented, although hang-gliding and solar-powered aircraft like the *Solar Challenger*, which flew across the Channel, must also be leading contenders in the energy-efficiency stakes. A touring bike can carry ten times its own weight — and runs 1600 km (1,000 miles) on a thimbleful of oil.

Ironically, the use of bicycles has declined considerably in recent years, despite their image as *the* green mode of transport. A key reason has been the high accident rates suffered by cyclists forced to share road space with cars, buses and lorries.

Public transport

Public transport, usually a more fuel-efficient and environment-friendly way of travelling, has been languishing in the Age of the Car. Bus and rail services have both been declining. The number of journeys made by rail passengers in Britain fell by almost 10 per cent between 1980 and 1986–7, from 760 million to 689 million, and the rail network shrank by more than 5 per cent over the same period, from 17,645 km to 16,670 km (11,030 miles to 10,420 miles). In 1985–6, buses or coaches carried some 5.6 billion passengers on local services in Great Britain, down 21 per cent on the 1976 figure.

Although travelling by rail is energy-efficient, unfortunately this is not the only consideration for the traveller. Reliability and convenience also count. Over the past 25 years, as a result, we have made increasing use of the two most energy-intensive forms of travel. These are the private car and air travel.

The Rise of Road Travel

- By 1985, 9 out of 10 km travelled by passengers in Britain were travelled by road.

- The distance covered by all motor vehicles reached nearly 300 billion km (187.5 billion miles) in 1986, of which some 100 billion km (62.5 billion miles) were attributed to road haulage.

- Partly as a result, public transport fares have soared, while the standard of service has often fallen.

The move towards fewer, bigger shopping centres, work-places, hospitals and schools has further fuelled the rise of car ownership. It also further disadvantages those who do not have access to a car. At the same time, the shift of much of Britain's freight traffic from rail to road has both accelerated the decline of the railway system and increased congestion on the road network. In addition to the accidents they cause, and the noise and air pollution they create, heavy lorries cause an estimated £600

TRANSPORT: FACTS YOU NEED TO KNOW

Mode of transport	Passenger kilometres in 1961 (1000 million)[1]	Passenger kilometres in 1985 (1000 million)[1]	% of energy consumed in the transport sector 1985 (excluding freight)
	142	432	80 (cars, buses and coaches)
	67	42	
	39	36	2
	1[5]	4[5]	15[5]
	10	5	

1. Source: Department of Transport Central Statistical Office.
2. Prices at a constant 1980 equivalent.
3. Expenditure on transport as a percentage of total consumer expenditure: 1963 = 11.3 per cent; 1985 = 15.4 per cent.

Consumer expenditure per head on transport (£s per week 1980 prices) 1963[2][3]	Consumer expenditure per head on transport (£s per week 1980 prices) 1985[4]	% of total freight carried in 1985
£2.43	£5.97	
£0.91	£0.46	
		60
£0.37	£0.39	8.8[6]

4. Prices at a constant 1980 equivalent.
5. Domestic scheduled journeys only.
6. Down from 15 per cent in 1975.

million worth of damage to Britain's roads and bridges every year.

Anyone who wants to see more investment in a green future should support public transport — and lobby public transport operators to ensure that standards of service are raised. Operators must recognize, however, that they cannot rely on the automatic support of Green Consumers: they must compete for their custom with services which are convenient, cost-competitive and pleasant to use.

Government support is essential to ensure that public transport can operate competitively. Transport 2000, an umbrella lobbying group composed of environmental and transport organizations, stresses that the Government should recognize the importance of public transport by:

- Removing the distortions in the tax system — such as company cars, and low taxes on the heaviest lorries — which unreasonably favour the private motorist and the road haulier. It is estimated that company car 'perks' cost Britain more than half as much again as all subsidies for all forms of public transport. The situation has improved somewhat since the March 1988 budget, however.

- Providing more support for local bus and rail fares, and more investment to bring local public transport up to the best continental standards.

- Recognizing the importance of walking and cycling by supporting the provision of safe, convenient and pleasant facilities for pedestrians and cyclists.

- Ensuring that new developments are planned in such a way that people do not need to own a car.

- Encouraging industry to locate near rail and water freight networks, so that they can be used cheaply and easily.

Company Cars: A Polluting Perk

Firms first began to give their employees cars, on a large scale, in the 1970s, not to make business more efficient but to exploit tax concessions and bypass Government pay restraint policies.

This wheeze has developed into a £2 billion-a-year annual subsidy for private motoring. About 45 per cent of new cars are now registered in company names, although it is estimated that nearly 60 per cent of new cars may effectively be company cars.

Given that around two million of Britain's cars, or one in eight of the total, are company cars, the well-respected transport consultancy TEST have estimated that company cars account for about 20 per cent of vehicle exhaust emissions in Britain. If you are offered a company car, ask your employer for the cleanest model on the market — and suggest that everyone is at least offered the option.

The Car

We all want to go back to Nature, as the saying goes, but we want to go back in a car. The number of new cars sold reached a record 12.37 million in Europe in 1987, up 6 per cent on the previous year. In the UK, there were 18.5 million new cars on the road (one for every three people of all ages), 15 per cent of households owned at least two vehicles and the car accounted for about 80 per cent of the average family's weekly transport expenditure.

When assessing the environmental effects of a car there are four particular issues which the Green Consumer should consider:

Losing ground

On the basis of Friends of the Earth estimates that each mile of motorway takes up at least 26 acres of land, it looks as though Britain has lost nearly 50,000 acres (200 sq km) of land under motorways. By 1986, Britain had some 374,000 km (233,750 miles) of road of all classes, of which 2,956 km (1,847 miles) were trunk motorways. The car, whether we like it or not, is one of the key factors which has shaped — and continues to reshape — our world.

Newer motorways, like London's M25, consume even larger areas — because of their design and, particularly in the M25's case, their greater number of intersections. But even much smaller roads can cause major controversy, where they run through environmentally sensitive areas.

Fuel efficiency

Consumer pressure has been a key factor behind the trend towards more fuel-efficient cars. Fifteen years ago, with the world still reeling from the shock of the first OPEC oil crisis, the motor industry was slowly forced to recognize that it would have to junk its gas-guzzlers and produce more thrifty cars. Its eventual success is reflected by the fact that the total amount of vehicle fuels consumed in the leading car-producing nations fell by 4 per cent between 1972 and 1982, even though the number of cars in use jumped by a third. But we still need enormous quantities of fuel to keep us on the move:

- Some 2.8 billion tonnes of oil and oil products, including petrol, are used in Britain each year, half for transport.

- Even today, the average car takes the energy equivalent of 1,500 litres (335 gallons) of oil to manufacture and uses at least 10,000 litres (2,250 gallons) of fuel before it is scrapped or dumped.

The fuel efficiency of new cars is now a key selling point and car designers have achieved a great deal in the fuel efficiency field. The car industry's challenge for the 1990s will be both to maintain (and improve upon) these achievements and simultaneously to produce cars that are safer, cleaner, quieter and longer lasting. The challenge for the Green Consumer will be to help persuade the industry that cleaner, quieter and longer-lasting cars are what the customer wants.

Pollution

As factories, power stations and other industrial sources of air pollution are cleaned up, motor vehicles have emerged as one of the worst offenders in all industrial nations. Despite tighter environmental regulations and improvements in fuel economy over the last 15 years, more people now own more cars, and drive them further each year. So, in spite of attempts to cut car emissions, the volume of most pollutants produced continues to grow. Cars produce five major forms of air pollution:

- **Hydrocarbons (HCs)**. These are largely responsible for the photochemical smogs which choke cities like Los Angeles. Such smogs can cause breathing distress, asthma attacks and help trigger heart failure. Road vehicles contribute about a quarter of Europe's total of 550,000 tonnes of HC emissions. Other major sources include industrial solvents and plants.

- **Nitrogen oxides (NOx)**. Produced by all combustion processes, from power stations to motor-scooters, NOx emissions are implicated in photochemical smogs and acid rain problems.

- **Carbon monoxide (CO)**. If you decide to commit suicide by channelling your car's exhaust emissions into your car or garage, it is the CO in those emissions which will kill you. Motor vehicles contribute about 83 per cent of total CO emissions in the UK, estimated at around 4.5 million tonnes. These emissions have increased by 15 per cent over the past decade because of increasing road traffic.

- **Particulates**. Road vehicles have overtaken the coal

fire as the major source of black smoke and particulates in urban areas. Black smoke not only affects visibility, but is also implicated in the onset of cancer and other diseases, and blackens buildings and clothes. Furthermore, it can cause extensive damage to plants. About 80 per cent of London's black smoke now comes from vehicles, with diesel-engined buses and taxis the main culprits.

● **Lead**. Among the most ubiquitous of pollutants, lead damages the brain and central nervous system. Children are particularly vulnerable because their nervous systems are still developing. Lead is the one pollutant where there is real hope for a reduction. Emissions from petrol-engined road vehicles fell from 7,400 tonnes in 1975 to 6,400 tonnes in 1985. A further 50 per cent cut followed the introduction of low-lead petrol.

What is being done — and what could be done — to control these pollutants?

Unleaded petrol

Petrol is a blend of up to 400 hydrocarbon chemicals. The exact recipe is juggled to produce varying levels of fuel economy or performance. Every litre of normal petrol that you put in your car contains a range of additives, including *lead* (used to stop your engine 'knocking' or 'pinking') and *lead scavengers* (which prevent the lead sticking inside the engine).

Lead was first added to petrol in the 1920s. As a lubricant, it also helps improve the durability of exhaust valves and seats. But lead in petrol inevitably meant lead in a car's exhaust emissions, and that meant lead — a great deal of it — in the environment.

Lead is highly toxic, particularly to pregnant mothers and children. Unfortunately, too, it does not break down naturally in the environment — which is why it is used to cover church roofs. The lead spewed from our exhausts each year simply adds to the lead already in the environment.

The British Government has already taken some important

steps to deal with this problem. In 1981, for example, it agreed that from 31 December 1985 the maximum amount of lead permitted in petrol should be cut by just over 60 per cent, from 0.4 to 0.15 grams per litre. At the time, the motor industry argued that if lead levels went any lower it would result in engine damage. New engines, however, have been designed to run without any lead whatsoever.

Following a strikingly effective campaign by the Campaign for Lead Free Air (CLEAR) to force the Government to introduce unleaded petrol, the UK helped push the European Community into ruling that all Member States should make unleaded petrol available by 1989 — and should encourage its widest use. In Britain, **Esso** has been the market leader in unleaded petrol.

In 1986, 5 per cent of European petrol sales were unleaded, but there were wide differences between countries. In West Germany, 80 per cent of filling stations were selling unleaded petrol. All Dutch filling stations had phased out regular leaded fuel. Nearly every station in Sweden, Norway, Denmark, Switzerland and Austria had an unleaded pump. But in Britain only 1 in 40 filling stations had an unleaded pump by late 1987 — and unleaded petrol then accounted for only 1 per cent of sales. In France, Belgium and Italy the position was even worse, with only 1 in 50 stations offering unleaded petrol.

As an incentive to the British consumer, the Government cut the price of unleaded fuel by 5p, to put it on an equal footing with ordinary low-lead petrol. Scandinavian countries, however, had made it cheaper, recognizing that the consumer had to go further afield for unleaded petrol. West Germany beat other EEC countries to the draw again when it banned all leaded two-star petrol from February 1988 — a move which would cut lead emissions by 2,000 tonnes a year. In the March 1988 budget, the British Government cut the duty on unleaded fuel further — so it is now *cheaper* than leaded fuel.

Consumers certainly should make the effort to find and buy unleaded petrol. Many potential suppliers are waiting to see if there is sufficient demand for the product. **JET Petrol**, for example, do not yet supply unleaded fuel in Britain — although they produce it for export.

JET carried out a survey early in 1988 which concluded that the

LEADING UK SUPPLIERS OF UNLEADED PETROL

	Number of sites selling unleaded Oct 1986[1]	Number of sites selling unleaded Oct 1987[1]	% of company's total sites selling unleaded in 1986	% of company's total sites selling unleaded in 1987	Total number of sites in 1987 (leaded/unleaded)[2]
Esso	92	155	3.18	5.55	2,794
Mobil	3	119	0.37	14.67	811
Texaco	24	101	1.82	7.66	1,318
Shell	0	56	0	1.85	3,026
BP	39	54	1.81	2.51	2,153
Fina	0	14	0	1.76	793
Gulf	0	5	0	1.47	341
Total	0	3	0	0.48	621

1. Figures exclude Northern Ireland which had 9 stations selling unleaded fuel in 1986 and 12 in 1987. Source: UK Petroleum Industry Association
2. Source: Mintel

information available to consumers was very inadequate. Significantly, the survey found that 55 per cent of motorists and a surprising 40 per cent of dealers' staff did not know whether their cars could run properly on unleaded fuel or, worse still, gave the wrong answer. Of the dealers who gave the right answer, a third took longer than five minutes to find the information. JET therefore concluded that it would not pay to convert the pumps at their 1,200 filling stations to supply unleaded until the public is better informed and demand picks up.

By early 1988, unleaded petrol was being sold at around 3 per cent of filling stations — and was being purchased by less than one half of 1 per cent of drivers. Yet 10 per cent of the cars then on the road could have run perfectly happily on unleaded fuel, while a further 15 per cent would have needed only a minor engine modification to enable them to do so.

Ironically, a survey reported by Which? at the same time found that two-thirds of motorists felt strongly that the use of unleaded petrol in new cars should be compulsory. Over three-quarters of drivers who had never used unleaded petrol said that they would if it cost the same as leaded petrol. It already did, of course, but most drivers still believed it cost more and there is no question that the car industry itself has been partly to blame. As the Which? survey concluded, 'you can't always rely on what dealers tell you about your car'.

The British Government announced in November 1987 that all new cars would use unleaded by October 1990. Junior Environment Minister Colin Moynihan also announced that the Government itself would order such cars in future. He had had his own private car, a **Ford** *Sierra*, converted to run on unleaded at a cost of just £13.50. The Prime Minister's **Jaguar** *4.2*, on the other hand, would only run on leaded fuel. Tackled on the subject, **Jaguar** said in late 1987 that its cars should be able to run on unleaded petrol 'in about 12 months'.

Senior Ministers had been issued with **Rover** *820*s or **Ford** *Granadas*, which could either use unleaded petrol or easily be converted to it. Junior Ministers, however, were using **Austin** *Montegos*, which could only run on leaded fuel.

Some Japanese manufacturers were already streets ahead of British manufacturers like Rover. **Honda**, for example, had announced in 1986 that all Hondas imported into the UK since 1972 could run on unleaded petrol. (Some models may need modifications.)

It is worth stressing that companies can also act as Green Consumers when buying their car fleets. But they should not expect an easy ride. The Body Shop, for example, operates a 'Buy British' policy and found that no British make of car suitable for its needs would run on unleaded fuel. Given that almost three-quarters of Britain's car fleet is made up of company cars, Green Consumers using — or about to be offered — a company car should lobby their employers to ensure that they take environmental considerations into account when choosing between competing models. A few more company fleet operators quizzing Rover on using lead-free fuel in its cars could make all the difference.

If you want to find out whether your current car — or preferred next buy — can run on unleaded petrol you should contact: **The Campaign for Lead Free Air (CLEAR)** (also provides free list of all UK filling stations offering unleaded petrol), or **The Society of Motor Manufacturers and Traders**. The **Department of Transport**'s new car fuel consumption booklet also tells you which car models take unleaded petrol.

Catalytic converters

A catalytic converter is a device which cleans up car exhaust emissions. In the tenth of a second that it takes exhaust hydrocarbons, carbon monoxide and nitrogen oxides to pass through an autocatalyst built into a car's exhaust system, 90 per cent are turned into less harmful carbon dioxide, nitrogen and water vapour.

Currently, catalytic converters are not used in Britain, although the world's leading manufacturer of autocatalysts is a

Should I switch to diesel?

Diesel cars are more energy efficient in urban conditions, and tend to last longer, but they also produce much of the dark smoke which can make walking around cities so unpleasant. About 80 per cent of the dark smoke in London's air comes from vehicles, most of it from diesel engines — particularly from buses, lorries and taxis.

Only 1–2 per cent of UK cars currently run on diesel, although around 4 per cent of new cars are diesels. Diesel engines normally emit much less carbon monoxide and hydrocarbons than petrol engines. They are also lead-free. But they produce more particulate pollution, smoke and odours, twice as much nitrogen oxides and six times more sulphur dioxides than petrol engines. There is concern, too, that substances called polycyclic aromatic hydrocarbons in diesel emissions could cause cancer. Diesels are also noisier.

Overall, however, diesels still come out well — as long as you are not involved in a great deal of motorway driving. But if you buy a diesel car, make sure it is regularly serviced. Big diesel vehicles like buses and lorries ought to be fitted with soot traps, while all diesel vehicles ought to be tested at least once a year to check their exhaust emissions. This is particularly true of buses, whose pollution output can be appalling!

Top-selling diesel cars in Britain are made by **Ford** (*Escort, Fiesta, Orion* and *Sierra*), **Peugeot** (*205, 305, 309*) and **Citroën** (*BX*).

UK company. One reason why the West Germans have been so quick to use unleaded petrol is that leaded fuel 'poisons' catalytic converters. Twenty per cent of new cars registered in Germany in 1987 were fitted with three-way catalysts.

There are three main types of autocatalyst:

- **Oxidation catalysts** are particularly effective in controlling carbon monoxide and hydrocarbons.

- **Three-way catalysts** provide the best way of simultaneously controlling hydrocarbon, carbon monoxide and nitrogen oxide emissions.

- **Diesel catalysts** help to control the hydrocarbon emissions which make diesel vehicles so odorous and smoky.

Under new EEC air pollution rules due to be enforced in Britain in the early 1990s, small cars (under 1.4 litres) will need retuning, medium cars (between 1.4 litres and 2.0 litres) will need simple oxidation autocatalysts, and larger cars (above 2.0 litres) will need full, three-way catalysts.

By the end of 1987, however, no British car sold in Britain had yet been fitted with an autocatalyst. Yet there were already over 100 catalyst-equipped West German car models. A key reason why West Germany decided to insist on the use of three-way catalysts was the growing evidence that hydrocarbons and nitrogen oxides from car exhausts are helping to destroy the country's forests. Faced with such evidence, German motorists bowed to the inevitable.

The first catalyst-equipped car on Britain's roads was Japanese, **Toyota**'s *Celica* GT-4, introduced in 1988. This was doubly ironic, given that a British company, Johnson Matthey Chemicals, is now the world's largest manufacturer of the catalytic converters which have been used to clean up car exhausts in the USA, Japan, West Germany, Sweden and Australia.

The cost of fitting an autocatalyst in Britain, if they were readily available, might be around £200 – £300. Yet in Europe companies like **Fiat**, **Volvo**, **Mercedes** and **Nissan** have begun to offer catalyst-equipped cars at no extra cost. Belatedly, **Rover** is now producing cars fitted with autocatalysts for the West German market.

Lean burn engines

The British motor industry dislikes catalytic converters. It argues that for smaller-engined (up to 2 litre) cars, so-called 'lean burn' technology will provide the best answer, both environmentally and economically. By using sophisticated electronics, improved engine management and modified cylinder heads, lean burn engines burn more air and less fuel. With the latest technology, up to 24 parts of air can be burned for every one part of fuel.

Lean burn engines not only cut carbon monoxide and hydrocarbon emissions, but are also typically between 10 per cent and 15 per cent more fuel-efficient. Catalytic converters, by contrast, involve a small energy penalty. The fuller combustion achieved in a lean burn engine results in the destruction of potential air pollutants. If lean burn engines are used on cars of 1.4 – 2.0 litres, however, they might actually *increase* the output of hydrocarbons and nitrogen oxides at higher speeds.

A test programme run by the West German motoring industry on **Peugeot**'s lean burn *1.6 GTI* and **Volkswagen**'s *Golf GTI* equipped with an autocatalyst found that at 19 – 25 mph (30 – 40 kph) the Peugeot produced 5 times more nitrogen oxides (NOx) and 30 times more hydrocarbons (HCs) than the VW, while at 90 kph (55 mph) it produced 240 times more NOx and 25 times more HCs. If all European vehicles of this size were to be fitted with such engines, NOx emissions could increase by 1.5 million tonnes a year, HC emissions by 500,000 tonnes and CO by 2.2 million tonnes.

Volvo, which has long pioneered in the 'clean car' field, has succeeded in meeting tough emission standards without having to install autocatalysts on many of its models. Exhaust gas recirculation is used on *200/700 Series* Volvos to cut NOx emissions. For cars sold in Sweden and West Germany, however, Volvo still has to use a three-way catalyst on its turbo models.

The conclusion: even if lean burn technology does become widely available, autocatalysts will still be needed on many models.

Low solvent paints

Painting a single car can involve the release of 12 – 15 litres (21 – 26 pints) of solvent into the atmosphere, helping to cause photochemical smogs and forest damage. This problem can be

Volvo: On the road to clean cars

Volvo has long had a reputation for designing safer cars. It has also invested a great deal of effort in producing cleaner cars. Most Volvos, for example, can run on unleaded petrol. The exceptions are the turbo models in the 200 and 700 ranges and the 240GL with the 200E engine.

Although in the UK in 1988 you couldn't buy a Volvo fitted with an autocatalyst, 70 per cent of the cars Volvo sold world-wide were fitted with autocatalysts. Because of Europe's later start in introducing unleaded petrol, only 40 per cent of Volvos sold in Europe were fitted with autocatalysts. The company says that it is 'just waiting for the broad introduction of unleaded petrol on the UK market in order to offer Volvo cars with catalytic converters'.

All silver metallic 200 and 700 range Volvos sold in Britain are painted with **ICI**'s *Aquabase* water-based paints. The company plans to use Aquabase on a growing proportion of its cars, including those with non-metallic colours. The use of Aquabase, which cuts solvent emissions, has also helped cut the overall quantities of paint used — bringing a further cut in solvent emissions.

Among other environmental improvements under way within Volvo, its manufacturing facilities are switching from oil to natural gas (cutting sulphur dioxide emissions by 80 per cent) and are using waste heat from a nearby BP refinery. Some of Volvo's own petrol stations are also being fitted with new pump nozzles which cut petrol vapour discharges by 95 per cent.

By no means finally, **Volvo Concessionaires** (who import Volvos to the UK market) have sponsored a number of rare breed survival projects. In return, the conservationists use Volvo estate cars when appearing at county shows!

cut by around 60 per cent if the Aquabase painting system, developed by **ICI**, is used. **Volvo**, in fact, was also the first car-maker in Europe to adopt this less polluting method of painting vehicles (see box). The company uses Aquabase on about 15 per cent of its output.

Instead of using conventional solvents, Aquabase provides a range of water-borne metallic paints. Although they take longer to dry, they provide an equally good finish and service life. Other manufacturers have been relatively slow on the uptake, although **GM Opel** and **Volkswagen** are planning to switch to Aquabase. British car manufacturers are less keen, because they are not building major new plants — and so find it difficult to incorporate the new drying facilities needed.

CFC-free aerosols

Garages sell a wide range of aerosols, from corrosion preventatives and de-icers, to engine starters, paints and polishes. Below is a selection of brands which are CFC-free.

DE-ICERS

Briggs	De-Icer
British Products	Sarmex Spray De-Icer
Domestic Fillers	Big D De-Icer
Duckhams	BP De-Icer
Duckhams	Duckhams De-Icer
E. R. Holloway	Gnome
Holt	Icemaster De-Icer
Holt	Turtle Wax Standard De-Icer
Hycote	De-Icer (Water-Free)
Hycote	De-Icer (Fast Action)
Spectra	De-Icer
Texaco	Windscreen De-Icer

ENGINE CLEANERS

Action Can	Action Can 2
Action Can	JPS Tune Up Formula
Briggs	Carb Cleaner
Briggs	Engine Lacquer
Briggs	Emulsifiable Degreaser
English Abrasives	Gunk Automotive Spray
English Abrasives	Gunk Foam

Holt	Foambrite
Holt	Spray DeCoker
Spectra	Engine Cleaner

ENGINE STARTERS

Briggs	Engine Start
Holt	Cold Start
Holt	Damp Start
Holt	Wet Start
Hycote	Start It
Keen	Keen Aquanol
Loctite UK	Loctite Permatex Engine Start
Spectra	Everstart
Spectra	OK Spray
Start-Pilot	Gasomatic
Start-Pilot	Viso-F (refill for Viso-F cold start unit)
Unipart International	Tech 2000 Wet Start

GLASS AND WINDSCREEN CLEANERS

Applied Chemicals	Hard Surface Cleaner
Briggs	Mixra
Dynaglaze	Glass Cleaner
Hycote	All Seasons Screen Wash
Hycote	Clear View Winter Screen Wash
Hycote	Glass & Screen Cleaner
Unipart International	Tech 2000 Glass Cleaner
Unipart International	Tech 2000 Anti Mist Spray

LUBRICANTS AND PENETRATING OIL

Action Can	WD40
Amway	Wonder Mist
Briggs	Loos'n It
Burmah-Castrol	DWF
Eezit	Eezit Penetrating Oil
English Abrasives	Plus Gas Formula A
Holt	Rubber Lubricant
Holt	Rustola Penetrating Oil Spray
E. R. Howard	3-in-1 Oil Spray
E. R. Howard	Expert
Hycote	Motor Chain Lube

Keen	Keen Aquanol
Loctite	Loctite Permatex D.L.F.
Loctite	Loctite Permatex Disc Brake Quiet
Simoniz	Workmate
Spectra	Liquid Spanner

POLISHES

Dynaglaze	Spray Polish
Dynaglaze	Back to Black
Holt	Turtle Wax Super Aerosol Wax
Keen	Keen Furniture Polish
Simoniz	Trim and Tyre Shine
Vauxhall	Silicospray

PRIMERS AND AUTO FINISHES

Briggs	Matt Black
Holt	Dupli-Color Autospray Touch Up
Holt	Dupli-Color Special Service
Holt	Dupli-Color Panel Spray
Hycote	Hammer Finishes
Hycote	Matched Colour Spray Paints
Hycote	Very High Temperature Paints
Hycote	Vinyl Paints
Spectra	Primer (White, Grey, Red Oxide)
Spectra	Gloss (Black, White)
Spectra	Decorative Gold Paint
Spectra	Heat Dispersant Paint
Spectra	Matt Black
Spectra	Satin Matt Black
Spectra	Hammer Finish (all colours)
Spectra	Clear Lacquer
Spectra	Plastic Primer Kit
Suzuki	Suzuki Touch & Go

Going to Waste

The ordinary motorist generates a fair amount of waste over a year's driving. There are waste batteries, oil, brake fluids, antifreeze, tyres and so on. Some of these are recyclable, some not (see the accompanying chart).

WHAT TO DO WITH THE WASTE FROM YOUR CAR

Product	Hazardous ingredients	Hazardous properties	Disposal recommendation
Anti-freeze	Ethylene glycol	Toxic	Do not pour on the ground — pour down a household drain*
Transmission fluid	Hydrocarbons, mineral oils	Flammable, toxic	Recycle — take to your garage
Brake fluid	Glycol ethers, heavy metals	Flammable, toxic	Dispose of very carefully*
Used oil (sump oil)	Hydrocarbons (eg benzene), heavy metals	Flammable, toxic	Recycle (see page 128)
Batteries	Sulphuric acid, lead	Corrosive, toxic	Recycle (see page 129)

*Ideally, products that need to be disposed of very carefully should be disposed of by a hazardous waste collection van, but there are virtually none in existence. It is better to pour the waste down a household drain than an outside drain as it will be treated by the sewage works in the first case, whereas in the second it can enter the surface water.

Source: Environmental Hazards Management Institute (see p. 201 for address)

Sump oil

It is illegal to pour sump oil down the drain. If you do so, it can lead to water pollution.

An estimated 79.6 million litres (17.5 million gallons) of waste oil are generated in Britain by private motorists every year. Industry sources suggest that around 12 million gallons of waste oil are collected each year from Civic Amenity Sites. What happens to the rest?

If you are a DIY motor mechanic, take waste oils to your local Civic Amenity Site. If there is no waste oil collection point, ring your local council and ask them to provide one. Central government has shown little interest in reclaiming sump oil, but the **Chemical Recovery Association** has been considering a campaign to persuade garages to set up oil collection points. If your local garage does not have one, ask it to consider setting one up and meanwhile find the nearest garage that does. Don't dispose of sump oil by any other means.

Scrap tyres

Each year we bury millions of scrap tyres. Some 31.2 million car and lorry tyres wore out during 1986, for example, a 19 per cent rise on the 1974 figure. About 9.5 million tyres are used each year as fuel in industrial boilers and cement kilns, or exported. But around half of the scrap tyres generated in Britain are simply buried in landfill sites, where they can lead to fires, subsidence or water pollution.

This is an extraordinary waste of resources. Japan only land-fills 1 per cent of its scrap tyres, while West Germany landfills 11 per cent. And the problem in the UK is getting worse.

Although an estimated 35 per cent of car tyres and 60 per cent of truck tyres are suitable for retreading (the process by which scrap tyres are turned into new tyres), UK retreading rates are only 14 per cent for car tyres and 27 per cent for lorry tyres.

It is common knowledge that some of the sub-standard scrap tyres, which are not suitable for retreading, are exported to the Third World for use on vehicles. Falling rubber prices have made rubber recycling less attractive, while the drop in world oil prices has made tyre pyrolysis — which uses controlled burning to extract usable hydrocarbons from the rubber — uneconomic. Until new recycling technologies penetrate the UK market, there seems to be little that the ordinary motorist can do to make sure that more tyres are recycled — except to help lobby the Government.

Batteries

Because of their high lead content (55 per cent), most lead batteries used in cars are recycled. The polypropylene in the battery case is sent to plastic recycling firms. The ebonite rubber casing found on older batteries is used as a furnace fuel. Ask your garage or car mechanic what will happen to your battery and — if necessary — try to persuade them to have it recycled.

INDICATORS OF ENVIRONMENTAL PERFORMANCE AMONG LEADING EUROPEAN CAR MANUFACTURERS

Company[1]	% of sales in Western Europe 1987[2]	Number of cars sold in Western Europe 1987[3]	% of 1987 models able to run on unleaded petrol[4]	Aquabase paint?[5]
Volkswagen	15	1,855,500	96	✓
Audi			91	
Seat			70	✓
Fiat	14.2	1,756,540	72	
Alfa Romeo			100	
Lancia			45	
Ferrari			0	
Peugeot-Citroën	12.1	1,496,770	50	
Citroën			65	
Talbot			100	
Ford	12	1,484,400	97	
General Motors	10.7	1,323,590		✓
Vauxhall-Opel			100	
Renault	10.6	1,311,220	100	
Daimler-Benz	3.5	432,950	100	
Mercedes				
Austin Rover	3.4	420,580	10	
Nissan	2.9	358,730	86	
Toyota	2.8	346,360	100	
BMW	2.4	296,880	68	
Volvo	2.2	272,140	80	✓ (see box on p 124)
Mazda	1.9	235,030	86	
Mitsubishi	1.2	148,440	83	
Honda	1	123,700	100	
Others	4.1	507,170	-	

1. Most of these companies are able to adapt their cars to fit catalytic converters, if they take unleaded petrol. Almost all models of

Mitsubishi and Nissan cars are fitted with catalytic converters in West Germany, for example.

2. Source: industry estimates, *Financial Times*, 18 January 1988.

3. Based on the percentages.

4. Percentage of car models (not diesel) included in the Department of Transport's *New Car Fuel Consumption* booklet, 1987, which can take unleaded petrol, including those that need a minor alteration ('refer to dealer') — improving all the time.

5. These are the companies that are in discussion with ICI about their Aquabase paint range. Volvo uses Aquabase paints on many of their silver models manufactured in Europe. It is still a new technology and could be used by other companies shortly. Note: other paint manufacturers are now introducing water-based paints.

Source: *Automotive Industry Yearbook*, 1987

GREEN CONSUMER RECOMMENDED BUYS

In an ideal world, it would be best if we didn't run cars. But if you need one, then it makes sense to buy a model with a good environmental performance — and to keep it regularly serviced.

Environmentally desirable features are now offered on a wide range of cars. For example, if you have money to burn you can buy a four-wheel-drive, 315 kph (197 mph) 'supercar' which runs on unleaded petrol! The **Porsche** *959* costs £145,000. If, however, you are looking for something a little cheaper and more fuel-efficient, study our tables.

As far as ability to run on unleaded fuel goes, **Austin Rover** has the worst record. Manufacturers who have ensured that all their models can run on unleaded fuel include (in some cases only if converted) **Daimler-Benz (Mercedes)**, **Honda**, **Renault**, **Toyota** and **Vauxhall-Opel**.

Overall, the **Nissan** *Micra* emerged from our survey as the car with the best performance. Other good buys include the **Fiat** *Panda 750L* and *Uno 45 Formula*, the **Peugeot** *205*, the **Renault** *5 Campus* and *9/11*, and the **Vauxhall** *Nova*. Elsewhere, the survey reveals a somewhat confused picture. For example, some cars with a good fuel economy rating, like **Rover**'s *Mini City E* and the *Metro City*, cannot run on unleaded petrol.

In the medium-sized range, reasonable buys include the **VW** *Polo* and the **Toyota** *Corolla*. In the larger engine sizes, leading

IF YOU ARE GOING TO BUY A CAR . . . .

Model	New car price — cheapest in range (£s)[1]	Fuel consumption		Lead-free?[3]	Reliability[4]
		Engine size (litres)	mpg[2]		
Alfa 33	8,199	1.5Ti	35	R	
VW Polo	5,129	1.05	39	E	✓
VW Golf/Jetta	7,125	1.3	36	E	✓
VW Passat (pre-June 1988)	–	1.6	33	E	
VW Scirocco GT	8,715	1.6	33	E	
Audi 80	10,499	1.8E	31	E	
Audi 100	12,769	1.8	34	R	o
BMW 3 Series	10,400	1.8	31	R	✓
Citroën AX 11RE	4,688	1.1	41	R	
Citroën BX 14E	6,640	1.4	37	L	o
Fiat Panda 750L	3,999	.75	45	E[5]	× ×
Fiat Uno 45 Formula	4,704	1.0	48	E[5]	o
Fiat Regata 85 Super	6,899	1.5	35	R	× ×
Ford Fiesta Saloon	4,810	0.9	38	R	✓
Ford Escort/Orion	6,903	1.1L	37	R	o
Ford Sierra/Sapphire	8,245	1.6	32	R	×
Ford Granada	11,414	2.0L	29	R	×
Honda Civic	6,850	1.3DX	37[6]	R	✓ ✓
Honda Accord Ex	9,990	2.0	34	E	

Jaguar XJ (pre-Oct. 1986)		4.2 auto	18	L	
Mazda 323	6,399	1.3LX	37	E	
Mazda 626	8,179	2.0GLX	27[6]	E[7]	✓✓
Mercedes-Benz 190E	13,850	2.0E	31	R	✓
Nissan Bluebird	8,297	1.6LS	34	R	✓✓
Nissan Micra	5,076	1.0LS	46	R	✓✓
Nissan Cherry	–	1.3	39	?	
Nissan Sunny	6,685	1.3L	39	?	✓
Peugeot 205	4,895	1.1XL/GL	40	E	o
Peugeot 305	7,695	1.4GL	34	?	
Peugeot 505	10,850	2.0GR	26	E	
Talbot Horizon	–	1.1LE	37	?	
Renault 5 Campus	4,820	1.1	44	R	x x
Renault 9/11	5,960[8]	1.1	42	R	
Renault 25	11,580	2.1GTX	31	R	x
Mini City E	4,098	850	41	L	x
Metro City	4,802	1.0	41	L	x x
Maestro City	5,965	1.3	37	L	x x
Montego	7,408	1.6	34	L	x
Rover 200	7,676	213	38	E	o
Rover 800	12,489[9]	820si	31	E	x x
Saab 900	9,795	2.0	27	E	
Toyota Corolla	7,299	1.3GL	34	E	✓

Model	New car price — cheapest in range (£s)[1]	Fuel consumption Engine size (litres)	mpg[2]	Lead-free?[3]	Reliability[4]
Vauxhall Nova	4,772	1.0	41	R	✔
Vauxhall Chevette	–	1.3	33	?	
Vauxhall Astra/Belmont	5,948	1.3L	38	R	o
Vauxhall Cavalier	7,444	1.3	34	R	o
Volvo 300 340DL	6,825	1.4	34	E	o
Volvo 200 240DL	10,425	2.1	25	E	o
Volvo 700 740GL	12,095	2.3	26	E	o

1. **New car price**: Source: *Which? Car Buying Guide*, 1988, as at April 1 1988. This price is for the most basic model of that car range, ie 3-door rather than 4-door, or 4-door rather than 5-door. No price is listed for cars which are no longer in production.

2. **Fuel consumption mpg**: Source: *Which? Car Buying Guide*, 1988. Average mpg from owners' reports in *Which?* survey. If the car model is too new for owners' reports, we have used *Which?* test results. This applies to: Audi 80, Citroën AX11RE, Honda Civic, Mazda 323, Mazda 626, Nissan Bluebird and Toyota Corolla.

3. **Lead-free?**: Source: Department of Transport booklet *New Car Fuel Consumption*, which includes 'Use of Unleaded Petrol'.

    L = Leaded petrol only

    R = Refer to dealer before using unleaded petrol. Adjustments can be made so that your car can take either leaded or unleaded petrol.

    E = Either leaded or unleaded petrol without alteration

4. **Reliability**: Source: *Which? Car Buying Guide*, 1988. These rankings are based on owners' reports for recent (1986/7) cars. They include breakdowns, faults, problems and days off the road.

    ✔✔ = Better than average

    ✔ = Looking good

    o = Average

    x = Looking poor

    x x = Worse than average

5. Most other Fiat models R.

6. Mpg as per *Which?* tests rather than owners' reports.

7. E except on fuel injection models.

8. Price for Renault TC.

9. Price for Rover 800 820 E.

contenders include **Ford**'s *Orion* and *Sierra*, **Honda**'s *Accord* Ex, the **VW** *Golf* and *Jetta*, and the **Volvo** *200* and *700* series.

The Car of the Future

It has proved difficult to recommend any car as the 'Green Car'. A car like **Fiat**'s *Uno*, which looked a reasonable candidate, proves, for some models, unable to run on unleaded fuel. But the pace of innovation is extremely rapid in companies like Fiat, so it is worth asking your dealer for the latest facts.

Fiat, too, have pushed small car technology ahead with their *Tipo*, introduced in 1988. The company invested £1 billion in this new family car, in the hope of toppling the **VW** *Golf* from its perch. A novel feature of the *Tipo* is that it is fitted with a corrosion-free galvanized iron bodyshell.

Diesel cars generally offer better fuel economy and also tend to last longer. Their share of the UK car market was expected to reach around 5 per cent during 1988, much lower than the 26 per cent share achieved in Belgium by 1985, 22 per cent in West Germany and 15 per cent in France.

Expect to see more add-on environmental protection features in the 1990s. For example, a prototype of **Opel**'s *Ascona*, the counterpart of **Vauxhall**'s *Cavalier*, has been fitted with an on-board canister filled with absorbent carbon — to see whether it cuts the amount of smog-promoting hydrocarbons escaping from the engine. It does, cutting evaporation of fuel by 90 per cent, and it could be fitted to new cars for between £10 and £20. Such end-of-the-pipe solutions are not ideal, however. They increase the price (and weight) of the car, and can depress performance.

Although there has been considerable interest in the potential of electric cars, these are still some way down the road. Sir Clive Sinclair's ill-fated *C5* was to have been followed by a *C15* electric family car, which now looks unlikely to leave the drawing board. Although **BMW**'s prototype electric car, the *Elektro*, is pollution-free, its range is limited to 100 km on an overnight charge. Worse, the sodium sulphur batteries BMW is using operate at very high temperatures and have to be carried in the car's boot in a giant vacuum flask.

Another, more likely long term fuel is hydrogen, which can be produced using solar energy, can be burned in an engine pretty much like those in use today and produces much cleaner emissions. But a hydrogen-powered car will need a petrol tank twice as big as those we are used to — and the ultra-low temperature fuel injection system likely to be required could double the cost of an engine.

The car of the not-too-distant future could be made of immensely strong composite plastics. Even its wheels, brakes and suspension will probably be made from high-performance plastics, to reduce weight and increase fuel efficiency. 'Low drag' body designs should make it possible to achieve an overall fuel consumption of around 25 kpl (70 mpg) — rather than the 18 kpl (50 mpg) returned by current models.

The engine itself will be made from a lightweight ceramic material which enables fuel to burn at higher temperatures, offering better fuel efficiencies and much cleaner emissions. Clearly, the 'Green Car' is not a total mirage, but there would be environmental question marks even here. Once the car of the not-so-distant future had reached the end of its life, for example, would its many different types of plastic be recyclable and recycled?

ACTION CHECKLIST

1. **Walk, cycle or take public transport wherever possible. Shop locally when you can**.

2. **Share your car or join a car pool. Alternatively, if you only need a car periodically, hire it**.

3. **Buy a 'green' car**. Remember that automatics are heavier on fuel. Before you buy, check with the dealer and/or manufacturer on your car's:

- energy efficiency
- pollution performance
- ability to take unleaded petrol
- life expectancy.

4. **Maintain your car carefully**. One million cars are scrapped each year, many of them needlessly. To keep your car in good health, have it tuned regularly and watch out for rust. Your car will waste fuel if poorly tuned or if the carburettor is incorrectly set. Make sure the cooling system thermostat is working. If it isn't, your engine's efficiency will be hit.

5. **Fit radial tyres**, which cut tyre drag. This can give you a 6 – 8 per cent fuel saving. Be careful to keep your tyres properly inflated.

6. **Drive carefully**. Avoid sudden acceleration and braking. If you cut your speed from 112 kph to 80 kph (70 mph to 50 mph), you use around 30 per cent less fuel. Aggressive driving leads to considerably higher fuel consumption and more pollution. The output of polluting nitrogen oxides, for example, doubles between 88 kph and 160 kph (55 mph and 100 mph).

7. **Buy unleaded fuel whenever possible**. Note: diesel has never contained lead, although diesel emissions can cause other environmental and health problems. Diesel vehicles can be more fuel-efficient in urban conditions, but should be fitted with autocatalysts.

8. **Use a reputable garage** for servicing. Ask what happens to the used brake fluids, batteries and sump oil they replace. If you buy chemicals for your car in the garage shop, think before you buy. For example, if you want to defrost the windscreen, use a scraper or warm water. If there is no alternative to an aerosol, buy CFC-free brands.

9. **Join one or more lobbying organizations**. The first step could be to contact **Transport 2000**, an

umbrella lobbying group whose members include
other organizations active in this area — including
the **Civic Trust**, the **Council for the Protection of
Rural England**, **Friends of the Earth** and
Greenpeace.

USEFUL ADDRESSES

Campaign for Lead Free Air (CLEAR), 3 Endsleigh Street, London
WC1H 0DD. Tel: 01-278 9686

Chemical Recovery Association, Kendal, Barnhill Road, Ridge,
Wareham, Dorset BH20 5BG. Tel: 0299 827100

Society of Motor Manufacturers and Traders, Forbes House, Halkin
Street, London SW1. Tel: 01-235 7000

Transport 2000, Walkden House, 10 Melton Street, London NW1 2EJ.
Tel: 01-388 8386

THE ELECTRICAL SHOP

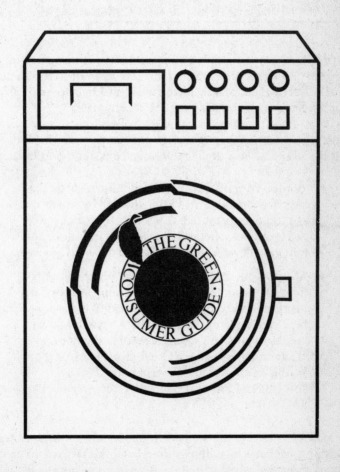

At the flip of a switch, we can illuminate a Christmas tree, a house or a city. Each year, the resulting acid rain makes it more difficult for the Norwegians to track down a healthy Christmas tree to ship for the celebrations in London's Trafalgar Square.

If you find it hard to spot the link between the way you use energy at home and the plight of the environment, and in particular the health of Scandinavian forests, consider the following:

- Ten 100 Watt light bulbs used continuously for one hour are equivalent to 1 kWh, the unit by which electricity is measured. One kWh of electricity gives you 3 gallons of hot water, 2 hours of ironing or 20 minutes of heat from a 3kW radiant heater.

- About 78 per cent of our electrical power comes from coal, with the rest mainly coming from nuclear plants (16 per cent) and oil (5 per cent). For every kWh you use in the home or office, Britain's power industry emits 10.1 grams of sulphur dioxide and 3.1 grams of nitrogen oxides from coal-fired stations — plus an appropriate share of the emissions, effluents and wastes produced by nuclear and oil-fired plants.

Most of us tend to think of 'white goods', such as fridges and washing machines, as pollution-free, but this is far from the case. Apart from the raw materials and energy consumed in their manufacture, and the pollution produced as a result, many of our

AIR POLLUTION FROM 'WHITE GOODS' IN THE UK 1986

Appliance	% of UK households owning appliance in 1986[4]	Actual number of households owning appliance[4]	Sulphur dioxide (SO₂) emissions caused assuming 1 machine per household and average use (tonnes)	SO₂ emissions as percentage of total CEGB SO₂ emissions — 2.6 million tonnes in 1986	Nitrogen oxide (NOx) emissions caused, assuming 1 machine per household and average use (tonnes)	NOx emissions as percentage of total CEGB NOx emissions — 783,000 tonnes in 1986
Cookers (freestanding)[1]	37%	7.65 m	66,454	2.55	20,459	2.6
Washing machines (automatic)[2]	86%	17.80 m	36,170	1.39	11,136	1.42
Tumble driers[3]	31%	6.42 m	19,568	0.75	6,025	0.77
Dishwashers (the fastest growing category)	7%	1.45 m	7,366	0.28	2,268	0.29
Refrigerators (1 door)	58%	12.00 m	36,576	1.4	11,261	1.44
Fridge-freezers (2 door)	43%	8.90 m	67,818	2.61	20,879	2.67
Freezers	38%	7.86 m	59,893	2.3	18,440	2.35

1. Also sold were 411,950 built-in ovens, 265,460 built-in hobs and 512,860 cooker hoods.
2. Also sold were 156,460 twin tub washing machines.
3. Also sold were 188,020 spin driers.
4. Source: AMDEA. 20.7 million households in the UK.
All figures relating to SO₂ and NOx emissions are calculated by SustainAbility.

household machines continuously consume electricity. Indeed, the typical fridge-freezer produces over 13 kg (30 lb) of acid pollution a year, and as much as a sixth of a tonne over a 10-year working life.

Mercifully, the growing interest in the energy efficiency of products is beginning to have a real impact on the amount of pollution we produce. British Coal, for example, wins around 500,000 tonnes of new business each year, in the form of orders for coal from new customers, but loses sales of about 200,000 tonnes each year because of the energy efficiency measures taken by some consumers.

We use energy much more efficiently than we did even 15 years ago. For example, it now takes 80 per cent less energy to heat the average home's hot water than it would have done in 1970. Often, however, these improvements are outweighed by the power consumption of the growing number of machines which we have in our homes.

But which of these machines are the most polluting? Clearly, they are going to be the ones that are the most power-hungry. Electrical appliances, in fact, can be divided into three main groups.

- *Motor-operated appliances*, such as vacuum cleaners, use relatively little power. A vacuum should give you around two hours of hoovering for 1 kWh of electricity.

- *Heating appliances*, such as radiant heaters, use more power — around 1 kWh per bar per hour.

- *Machines which combine both a motor and heating element*, such as washing machines. The weekly wash for a family of four, according to the Electricity Council, consumes 5 kWh of power.

Hot Water Systems

On average, about twenty pence out of every pound you spend on energy goes on water heating. Choose the wrong heating system and you will not only waste fuel and money, but also contribute more than your share to problems like acid rain, coastal oil pollution and the spread of nuclear power stations.

Boilers

Today's boilers are much more energy-efficient than yesterday's. More than 3 million British homes have boilers over 10 years old. If all these boilers could be updated, the fuel savings could be equivalent to 5 per cent of total domestic energy consumption. You can save up to 35 per cent of your fuel bills by replacing your boiler and fitting up-to-date controls.

Gas-fired boilers are more energy-efficient than electrical ones, in primary energy terms, and they have the edge environmentally. They emit no sulphur dioxide and less nitrogen oxides. The choice of boiler is very important. A modern gas condensing boiler is likely to be more than 90 per cent efficient, whereas older systems were perhaps 65 per cent efficient. Such boilers extract more heat from the waste flue gases by allowing them to condense in the boiler. The higher cost of condensing boilers makes them more suitable for medium-sized and large houses.

Boilers are most efficient when running flat out. If you have invested in high levels of insulation (see pages 51 – 3), be careful that you pick a boiler which is fairly closely matched to your likely heat and hot water needs — rather than simply to the size of your house or flat.

Hot water tanks

Whether or not you are buying a new boiler, have a look at your hot water tank. Check that it is fitted with a jacket — and that the jacket is adequate. It should meet the current British Standards specification (BS 5615: 1978). A purpose-made jacket will cost from around £7, but you are likely to save this much on your fuel bills within a few months. If you previously had no jacket on the tank, you could save anywhere between £30 and £80 a year. Many new tanks now come with built-in insulation. If you also

Check the Label

There is no national energy-efficiency labelling scheme for products or homes operated by the electricity and electrical products industry. We think there should be.

New equipment like washing machines and dishwashers should carry labels showing both the energy cost (in kWh) for full and economy wash programmes, and the hot and cold water use (in litres). The expected cost of running electric ovens, fridges and freezers should also be shown on the label. The size of most of these items means that they can comfortably carry a reasonably sized label.

Manufacturers could significantly reduce the energy consumption of most electrical appliances if there was real pressure to do so. However, marketing departments do not see energy efficiency as a priority. Consumers generally do not consider the energy consumption rating of a product when deciding whether — and what — to buy. This is particularly true in the case of mowers or vacuum-cleaners, where the manufacturer is much more likely to advertise a product as 'powerful' — which generally means that it uses more energy.

The British Standards 'kitemark' on a product provides some assurance that it has been tested not only for performance and safety, but also for energy efficiency. The **Eastern Electricity Board** has run a pilot labelling scheme in its showrooms and the **John Lewis Partnership** labels the white goods it sells to tell the consumer how much each appliance is likely to cost to run for a year. Appliances made by firms who belong to the **Association of Manufacturers of Domestic Electrical Appliances (AMDEA)** are more likely to be labelled than are cheap imports.

On gas appliances, check the gas input and heat output rates shown on the appliance's data plate. For solid fuel appliances, British Coal runs the **Domestic Solid Fuel Appliances Approval Scheme (DSFAAS)**, originally set up in the 1940s to ensure 'appliances fit for heroes'.

New homes should also be labelled. The Milton Keynes Energy Cost Index, which is the equivalent of a miles-per-gallon rating for homes and other buildings, should be used nationwide (see page 166). The Index is presented as a figure between 90 and 250: the lower the figure, the lower the house's likely running costs.

But when we asked the Energy Efficiency Office what labelling schemes it operates, a spokesman told us that the EEO is 'fairly sceptical about energy labelling schemes for buildings, although the Building Research Establishment is continuing to work in this area'. This is unfortunate, particularly given the fact that the annual cost of space and water heating in many of the homes shown at the Milton Keynes Energy World Exhibition in 1986 was less than £100 — compared to around four times that amount for the average British home.

Whereas a normal home might have a rating of 170, the Energy World homes were designed to achieve 120. But further improvements are possible: Scandinavian homes have to be built to meet a 100 rating. Remember, too, that such an energy index is very much like the fuel economy rating on a car. The actual level of energy efficiency you achieve will very much depend on how you drive your car — or home.

Consumers should insist on energy-efficient homes and appliances, not only for the environment's sake but because it will save them money. If consumer pressure is there manufacturers will respond. The gas industry, for example, has recently begun to advertise Gas Warm Energy Conscious Homes — with some 75,000 new homes of this type for sale up and down the country.

lag the hot and cold water pipes in your loft, you could cut the amount of energy you use for water heating by over a third.

Thermostats and taps

Turn the hot water thermostat down to 60°C (140°F), or less. Make sure that hot water taps are turned off properly, especially if you are going away. In a single day a fast-dripping hot tap can waste enough hot water to fill a bath. Remember, too, that washing dishes or hands under a running hot tap is costly: try to use a bowl, or put the plug in the sink or basin.

Showers

Contrary to what you may think, a shower uses about half the hot water used by a bath, and the water is generally heated to a lower temperature. Make sure that you have not got the water in the tank so hot that you have to add cold water to avoid scalding yourself.

Economy 7

If you use electric storage heating or water heating, think about Economy 7. This tariff takes advantage of 7 hours of night-time electricity at less than half the cost of the standard domestic tariff. Which? concluded that 'it is always worth changing to Economy 7 if an immersion heater is your only means of water heating'. It may be worth switching even if you don't have an immersion heater.

The seven hours of cheap electricity can quickly offset the higher standing charge and day unit rate, where this applies. By spreading power demand through the 24-hour day, Economy 7 can have environmental advantages — by shrinking peak demand and cutting the need for new power stations.

Heating your Home

Most of your fuel bill goes on heating your home. The first step is to make sure that it is properly insulated (see The Hardware and

DIY Store). Once that is attended to and you have picked an energy-efficient boiler system, consider the following steps.

Radiators

Check that your radiators are not blocked by furniture. If they are, it could be bad for both your heating bills and your furniture. Never hang curtains directly over radiators, a sure recipe for heat loss through windows. Another trick is to fix aluminium foil behind any radiators which are hung on outside walls. This will reflect heat back into the room. You can buy special foil for this, although ordinary kitchen foil works almost as well. (But remember that aluminium foil is itself an enormously energy-intensive product: see *The Supermarket*).

Time switch

Keep your heating under control. If you have central heating, make sure that it is only on when you need it. If you are worried about your water pipes freezing while you are away, you only need to leave background heating on when it's really cold.

Thermostatic controls

A thermostat will control energy consumption. It is a simple job for an electrician to fit one. It will cost you about £15 to buy and perhaps £40 to install.

If you are installing only one thermostat, put it in your most frequently used room — away from draughts, direct sunlight or local heat sources such as TVs or lamps. It is also possible to have thermostats fitted to individual radiators, enabling you to control the heat in each room independently. Once you have one or more, turn down room thermostats by a few degrees to around 20°C or 68°F. Many people find 18°C (65°F) perfectly comfortable when they are moving about the house.

Heating bills can be cut by around 8 per cent if you cut the room temperature by 1°C. But make sure not to overdo it. Remember that the sick, the young and old people all need a warmer environment. Ideally, install either a time switch or programmer, which is a little more sophisticated and allows your water and space heating systems to operate independently. Remember to adjust the settings on your programmer as the weather changes.

Small fires

1.2 million electric fan heaters were sold in Britain in 1987 alone. Check whether you could use off-peak electric heaters or gas fires instead. They might be more convenient and they would certainly be cheaper to run, because they consume less energy.

Solid fuel fires

Keep open grate fires filled, when burning, with a 7 – 10 cm (3 – 4 inch) layer of fuel and regulate the burning rate by the careful use of the air control at the front. Use the poker sparingly and gently: a long thin poker is best when clearing ash between grate bars without losing unburned fuel. Smokeless fuels are covered in *The Hardware and DIY Store*.

Cooking

Gas or electricity?

Your cooker is one of the most energy-hungry machines in your home. The first thing to say here is that, although gas cookers may be somewhat more expensive to buy, they are more energy-efficient than their electric counterparts. (But be aware that pilot lights often consume considerable amounts of gas. On most models you can turn' them off and use matches. Alternatively, ensure your cooker has an electric ignition system.) Tests by *Which?* have also shown that electric cookers cost about three times as much to run as gas cookers. Electric grills are particularly power-hungry, because of their longer warming up time.

Nonetheless, we bought nearly 600,000 free-standing electric cookers in 1987, 405,000 built-in electric ovens and 243,000 built-in hobs. *Which?* have abandoned their attempts to rate different cookers on the basis of their energy efficiency, because the different sizes and capacities of cookers make it extremely difficult to come up with realistic comparisons. But once you have bought your cooker, whatever fuel it uses, there are some basic, common sense ground-rules which will improve its energy-efficiency.

- Try to cook more than one dish at a time. Using the oven full saves energy. If you are cooking something small, use the grill.

- Pick a pan which just covers the cooker ring. If you are using gas, adjust the flame to suit the size of pan.

- Remember to put lids on saucepans and turn the heat down once the contents have boiled.

- Don't use too much water and don't over-cook food. If food is cut up small, it cooks faster and more evenly.

Microwave ovens

In 1980 1 per cent of homes had a microwave. By 1987 over a third of homes had one. By accelerating cooking times, microwaves can save a great deal of energy. At the same time, however, the growing use of convenience foods which microwaves help encourage often means that there are more packaging materials to throw away: the box, the disposable dish, and the plastic wrap or paper towel you use to cover the food while it's being microwaved.

Kettles

Do not fill your kettle with more water than you need. Switch off the kettle as soon as it boils — or, better, buy a kettle with an automatic cut-out. Also make sure that your kettle doesn't start to 'fur up', which means that it takes longer to boil. Descale your kettle regularly (rinse it well afterwards). Low-cost descalers can be found in household and hardware shops.

Washing Machines and Tumble Driers

Five per cent of homes had a fully automatic washing machine in 1969, a proportion which grew more than 10-fold to 59 per cent by 1986. In 1987 alone, 1.9 million were sold. Washer driers are also doing well, with nearly 700,000 sold in 1987. And, while only 1 per cent of British homes had a tumble drier in 1969, 28 per cent of homes had one by 1986. Some 699,000 were sold in 1987, a further 7 per cent increase.

Not only do more of us own such machines but we use them more often. So their environmental performance is crucial. Key considerations are water and energy consumption.

It is obviously better to wait until you have a full load of clothes before using your washing machine. If you do not have enough for a full load, use an economy or half-load programme, if your machine has one. This cuts down on the amount of water and detergent needed, though usually not much on electricity. It is even more important to run your machine on the programme best suited to your fabrics. People often use too hot a wash when a lower programme would economize on electricity. Remember that cold-fill washing machines (those that heat water within the machine itself) may use twice as much energy as hot-fill, although the latter are obviously drawing hot water from your domestic hot water system — effectively hiding a key component of their power needs. In general, however, it is more energy-efficient to run on hot-fill than cold-fill, especially if your domestic water is heated by gas or solid fuel.

GREEN CONSUMER RECOMMENDED BUYS

Given the different capacities of the various washing machines shown in the table, coupled with the fact that we are looking at

CHOOSING AN ENERGY- AND WATER-EFFICIENT WASHING MACHINE

(Unless otherwise stated the machines in this chart can run on either hot or cold fill)

FRONT-LOADING MACHINES

Brand	Prices as quoted by John Lewis May 1988 (£s)	Maximum load (kg)	Maximum spin (rpm)	Which? tested (✓ ✓ = Which? recommended) Jan. 1988 issue	Energy use on HLCC1 programme (cotton, all whites) (kWh)[1]	Energy use on HLCC4 programme (colour-fast synthetics) (kWh)[1]	Cold water use on HLCC1 (litres)[2]	Hot water use on HLCC1 (litres)[3]	Total water use on HLCC1 (litres)[4]
AEG 561 W	335	5.0	850	✓	1.5	0.6	85	18	103
Ariston A 836	out of production	4.5	800	✓	1.4	0.8	?	18	?
Bendix Autowasher 71868	not stocked	4.0	500	✓	2.6	0.8	75	9	84
Bendix Autowasher 71468	not stocked	4.0	800	✓✓	2.8	0.5	95	18	113
Bendix Autowasher 800 71668	265	4.0	800	✓✓	1.6	0.2	67	23	90
Bendix Autowasher 71968	325	2.5	550	✓✓	1.5	0.5	64	0	64
Bosch V 454[5]	345	4.5	800	✓	1.5	0.5	84	17	101

CHOOSING AN ENERGY- AND WATER-EFFICIENT WASHING MACHINE (continued)

FRONT-LOADING MACHINES (continued)

Brand	Prices as quoted by John Lewis May 1988 (£s)	Maximum load (kg)	Maximum spin (rpm)	Which? tested (✔ = Which? recommended)	Energy use on HLCC1 programme (cotton, all whites) (kWh)[1]	Energy use on HLCC4 programme (colour-fast synthetics) (kWh)[1]	Cold water use on HLCC1 (litres)[2]	Hot water use on HLCC1 (litres)[3]	Total water use on HLCC1 (litres)[4]
Candy Compact Aquamatic 3	?	2.7	550	✔	0.9	0.6	32	10	42
Candy D4 – 104X	299	4.5	1000	✔✔	1.6	0.8	68	24	92
Electrolux WH 1125	?	4.5	1100	✔✔	1.3	0.8	85	20	105
Hoover Logic 800 A3622	253	5.0	800	✔✔	1.3	0.8	85	20	105
Hoover Logic 1200 A3628/30	335	5.0	1200	✔	1.4	0.5	81	19	100
Hoover Logic 1300	354	5.0	1300	✔✔	1.3	0.4	91	19	110
Hotpoint[6] Electronic 9520	?	4.1	800	✔✔	1.6	0.5	68	20	88
Hotpoint Electronic 9540	?	4.1	1000	✔	1.7	0.6	68	21	89
Hotpoint Electronic 9551	?	4.1	1000		1.6	0.7	74	21	95
Indesit W 823	?	5.0	800	✔✔	1.7	0.9	73	20	93
Indesit Omega W 1130	285	5.0	1100	✔	1.8	1.1	78	17	95
Philips De Luxe AWB929	275	4.5	850	✔	1.8	0.8	96	19	115
Philips Elite AWB949	325	4.5	1000	✔✔	1.6	0.7	96	18	114

Servis Quartz Plus 6032	345	4.0	1000	✓	1.8	0.6	75	25	100
Servis Quartz Plus 6033/5	335	4.0	1000	✓	1.8	0.6	75	25	100
Zanussi FL 812	275	4.5	800	✓✓	1.8	1.0	86	20	106
Zanussi FL 1023	335	4.5	1000	✓	1.5	1.0	80	20	100
AEG Lavamat 2060 Turbo (cold fill only)	770	5.0	1100	✓✓	2.5	1.0	106	0	106
Ariston 1258CD	383	4.5	1100	✓	1.6	1.0	99	26	125
Bosch V 694	595	5.5	900	✓	2.2	0.5	107	16	123
Candy Turbomatic 38 WD	385	4.5	1000	✓✓	1.6	0.6	69	22	91
Electrolux WD 1034	399	4.5	1000	✓	1.5	1.0	77	18	95
Zanussi WC1012	430	4.5	1000	✓	2.5	1.0	98	22	120

1. Amount of energy used in one wash. These figures are from unpublished data supplied by the Consumers' Association (April 1988) and are based on their tests.
2. Amount of cold water used in this wash (HLCC1) when tested by the Consumers' Association.
3. Amount of hot water used in this wash (HLCC1) when tested by the Consumers' Association.
4. Total amount of water used in HLCC1 wash.
5. All Bosch washing machines use a cast iron counterweight instead of concrete in their drums. Bosch say this prolongs the life of the machine to 10 years (normal life estimated at 5 years).
6. Hotpoint model numbers are due to change but the machines will be the same.

the machines in terms both of their energy- and water-efficiency, a range of possible 'best buys' emerges. Machines which we would recommend that the Green Consumer considers are: the **Bendix** *Autowasher 800 71668* and *71968*; the **Electrolux** *WH 1125*; **Hoover**'s *Logic 1300*; and the **Hotpoint** *Electronic 9520*. Among front-loading machines with integral driers, the **Candy** *Turbomatic 38 WD* would seem to be the front-runner.

One range not included here (because we did not have the relevant information when compiling the table) is the **Zanussi** *Jet Master* series. These machines incorporate a microprocessor-based control system that automatically adapts the amount of water used to the size of the load. Zanussi also claims that the machine cuts detergent use by about 40 per cent on a full load. If the company's claims are true, Zanussi's washing machines would seem to be an 'intelligent' choice for the Green Consumer.

Tumble driers

By far the most energy-efficient method of drying your clothes is, of course, to hang them out on the line. But if this is not possible, you may decide to use a tumble drier. A typical machine will dry 4 kg (9lb) of cotton garments and towels for around 2.5 kWh, or an equivalent load of synthetics for around 3 kWh.

Dishwashers

The dishwasher sector has seen rapid growth in recent years. After 25 years of sluggish sales, outstanding growth of more than 27 per cent took British sales through the 400,000 mark for the first time in 1987.

When this is compared with figures of 40 per cent in the United States, 36 per cent in Sweden and 29 per cent in West Germany, future growth seems likely. Our kitchens tend to be smaller,

CHOOSING AN ENERGY- AND WATER-EFFICIENT DISHWASHER

(Manufacturers usually recommend cold-fill use. See washing machines page 150)

Brand	Prices as quoted by John Lewis, May 1988 (£s)	Capacity (no. of place settings)	Which? tested (✓✓ = Which? recommended) Nov. 1987 issue	Water use on normal programme (litres)	Electricity cost per cycle at an average of 5.4p per kWh (Which? Nov. 1987)	
					Normal programme	Economy programme
Ariston Aristella LS814	not stocked	14	✓✓	49.1	13p	11p
Bendix Super Twelve 78268	345	12	✓	?	14p	11p
Bosch S610	425	12	✓	28	11p	10p
Bosch S4102	325	12		25		
Candy Sylenma 650	280	12	✓✓		9p	5p
Creda Debonair Super Deluxe 17901 (hot and cold fill)	out of production	12	✓	43	12p	8p
Hoover Cristaljet D7156	310	12	✓	64	12p	11p
Hoover Cristaljet D7158	290	12		64		
Hotpoint 7810W	295	12	✓✓	33	11p	11p
Philips ADG 664	340	12	✓	22	9p	8p
Servis 4145 Deluxe	299	14	✓	42	11p	6p

CHOOSING AN ENERGY- AND WATER-EFFICIENT DISHWASHER (continued)

Brand	Prices as quoted by John Lewis, May 1988 (£s)	Capacity (no. of place settings)	Which? tested (✔✔ = Which? recommended) Nov. 1987 issue	Water use on normal programme (litres)	Electricity cost per cycle at an average of 5.4p per kWh (Which? Nov. 1987)	
					Normal programme	Economy programme
Zanussi DW40	330	12	✔	30	10p	9p
Zanussi DW65 TCR	355	12		20.5		
SMALL DISHWASHERS						
Bendix 78868	225	4	✔	?	5p	4p
Servis Secret Compact 4400	215	4	✔✔	17	7p	3p

however, which can make it more difficult to fit in a dishwasher. In addition, consumers here have so far tended to prefer to spend their money on microwave ovens and video recorders.

Key environmental question-marks over dishwashers are the use of energy and water, as the chart shows. The average cold-fill dishwasher uses around 2 kWh of electricity for a full load. Generally, the question of detergent use is less significant, since a dishwasher is likely to use little more than conventional styles of washing up. But be careful not to use too much detergent — and remember that manufacturers of both machines and detergents are more likely to encourage you to use too much than too little. If your dishes are only slightly soiled, try using the economy wash. It is certainly worth testing out the different programmes to see if your dishes are still clean on a shorter, more energy-efficient programme.

GREEN CONSUMER RECOMMENDED BUYS

Best buys, in energy terms (using the economy programme) and on the basis of running costs calculated by *Which?*, are the **Candy** *Sylenma 650*, the **Creda** *Debonair Super Deluxe 17901*, the **Philips** *ADG 664* and the **Servis** 4145. As far as small dishwashers are concerned, the **Bendix** and **Servis** models seem to come in neck-and-neck, depending on which washing programme you use.

Fridges and Freezers

Next, let's look at fridges, fridge-freezers and chest freezers. In 1987, we bought just over one million fridges, over 900,000 fridge-freezers and nearly 280,000 chest freezers. Key issues here are energy consumption and the use of chlorofluorocarbon (CFC)-based refrigerants. CFCs are also used to aerate some of the plastic foams used to insulate fridge and freezer cabinets.

At this stage of the game, however, there is little you can do

CHOOSING AN ENERGY-EFFICIENT FRIDGE OR FRIDGE-FREEZER

WORKTOP HEIGHT FRIDGES
(With frozen food compartment)

Brand	Prices as quoted by John Lewis May 1988 (£s)	Storage volume of fridge (litres)	Storage volume of freezer (litres)	Which? tested (✓ ✓ = Which? recommended) Jan. 1988 issue[1]	Approx quarterly running cost at 5.4p per kWh (Which? Jan. 1988)[1]	Quarterly cost per 10 litres storage[2]
Bosch KTL 173	330	140	20	✓	£5.80	36p
Hotpoint Iced Diamond 8214W	148	93	12	✓ ✓	£4.40	42p
Hotpoint Iced Diamond 8221W	179	93	11	✓ ✓	£4.40	42p
Lec R405S	124	92	6	✓ ✓	£5.10	52p
Lec R505S	124	113	9	✓ ✓	£5.00	41p
Zanussi ZR50/2	124	113	9	✓ ✓	£4.20	34p
Zanussi ZR54/3	185	123	22	✓ ✓	£3.90	25p

LARDER FRIDGES
(no freezer or frozen food compartment)

Brand	Prices as quoted by John Lewis May 1988 (£s)	Storage volume of fridge (litres)	Storage volume of freezer (litres)	Which? tested (✓ ✓ = Which? recommended) Jan. 1988 issue[1]	Approx quarterly running cost at 5.4p per kWh (Which? Jan. 1988)[1]	Quarterly cost per 10 litres storage[2]
Ariston MC140S	139	135		✓	£3.40	25p
Bosch KTR162	235	139		✓ ✓	£4.40	31p
Bosch KTR183	295	167		✓ ✓	£3.60	21p
Electrolux RF592	165	153		✓ ✓	£2.40	15p

Hotpoint Iced Diamond 8126W	not stocked	131		✓	£4.40	28p
Lec L505S	129	132		✓	£4.50	34p
Philips SRG193	197	132		✓	£5.90	44p
Zanussi ZR6L	205	161		✓	£3.30	20p
Zanussi ZR56/L	172	158		✓	£3.90	24p

FRIDGE-FREEZERS
(Single temperature control type)

Ariston RF225S	215	107	99	✓	£8.50	41p
Ariston DF230SB	205	198	59	✓	£8.20	
Bosch KSV2610	370	189	68	✓✓	£5.70	22p
Bosch KSV4310[3]	540	315	97	✓	£6.40	15p
Electrolux TR915A	255	98	102	✓	£7.10	35p
Electrolux TR925A	255	144	72	✓✓	£6.70	31p
Electrolux TR1125A	not available	195	103	✓✓	£8.00	27p
Hotpoint Iced Diamond 8633W	275	93	103	✓	£9.30	47p
Hotpoint Iced Diamond 8326W	225	164	62	✓	£9.00	40p
Philips ARG279/PH	255	108	101	✓	£8.40	40p
Zanussi ZS62/26[4]	233	163	61	✓	£7.80	24p
Zanussi ZF65/14	205	174	40	✓	£7.90	37p

1. Which? August 1987 issue for fridge-freezer section of this table.
2. This is an average across the whole appliance.
3. Revised model number from Bosch KSV4300.
4. Used to be Zanussi Z918/8R.

about the refrigerants or the insulation, apart from not buying fridges or freezers. You can certainly write to CFC-manufacturers like ICI and express your concern. But ICI tell us that it could be another 10 years before safe, effective alternative refrigerants are brought onto the market.

As far as energy consumption is concerned, a normal fridge will use anywhere between 1 and 2 kWh of electricity a day, while freezers tend to consume between 1.5 and 2 kWh a day.

GREEN CONSUMER RECOMMENDED BUYS

Using quarterly electricity costs as an indicator of the power station pollution likely to be caused in generating the current needed to run your fridge or freezer, the brand comparisons shown in the chart suggest that if you are looking for a fridge with a frozen food compartment, **Zanussi** are the people to go for. If you are looking for larger fridges, try **Electrolux** or **Zanussi**. And if you are looking for a fridge-freezer, consider buying a **Bosch**, **Electrolux** or **Zanussi**.

When buying and using a fridge or freezer, there are some important dos and don'ts to remember.

- Don't buy a fridge or freezer that is too big for your needs. This obviously wastes energy. Keep them at least three-quarters full for maximum operating efficiency.

- Always load or unload a fridge or freezer as fast as you can, so too much cold air does not escape.

- Let warm food cool before putting it in the fridge or freezer. Warm food and warm air can lead to a build-up of extra frost, which may make the fridge less efficient.

- Regular defrosting cuts running costs. Contrary to what you might think, frost build-up can make your fridge less — not more — efficient.

- If at all possible, site the fridge or freezer well away from your oven or boiler. At the very least, leave a good gap between them.

- Test the seal around the doors of fridges, freezers and ovens by closing the door on a thin strip of paper, checking that the paper is tightly gripped and does not slide easily. Worn seals can be replaced at fairly low cost.

Many of the statistics we have quoted in this section are based on *Which?* surveys. *Which?* tests the performance of machines against a wide range of criteria, although environmental criteria are not yet included. Check with the latest *Which?* survey to ensure that you have the latest general performance figures at your finger-tips.

Lighting

In most homes, lighting is not a major energy problem — although using the wrong light bulbs and keeping them on all day will certainly drive up your electricity bills. You can cut your bills and your energy consumption significantly by using fluorescent lighting or the new energy-saving bulbs, instead of ordinary filament light bulbs. Examples of these are the **Thorn EMI** *2D* light bulb and **Wotan** *Dulux EL*.

An ordinary 100W light bulb can use around £6 worth of electricity during its average 1,000-hour life. Fluorescent tubes and the new, compact energy saving bulbs use 75 per cent less electricity than ordinary filament bulbs for the same amount of light and can last five times as long. The compact fluorescent bulb is achieved by folding energy-efficient 'discharge tubes' into a manageable size. The extra cost of such bulbs, which fit into existing fittings, is soon paid for by the electricity saved. Where you are likely to have a light on for an average of 3 hours or more each day, it generally pays to use fluorescent or other energy-saving bulbs. Improved fluorescent light technology means that today's bulbs are much more pleasant to use than old-style fluorescent tubes. *Which?* suggests a number of points you should consider when fitting fluorescent lighting:

- The life of a fluorescent lamp depends on how often you turn it off and on. If you left a lamp on continuously, for example, it might last 150 per cent longer, whereas if you were to switch one off every five minutes, you might get just 20 per cent of the rated life.

- The life of fluorescent lamps is considerably reduced at low temperatures. If you are planning to use such a lamp outside or where temperatures may fall to near-freezing, enclose it in a glass fitting.

- Normal 'ballasts' — the heavy coils of wire used in fluorescent lamps — consume a certain amount of power. The latest electronic ballasts use less power, are lighter in weight and start the lamp almost immediately. They also eliminate the flicker so often associated with fluorescent lighting. Although they are more expensive, they can increase a lamp's efficiency by around 10 per cent, so you should see your money back in the long run.

- A final, common sense bit of advice: keep all bulbs and lamp-shades clean. The grubbier they get, the less light they emit.

The Electric Home

Our homes have been invaded by an enormous number of electricity-consuming machines. In 1980, for instance, only about 2 per cent of households had a video recorder. But by 1986 the figure had leapt to nearly 30 per cent.

Individually, many of the machines may only use the same

HOW MUCH ELECTRICITY DO YOU USE IN YOUR HOME?

Items asterisked are either of negligible wattage or can be battery operated. Where possible, it is always better to use mains electricity rather than a battery (see pp. 45–8). Items printed in bold are the most energy consuming. All figures relate to continuous use at full capacity, which is rarely the case for appliances such as irons, cookers and immersion heaters that are thermostatically controlled.

Kitchen Appliances and Equipment

Appliance	Average Wattage (1000 Watts used for 1 hour = 1 kWh)	Appliance	Average Wattage (1000 Watts used for 1 hour = 1 kWh)
Baby bottle warmer	100	Juice extractor	60
Blender	200	**Jug**	**2000**
Can Opener	60	**Kettle**	**2500 – 3000**
Carving Knife	100	Knife sharpener	40
Citrus presser	60	Liquidizer	(see blender)
Coffee filter	220 – 500	Microwave oven	600
Coffee grinder	100	**Milk warmer**	**1500**
Coffee percolator	750	Mincer	100
Coffee roaster	1000	Peanut butter maker	35
Contact grill	**1000 – 2000**	**Plate warmer**	**1000**
Cooker hood	130	Refuse compactor	250
Cooker (oven and hob)	**12000**	Rice boiler	600
Deep fat fryer	**2000**	**Rotisserie**	**2000**
Dishwasher	**3000**	**Rotary iron**	**2000**
Egg boiler	300	**Sandwich toaster**	**1000**
Food mixer	120 – 700	**Slicer and shredder**	**1500**
Food freezer	300	Tea maker	500
(*Wattage varies considerably depending on usage*)		**Toaster**	**1050 – 1360**
		Trolley (heated domestic)	560
Food processor	200 – 700	Vegetable peeler	150
Food server (trolley)	500	Waffle maker	200
Fondue set	500	Waste disposer	250
Grill	**2500**	Wine warmer	60
Ice cream maker	50	**Wok**	**2500**
Infra-red grill	**2000**	Yoghurt maker	25

Other Household Appliances and Equipment

Appliance	Wattage	Appliance	Wattage
Air freshener and purifier	40	**Clothes drier**	**2000**
Air conditioner	**5000**	Clock	*
Aquarium heater	75	Clock/Radio	*
Battery charger	10	Compact disc player	30
Blanket (under)	60 – 120	Computer (home)	30
Blanket (over)	150 – 350	Door chimes and bells	*
Cassette deck	30	Duvet	300

Appliance	Average Wattage (1000 Watts used for 1 hour = 1 kWh)	Appliance	Average Wattage (1000 Watts used for 1 hour = 1 kWh)
Facial sauna	100	Record player	75
Fan (desk)	20	Security and fire alarms	*
Fan extractor	75	Sewing machine	75
Firelighter	**1100**	Shaver	16
Glue gun	50	Shoe polisher	120
Hair rollers	500	**Shower unit**	**3000 – 6000**
Hair stylers	250 – 500	**Solarium**	**1400**
Hair drier	350 – 800	Spin drier	300
Hand drier	1500	Spray gun	75
Health lamp	150 – 400	Tape recorder	25 – 75
Intercom system	*	Television (black and white)	50
Iron	**1250**	Television (colour)	100
Ironing machine		Towel rail	120
(rotary or flat bed)	**2000**	Trouser press	35
Massager	600	**Tumble drier**	**2500**
Personal stereo	*	Typewriter	35
Pencil sharpener	*	Vacuum cleaner	500
Photographic enlarger	60	Video recorder	110
Polisher	400	Video disc player	50
Radio	*	**Washing machine**	**2500**
Radio/Recorder	*		

Power and Electrical Tools

Drill	250 – 500	Paint Remover	300
Drill sharpener	100	Sander	250
Engraving tool	160	Saw (circular and jig)	200 – 250
Garage doors	100	Screwdriver	200
Grinder, pump, planer	160	Tyre inflator	200
Pump	60		

Garden Tools and Equipment

Barbecue	**3000**	Compost shredder	60
Edge trimmer	from 150	Propagator	from 60
Fountain	40	Rotary tiller	from 250
Grass cutter (rotary)	from 280	Soil heater	from 60
Greenhouse ventilator	75	Watering equipment	from 100
Hedge trimmer	from 200	Weed remover	60
Lawn mower	from 250		

Heating Equipment

Convector	**1000 – 2500**	**Storage heater**	**2000 – 3000**
Fan	**2000 – 3000**	Towel rail	30 – 1000
Oil filled radiator	**500 – 2500**	**Immersion heater**	**3000**
Radiant	**500 – 3000**	**Water heating**	**1000 – 5000**

Source: Taken from the Electricity Council, Home Electric Information 1987.

amount of electricity as a light bulb, as the chart shows. But add them up, and you can see how the all-electric home can begin to cost the earth. Some leisure equipment can be very heavy on electricity, particularly barbecues (3,000W) and shower-units (3,000 – 6,000W).

The best advice is simply to limit the number of unnecessary electrical gadgets you buy — and to switch them off whenever you are not using them. You can also even consider buying an energy-efficient home — though that's an option that is still not open to many of us. Visit Milton Keynes's Energy Park and you can see the latest in energy-efficient housing. The city is likely to be the first to apply an energy cost index, generated using a computer, to help cut future fuel bills. The Milton Keynes Energy Cost Index allows architects and planners to assess the energy efficiency of all new buildings. The Index is calculated by computer software which takes account of the number of people and heat-generating machines, the orientation of a building, any shading by other buildings or trees, and the level of insulation.

Unfortunately, as the Energy Park's project manager put it recently, 'energy efficiency is market-invisible'. What he meant was that energy efficiency is still not the first thing prospective buyers think about when checking out a new home — indeed many people never think of it. The availability of an Energy Cost Index figure for all new homes would be a welcome step. Over its lifetime, the average house is going to use a great deal more energy than the average car, so home-buyers should insist on knowing how a particular house is likely to perform.

Longer term, there is also likely to be growing interest in 'smart' homes and 'intelligent' buildings. Japan and the United States are making the most progress towards buildings that use sensors to monitor their own energy use and the needs of occupants, and then automatically reprogramme domestic equipment to ensure that energy is not wasted.

Seven of Europe's leading makers of audio, video and domestic appliances are collaborating to produce equipment — from burglar alarms and central heating systems to dishwashers and video recorders — that can be operated automatically by a central control. The home of the future, it seems, will not only keep the family accounts up to date but will also ring the police in the event of an attempted burglary and the fire brigade or hospital in the event of a fire or accident.

ACTION CHECKLIST

1. Make sure you **know all the facts about energy saving**. Visit your local British Gas or Electricity Board showrooms. Many of the larger showrooms have specialist advice centres where staff can demonstrate equipment and give advice on energy saving.

2. If you want detailed advice on the measures appropriate to your own home, you may want to pay for a **home energy audit**. You may still find this service hard to track down, however. We tried the option suggested by the Energy Efficiency Office. The EEO says you can get a cheap home energy audit from **Energy Matters**. We tried calling them, but they failed to send any details.

3. For information on **home insulation and central heating controls**, get a free copy of *Make the Most of Your Heating* from the **Energy Efficiency Office**.

4. Saving energy is common sense — and common sense can help you cut your energy bills. **Turn off electrical appliances when you are not using them**.

5. **Check the energy consumption of new machines** or equipment that you buy. Don't just think of the things you buy frequently, like light bulbs. Machines like ovens, freezers and dishwashers, which we buy very rarely indeed, are the big energy consumers.

6. If you have already bought a washing machine or dishwasher, make sure that you **run them when they are full**, rather than half-empty. Otherwise use the economy programme.

7. **Products to avoid** include fan and convector heaters (a 2 kW convector heater uses 1 unit of electricity to give 30 minutes' warmth), infra-red heaters (a 1 kW model gives 1 hour for 1 unit) and radiant heaters (a 3 kW model gives 20 minutes' warmth for 1 unit).

8. **Remember, up-to-date boilers are much more energy-efficient**. Try to match the size of the boiler as closely as possible to your likely needs: big boilers are greedy.

9. However old your boiler, **fit a time clock/programmer, a central room thermostat, and a water cylinder thermostat**, and you can save as much as 30 per cent of your present heating costs. If you already have a time switch or programmer, but no thermostats, fitting them can save you 15 per cent of your heating bill. Reprogramme them when the weather gets warmer or colder.

10. **Always check the energy performance of new electrical equipment** before buying. If there is no label, ask your electrical dealer for information. If they are asked the question often enough, they will also be forced to lobby for labelling schemes!

USEFUL ADDRESSES

Energy Efficiency Office, Room 1312, Thames House South, Millbank, London SW1P 4QJ. Tel: 01-211 3000

Energy Matters, Energy Research Group, Open University, Walton Hall, Milton Keynes MK7 6AA. Tel: 0908 653335

THE SUPERMARKET

Organic fruit, vegetables, wines and champagne

Hormone-free meat

All part of the package

Low-impact detergents and cleaners

How green is your supermarket?

'Natural', 'additive-free', 'wholesome', 'high fibre' and 'no added sugar' have become watchwords of the supermarket industry. The industry's extraordinary race to get additives out of food and drink in recent years has been a dramatic illustration of how fast events can move once supermarkets are persuaded that they are in danger of missing a new consumer trend.

Interestingly, most such additives have not caused major health problems, other than allergies. Tartrazine, for example, a yellow colouring agent, produces only one adverse reaction in every 1,600 people exposed, far less than those affected by 'natural foods' such as milk, cheese, chocolate, shellfish and strawberries. But many supermarket and other retailing companies have sensibly removed artificial colours and flavours from their own brands of food and drink. They have also put considerable pressure on manufacturers to get additives out of their products, too. Their next challenge: the environment.

Our supermarket survey, which begins on page 225, compares the relative performance of the major supermarket chains in restocking their shelves to appeal to the Green Consumer. The issues covered range from food irradiation, through CFCs in products and packaging, to the availability of free-range eggs and organic produce. At the time of the survey, mid-1988, **Safeway** was ahead of the pack — and intending to increase its lead. But almost all the supermarkets were extremely helpful in supplying the information we requested, which is an indication of how seriously they now take such issues.

In the 1960s and 1970s, there was a massive upsurge of interest in 'wholefoods'. It is easy to forget what a profound impact this interest had; it created a new industry. Even the House of Commons now has a 'wholefood alternative' menu. The fast food industry is struggling to catch up.

But the challenge such companies face is becoming more difficult: now consumers are increasingly demanding organic food (see pp. 172–3) grown without artificial fertilizers and synthetic pesticides. Some of the more enlightened manufacturers are making real progress.

In the US, **H. J. Heinz** ordered American farmers to stop using 12 chemicals (all of which were still legal) on crops grown for its infant products. The concern was that babies, because of their low body weight and high consumption of fruits and vegetables, are particularly at risk if exposed to pesticide residues. Even so, these products cannot be described as 'organic'. But Heinz have recognized the edge that a good environmental image can give companies. In Britain, their £1 million Heinz *Guardians of the Countryside* campaign with WWF has proved a considerable success — both in conservation and in commercial terms.

Of course, some manufacturers have responded cynically by putting carthorses or other natural symbols on their labels, and claiming that their ingredients are 'natural'. Others have made a feature of the additives which are not in their products, many of which were not there in the first place, turning a blind eye to problem additives which are still included.

But there is no question that the food and drink industry has been rocked by consumer campaigns in favour of wholefoods, health foods and vegetarian foods and against additives, food irradiation and over-packaging — and by the success of recent environmental campaigns on such issues as CFCs in aerosols.

In West Germany, there are approaching 2,000 *Reformhaus* or *Naturkostladen* (Nature diet) shops, popularly known as 'bio-shops'. Food accounts for around half of their turnover, special diet foods for 14 per cent, herbal medicines for 21 per cent and natural cosmetics for 30 per cent. In 1982 they formed their own trade association, and are branching out into wholemeal bakeries, factories manufacturing 'biological' paint and solvent factories. And the Chernobyl and Rhine disasters have spurred interest in the new wave of so-called 'eco-supermarkets'.

The pace of development has been much slower in Britain, although it shows signs of quickening. The map is now dotted with 'green shops', from the **Little Green Shop** in Brighton (which sells **Rolith** household cleaning products, made in Belgium, Holland and Germany) to **Fairfields** — probably Britain's first 'green supermarket', which is due to open in Bristol during 1989.

What marks organic farmers out from the herd is the fact that they do not use artificial fertilizers, synthetic pesticides or feed additives.

Instead of relying on chemicals, they concentrate on building up healthy soils by using compost, animal manures, and crop rotations. Plants grown organically are better able to resist disease — which crop rotations also help to discourage. And foods grown organically are not only healthier for the land, but also are healthier for you, the consumer.

In the 1970s, you could only find organically grown produce in a small number of health food stores, but the organic sector has made astonishing progress in recent years. No longer is it seen as the preserve of 'cranks', indeed the supermarkets are now competing to break into the market. You can buy a growing range of organic produce, from fruit and vegetables, through cereals and biscuits, to fruit juices and wines.

The supermarket group which came top in our survey as far as the range of organic food available was concerned was **Safeway**, although **Asda**, **Gateway**, **Sainsbury** and **Waitrose** also stock organic produce.

Safeway took the initiative in extending its own-brand products into the additive-free market and then began offering a wide range of organically grown produce. Such produce tends to be more expensive, however, because of the time needed to convert land from chemical-based agriculture to organic methods, the higher labour inputs needed on organic farms, and the much smaller distribution systems available to organic suppliers — which have so far prevented them enjoying economies of scale.

Unfortunately, the word 'organic' on a food label can mean different things to different people. This variability in standards, in fact, has been a major problem both for genuinely organic producers and for consumers. There is a growing range of partially competing symbols, as illustrated below.

- The **Soil Association** symbol is the most widely recognized and is awarded to producers who do not allow the use of synthetic fertilizers, pesticides, growth regulators, antibiotics, growth stimulants or intensive livestock operations.

- **Organic Farmers and Growers** combines a marketing role with standard-setting and inspection. Standards are more permissive than Soil Association's. It has a second label, 'In Transition to Organically Grown', for those growers who have embarked on the process of weaning their land from chemical inputs — which takes a minimum of two years.

- The **Organic Growers Association** helps members switch to organic growing, and encourages them to apply for eventual Soil Association membership.

- Companies like **Jordans** produce a range of 'organic' and 'conservation grade' products, the latter denoting membership of the **Guild of Conservation Food Producers**, which allows the use of fertilizer compounds containing ground rock phosphate and potash.

Late in 1987, the Agriculture Minister announced the imminent introduction of a new UK register of Organic Food Standards, based on a voluntary code of practice, which would replace the competing 'organic' labelling schemes with a single scheme and label. It would certainly help.

If this chapter whets your appetite for organic foods, you may want to buy Alan Gear's *New Organic Food Guide* (Dent, 1987). It lists suppliers of organic foods, from small producers with a little surplus produce for sale to large 1,000 acre farms, from wholefood shops to supermarkets.

ALONG THE SHELVES

The Fruit and Vegetable Counter

Vegetables

Each year, the average Briton gets through 244 lb (110 kg) of potatoes; 85 lb (38 kg) of 'other vegetables', including 14 lb (6 kg) of peas; 13 lb (6 kg) of carrots; and just two ounces (56 grams) of asparagus. The range of vegetables available in supermarkets has expanded at a phenomenal rate. But there is a price to be paid. The Common Market destroyed 2.5 million tonnes of fruit and vegetables in 1987 alone, for example, to keep producers' prices up. Among the produce which was ploughed into the soil or intentionally spoiled were lemons, tomatoes, oranges, peaches, grapes, apples and cauliflowers.

There may be little we can do individually about food surpluses in the Common Market, but we can help push farmers into low-chemical styles of farming. With such huge agricultural surpluses now being produced across Europe, the fact that organic agriculture produces somewhat smaller yields may actually prove to be an advantage.

The whole supermarket ethos suggests that we should buy fruit and vegetables which are uniform in size, colour and taste — and with no imperfections. This not only pushes farmers towards chemical-intensive agriculture but also promotes an enormous amount of waste.

Even with chemically grown fruit and vegetables, a very large percentage is thrown away because it is irregular or blemished in some way. If you are eating produce which has been grown chemically, make sure that you wash it thoroughly before cooking or eating it.

Organic fruit and vegetables may well be less uniform and possibly even slightly damaged, but the many benefits of organic farming include reduced pollution by pesticides and nitrates and a wider range of fruit and vegetable species. You can buy a growing selection of organic fruits and vegetables in some of the supermarkets covered in our survey, including such exotica as organic avocados.

Although British farmers are unlikely to switch to avocado growing, it is still surprising that around 70 per cent of the organic produce currently sold in British supermarkets has been imported. The more organic produce you buy, however, the more likely it is that our own farmers will scent a profit and switch to no-chemical or low-chemical farming.

Wherever possible, buy fresh fruit and vegetables — rather than the canned or bottled varieties. Buy your produce loose, rather than pre-packed — particularly if foamed plastics are used in the packaging. And eat more raw food: this not only preserves the nutritional value of your food, but can also save energy which you would otherwise use in cooking.

Apples and pears

Since we joined the Common Market, the range of acceptable fruit and vegetables has shrunk. Take apples. The ubiquitous Golden Delicious is squeezing out many traditional types of apple. This not only reduces your choice as a consumer, but also results in single-crop orchards which are more vulnerable to pest attack — and are therefore more reliant on pesticides. If you can track down unusual varieties, do.

Mushrooms

Per head, we eat about 5 lb (2.3 kg) a year, mainly the cultivated variety. While mushroom farms can be a useful source of compost materials for gardeners, many of the materials emerging from modern mushroom farms could hardly be described as 'organic', since a range of chemical fertilizers and crop protection products may have been used.

Wild mushrooms can be a useful barometer of rising pollution levels. Acid rain in Europe has hit the supply of chanterelle mushrooms, for example, a much sought-after woodland delicacy. Once plentiful in The Netherlands, the chanterelle has been in steady decline.

Nuts

Buy as many brazil nuts as you possibly can. The nut grows on the *castanha do para* tree, whose range has been halved over the last decade as Brazil's tropical forests have been destroyed. The country's nut farmers have been forced to resort to armed struggle to protect their crops from migrants, who chop down the trees illegally for firewood. One exporter commented: 'We are on the way to killing the business'. The brazil nut farmers help to show a commercial return from trees left standing.

Olives

If you are looking for organic black olives or pickles, keep an eye out for the **Demeter**, **Eden**, **Infinity** and **Lima** labels.

The Dairy Counter

Milk

Like meat, milk can concentrate radioactivity. In the wake of the Chernobyl disaster, for example, the West Germans found themselves with 150 rail wagons of radioactive milk powder on their hands. But, for the moment, the radioactivity in milk and milk products is not the main issue when you load up at the dairy counter.

As a nation, Britons drink 33 million pints (18.8 million litres) of milk a day. Most of that milk is still delivered to our doorstep, a system which is unique in Europe. The bottles can be re-used up to 50 times, making the humble milk bottle potentially the most resource-efficient liquid container available. To ensure that more bottles get back to the dairy, **National Dairies** has launched a scheme of purpose-designed milk bottle banks in the Birmingham area, which use an elaborate system of tubes to ensure that milk bottles are not broken and can be re-used.

The amount of milk we drink (an annual average of 216 pints or 123 litres a head) has fallen by over 25 per cent during the last five years, however. There has also been a dramatic shift to low-fat milks, which now account for around a quarter of sales.

Hormones: Consumer and animal welfare groups have joined forces to attack the secrecy surrounding the testing of a new hormone increasingly used to boost the milk production of cows. Bovine somatotropin (BST) is just like the growth hormones produced naturally by cows, but it is produced by genetically engineered bacteria. It is believed to increase milk production from individual cows by about 20 per cent. Although the London Food Commission, an independent lobbying organization, is not arguing that BST will damage consumers' health, it believes that milk produced in this way should be identified on the label.

The real problems are likely to be economic and social: it has been estimated, for example, that US farmers will have to kill a million dairy cows in order to cut existing American milk surpluses. A Cornell University study concluded that, with BST-treated cows producing more milk, the US would need 25 per cent fewer cows and 32 per cent fewer dairy farmers! Since milk from BST-treated herds is not identified on the label, there is little you can do, but be aware of the issue.

Butter and margarine

The shift to low-fat diets has hit butter hard, helping to raise Europe's 'butter mountain' even higher. British butter consumption (9 lb 3 oz or 4.2 kg per head per annum) fell by just over 5 per cent in 1987. Between 1980 and 1987, it fell by an extraordinary 50 per cent. Meanwhile, sales of margarines high in polyunsaturates are growing 10 times faster than other margarines.

Cheese

Each year Britons eat 14 lb 5 oz (6.5 kg) of cheese per head, spending a total of over £770 million. There has been a renaissance in the making of traditional British cheeses, with enormous interest in 'real cheese'. At the same time, however, there has been a growing demand from vegetarians for cheese made with non-animal rennet.

Rennet, an extract from the stomach lining of cud-chewing

animals which contains the enzyme rennin, is needed for clotting milk to make curds. Usually taken from the stomachs of slaughtered unweaned calves, it can also come from lambs, kids, young pigs and even hares and rabbits. The alternatives are microbial rennet, called *mucor miehei*, and a range of enzymes extracted from plants.

Many processed cheeses (including **Kraft**'s *Philadelphia* brand) do not contain rennet. Almost every supermarket now offers a vegetarian Cheddar and **Safeway** offers *Soderasens*, a vegetable oil cheese made with skimmed milk, sunflower and soya oil, and vegetable rennet. (Safeway also offers organic cheese.) *Pencarreg* is a full-fat cheese produced to organic standards.

The specialist cheese suppliers are generally still streets ahead, however. Examples include **Cranks Wholefoods**, **Neal's Yard Dairy** (which offers vegetarian regional varieties, including herb-filled Jersey-milk Devon Garland, rich Exmoor, and Satterleigh) and the **Real Cheese Shop**. A mail order service is available from **Wells Stores**.

Eggs

Every Briton, we are told, eats 222 eggs a year. Despite the best efforts of the egg marketing people, however, the egg is undergoing a long-term decline in popularity. The medical evidence that eating eggs can boost your cholesterol level, increasing your heart-attack risk, hasn't helped. There is also some evidence from the US that chicken eggs (like duck eggs) can transmit the salmonella bacteria which cause food poisoning, especially if not cooked properly. But eggs are still an important part of most people's diet.

The answer here is to buy free-range eggs. An estimated 10 million free-range eggs are sold every week in Britain. As our survey shows, most supermarkets now stock them. The exceptions are **Bejam** and most **Spar** stores.

The key problem here is that different stores have different ideas on what constitutes a 'free-range' egg. Most deal with suppliers who meet EEC standards. But the EEC has four standards:

- **Free-range**: Under this system birds must have continuous daytime access to open-air runs mainly covered with vegetation and with a maximum stocking rate of 1,000 hens per hectare (405 hens per acre). Hen house conditions must comply with those for deep-litter systems (see below). So long as these requirements are met, however, poultry farmers can pack almost as many hens into their poultry houses as they like.

- **Semi-intensive**: Birds must have continuous daytime access to open-air runs mainly covered with vegetation and with a maximum density of 4,000 hens per hectare (1,619 per acre). Hen house conditions must comply with those for deep-litter systems (see below).

- **Deep-litter**: Birds are kept in hen houses with a maximum stocking density of 7 birds per square metre of floor space. At least a third of the floor space should be solid, covered with straw, wood shavings, sand or turf. And at least a quarter of the floor area should be used for the collection of droppings.

- **Perchery (barn)**: Eggs produced in this way, a variation of the deep-litter system, are called 'barn' eggs. It uses a series of perches and feeders at different levels to enable the farmer to cram in more birds — up to 25 hens per square metre.

Wherever possible, buy free-range eggs. If they are not available, then work your way down the list, avoiding the rather misleadingly titled 'barn' eggs if you possibly can.

Meanwhile, our preference for deep yellow egg yolks has persuaded most poultry farmers that the natural (and rather insipid) colour of the yolks produced by most chickens is not good enough. So they add such dyes as beta-apo-8-carotenal, caraphyll, xanthophyll and Tartrazine (E102) to the hens' diet. Even some free-range eggs may be dyed in this way.

A key point to remember when buying eggs is that they come in three main types of packaging. Worst are the spongey foam plastics, most of which still contain ozone-damaging CFCs. Also avoid the clear plastics. They may give you a good view of the eggs, but they are wasteful and do not biodegrade. The best choice by far: cardboard egg-boxes, which are not only biodegradable but are made from recycled paper. Almost all free-range eggs come in this form of packaging.

Hot and Cold Beverages

Britons on average drink eight cups of liquid (excluding tap water) a day, 3.7 of them tea and 1.6 coffee. More than 100,000 million cups of hot drinks are consumed each year in Britain, costing £1.2 billion. Coffee sales top £600 million and tea sales £550 million.

Coffee

Twenty years ago, Britons drank six cups of tea to every cup of coffee. Today, the gap has shrunk to two to one. The range of different coffees is illustrated by the fact that **Nestlé** market over 200 brands of coffee, ranging from freeze-dried to spray-dried, from mocha and java to decaffeinated. Decaffeinated coffee now accounts for nearly 10 per cent of the market. The market leader is *Café Hag*, produced by **General Foods**, which dates back to 1905 and was first introduced to England in 1955.

Unfortunately for the environment, coffee cultivation has led to widespread forest clearance around the world, and to the exhaustion of fragile soils. Because coffee plants are highly susceptible to certain pests and are grown in single crop 'monocultures', considerable quantities of chemicals have to be sprayed on them. Coffee-washing plants produce extraordinarily strong effluents, which pollute rivers in many countries. And the energy used in roasting, grinding and processing coffee is prodigious.

If you drink coffee, the best option is to order your coffee through a co-operative like **Traidcraft**. By cutting out the middlemen, they aim to ensure that a much higher proportion of your money ends up in the hands of those growing the coffee.

Tea

Prices of many teas rose following heavy Russian buying in the wake of the Chernobyl disaster, because their own tea crop was contaminated. But the disaster didn't make much of a dent in our annual tea consumption of about 6 lb 8 oz (2.9 kg) per head. Tea bags now account for over three-quarters of tea sales. We haven't yet come across either organic tea or organic tea bags!

Sales of herbal teas have been growing at around 25 per cent a year. They are widely available. The **London Herb & Spice Company**, claiming 60 per cent of the herb teas market, offers a morning herbal tea, *Morning Time*.

Fruit drinks

Consumption of fruit juices has risen enormously. This is good news in health terms, but it is still often difficult to distinguish real fruit juices from 'squashes' when buying cartons. And, whatever the case, the oranges, lemons and other fruit used by juice processors and squash manufacturers have to be grown somewhere.

Consider **Coca-Cola**, the biggest producer of orange juice. The Florida orange crop, on which the company has been heavily dependent, was recently devastated by blight and frost. So Coca-Cola began to cast around for somewhere else to grow fruit. Friends of the Earth claimed that the land Coca-Cola had bought to establish an orange grove project in Belize included virgin forest, home of endangered species like the Central American tapir and the Jabiru stork. Following widespread lobbying by environmentalists, Coca-Cola shelved the plan at the end of 1987 although it retains 50,000 acres for a possible scaled-down version of the original project.

Organic fruit juices are few and far between, mostly being produced locally from home-grown fruit. One or two suppliers are breaking through into the commercial market, like **Aspall**

Cyder, which offers an excellent apple juice. It can be found in some supermarkets, including **Safeway** stores. You can also buy it in many health food shops around the country. Other brands to look for when shopping for fruit and vegetable juices are **Eden** and **Biotta**.

Water

In the decade from 1977 to 1987, our bottled water consumption rose from 8.1 million litres to 137 million litres (1.8 million gallons to 30.4 million gallons). Strikingly, a typical bottle of supermarket water costs over 1,000 times as much as water from your kitchen tap. Most of the successful brands to date have been French, but there are a growing number of successful UK brands. Since such companies spend a great deal of money advertising the purity of the catchment areas from which they draw their

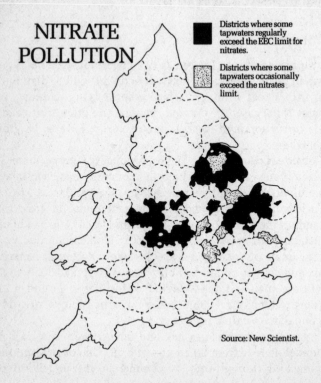

NITRATE POLLUTION

Districts where some tapwaters regularly exceed the EEC limit for nitrates.

Districts where some tapwaters occasionally exceed the nitrates limit.

Source: New Scientist.

water, perhaps they will help to defend — and improve — the quality of the water environment. It is perhaps worth mentioning, though, that the mere fact that water comes to you in a bottle does not guarantee that it is 100 per cent pure.

A variety of pollutants can find their way into the water we use to make coffee, tea or squashes. The nitrate used in fertilizers to make plants grow, for example, can also cause water pollution and illness in people who drink contaminated water. Every time a field is fertilized or ploughed, nitrate moves down towards the water supply.

Five million Britons receive tap water which breaches the legal limits set in the EEC Drinking Water Directive. The most affected areas are shown in the map. In the Yorkshire Dales, the Yorkshire Water Authority has been forced to deliver bottled water to some areas to protect babies from the nitrates in local water until a new water supply is tapped.

There is no need for people on a public supply to buy water filters or bottled water on grounds of health. Indeed, some water filters may actually lead to a deterioration of water quality if not used and maintained properly. Remember, too, that most filters don't remove all nitrates or lead.

In areas where water quality is low, a water filter can improve the taste of your tapwater, however — and clean it up a fair bit. Among the best (and cheapest) buys is the *Brita* jug filter, made in Germany. This uses an ion exchange cartridge, which has to be thrown away after filtering 60 – 100 litres (100 – 175 pints) of water. The Brita jug removes every trace of the bacterium *E. coli*, plus 97 per cent of the lead, 95 per cent of the copper, 80 per cent of the cadmium and all the chloride. But it does not remove nitrates, nitrites or fluorides, all of which can be found in our water to some extent.

Write to your local MP and water authority and ask them to support the campaign to clean up Britain's rivers and tap-water. The bill for cleaning up the nation's water is likely to be around £6 billion by the mid-1990s, costs which will increase our water bills — and help to promote the water efficiency measures discussed in *The Hardware and DIY Store*.

You might also think of backing Friends of the Earth's Charter for the Water Environment. Membership (see page 325) would cost you about the same as a cheap water filter! FoE is planning a series of annual reports on water pollution incidents in England and Wales. Or back the charity WaterAid. They aim to help provide Third World people with safe water and basic sanitation. Since half of the world's people lack access to them, with water-borne diseases killing 30,000 children every day, this is a critical area for charitable support.

The Meat Counter

Despite the fact that several million Britons now eat little or no meat, the meat consumption of the average Briton is high: a total of 135 lb (61 kg) of meat each year, about 42 lb (19 kg) of which are accounted for by beef and veal. The cruelties of mass production of meat are well documented. Several million Britons are now vegetarians or are switching to low-meat diets. For non-vegetarians, we look at the steps you can take to ensure that the meat you eat comes from animals that have been well cared for — and have not been stuffed with hormones and other chemicals. It is ironic that food-poor countries such as Ethiopia and Botswana are significant exporters of meat. In some Third World countries, including Brazil, cattle ranching has contributed very substantially to deforestation — and various tinned meats, including some of those produced by **Fray Bentos**, come from such sources.

Hormones and growth promoters

Early in 1988, **Marks & Spencer** banned livestock farmers from supplying any meat to its stores which comes from animals raised on growth-promoting antibiotics. **Waitrose** has taken the same step with pork suppliers. Neither, however, yet offers 'real meat' — which comes from animals raised on farms where their welfare is a primary concern and growth hormones and other synthetic growth promoters (including antibiotics) are absolutely forbidden.

This is an important issue for the consumer. Synthetic animal growth promoters have been used for more than 10 years. A

European Community ban brought into effect in 1986 prohibited the addition of growth hormones to animal feeds, or the implantation of slow-release hormone capsules.

Game

Legally or illegally, game has formed part of the British diet for centuries. In these days of intensively reared animals, it provides the most obvious source of free-range meat and poultry. Game animals and birds are highly unlikely to contain additives, but you should beware of buying game outside the legal season. Neither fresh nor frozen game can be sold more than 10 days after the close of the season, unless it is imported dead into the country.

Note, too, that some birds are protected at all times — including the Common Scoter, Garganey teal, Long-tailed duck, Scaup duck, Velvet Scoter and Whimbrel. It is also illegal to sell wild geese. See also Venison.

Pork

The average Briton eats 28 lb 7 oz (12.9 kg) of pork each year. Apart from questions of animal welfare, you may wish to avoid pork and pork products for the sake of your own health. As Maurice Hanssen, author of *E for Additives*, explains:

A pork pie can contain as much as 50 per cent highly saturated fat which is bad for the heart and arteries. A perfectly good pork pie could be made from reasonable ingredients but it is cheaper to make it with additives because less meat is then needed. The additives in the pie do little harm in themselves. The fat is made acceptable by a perfectly safe emulsifier. Added colour, which makes the fat look like meat, might cause a few people to have allergic reactions. The anti-oxidant, put in to prevent the fat going rancid, may be a natural one. And sodium glutamate, used as a flavour enhancer, may be all right in limited quantities. The pie could even have a wholemeal crust, but the additives in it deceive our senses and persuade us to eat too much fat. Even if the additives themselves are considered to be completely safe, the nutritional consequences are appalling.

Sausages

The ordinary British sausage has been described as 'fat-soaked bread'. 'Real sausages' are increasingly available, however, and are increasingly popular. **Selfridges**, for instance, has doubled sales of an old-fashioned sausage free of preservatives, delivered daily. For an alternative, try **Realeat**'s vegetarian sausages, the *Vege Burger* and the *Vege Banger*. Both are widely available through health food shops and supermarkets, and are also sold frozen or as mixes. **The Pure Meat Company** will also make 'real meat' sausages to your own recipe!

Veal

It took the animal welfare lobby 20 years to get rid of the barbaric system of rearing calves in crates for veal. Late in 1986, the Government announced that it would ban the use of veal crates. At the time, 10,000 calves were still being reared in this way. The Green Consumer should continue to avoid veal, however, particularly when eating abroad. It is still not at all clear that veal calves are being raised in acceptable conditions in the UK, let alone in countries where animal welfare is a much lower priority.

Venison

The culling of wild deer offers a number of ecological advantages, especially in areas where they have become a pest species. And the low intensity farming of deer in the Highlands is an excellent way of harnessing the resources of Scotland's poorer lands in an environmentally acceptable way. But deer farmers have found that their animals do much better on dairy and arable land. So expect to see more deer farming in the lowlands.

Some supermarket groups, including **Waitrose**, are selling venison from farmed deer slaughtered in abattoirs. The meat is processed into steaks, 'veniburgers', pâtés or sausages. But animal welfare groups are resisting deer farming ventures which slaughter animals in an abattoir, rather than having them shot on the farm by a licensed marksman. Given that deer are highly strung animals and unused to human management, there is a strong argument for coming up with a more humane method of slaughter than that afforded by the ordinary abattoir.

'Real meat'

Many Green Consumers who eat meat are switching to what is often described as 'real meat', produced by farmers who care for their animals properly and do not use growth promoters and other potentially harmful chemicals on their farms.

One of the leading suppliers is the **Real Meat Company**. The company provides high quality meat and meat products from animals kept in high welfare conditions and fed on feed containing no growth promoters or prophylactic medications. Their shop opened in Bath in 1986, selling 'Meat you can eat with a clear conscience'. The product range includes fresh beef and pork, bacon, ham, pork pies, sausages and chicken.

Another supplier is **Natural Farms**, which also offers meat reared without routine use of drugs, on farms where animal welfare is the highest priority. The animals are kept in free-range conditions, with shelter provided. No artificial colouring or preservatives are used in Natural Farms' sausages and bacon. Intriguingly, consumers are invited to see for themselves: tours are provided. Natural Farms offers beef, pork, poultry, lamb, venison, bacon, sausages and other meat products.

There were plans, at the time of writing, to launch a Pure Meat Association. Another supplier, the **Pure Meat Company**, was hoping to ensure that other like-minded producers adopted guidelines and standards covering all aspects of production, including organic pastures and residue-free cattle food. The Pure Meat Company offers bacon, ham and sausages which can be made to your own recipe — including recipes designed not to trigger allergies in sensitive children. It has two local shops but supplies anywhere in the country within a day.

Ask your supermarket or butcher to ensure that meat products are labelled with the method of production, for example 'factory farmed' or 'real meat'. None of the supermarkets we quizzed offered 'real meat', but the Real Meat Company's products are available through over 40 outlets in the South and South-west, including **Selfridges** in London.

The Poultry Counter

The demand for fresh poultry has doubled over the past 20 years, as consumers have switched away from red meat. Each year, the average Briton eats 28 lb (12.7 kg) of poultry meat, including 20 lb 12 oz (9.4 kg) of chicken and 6 lb 8 oz (3 kg) of turkey. Unfortunately, most of the poultry eaten in Britain now comes either from broiler or battery units. You do not have to be a member of **Chickens' Lib** to accept that the conditions in many battery units are inadequate. Luckily, however, most of the supermarkets interviewed in our survey now supply free-range chickens. These are raised with continuous daytime access to open-air runs (see page 179) and are kept for longer than battery hens. They should therefore be tastier, but there's no guarantee that their food has not contained antibiotics and growth promoters.

Eggs   See under The Dairy Counter.

Pâté de foie gras

This is pâté made from the livers of force-fed geese. The process, which the French call *gavage*, involves forcing up to 6 lb (2.7 kg) of salted fatty maize down the goose's throat every day.

In a trial in France, with 100 geese force-fed and 100 left to feed themselves, the force-fed geese produced more *foie gras*, but of a significantly lower quality. Challenged on the subject, the French Agriculture Ministry retorted that *foie gras* was not a matter for environmentalists.

Vegetarian pâtés

Instead of pâté de foie gras, try some of the growing number of vegetable pâtés available under the **Living Foods** and **Euvita** labels. **Vessen** also offers vegetarian pâté snacks, including herb, mushroom and sweet pepper flavours.

The Fish Counter

Fish eaters face some of the same issues as meat eaters — including the growing use of hormones. But, from a natural resources viewpoint, fish offer a much better way of converting feed into animal protein than do farm animals. Fish is also highly nutritious and contains many oils which are important for our health.

Hormones

Around the world, biotechnologists are looking for ways of boosting the productivity of fish farms. Some, for example, have been injecting growth hormones from chickens and cattle into young salmon — and have found that the fish grow up to 50 per cent faster than normal. Next, they plan to isolate and mass-produce the salmon's own hormone and inject that.

Fish farming is already worrying environmentalists, as is explained below, but consumers may also have longer term cause for concern. Connoisseurs say that the taste of farmed fish is distinctly inferior to that of wild fish. If fish like salmon are to become a staple item in our diet, as has chicken, this will simply be part of the price that we will have to pay.

Cod

The estimated weight of cod at large in the North and Barents Seas fell by around three-quarters between 1955 and 1982. Although there has since been a limited recovery, the evidence suggests that these fisheries are under severe stress.

The causes include natural factors, like falling sea temperatures and the failure to arrive of the shoals of capelin (on which cod feed) for several years, but over-fishing is also to blame. The use of large, technologically-advanced and capital-intensive factory trawlers has meant that small cod are vacuumed up alongside the larger fish. For the moment, however, it is probably going to be more effective to join organizations that lobby governments to impose — and enforce — strict fishing quotas than it is to boycott cod in the shop.

Fish fingers

Iceland continues to catch whales at a time when even the Russians have announced that they are going to stop commercial whaling. So in 1987 Greenpeace launched a boycott of fish fingers containing Icelandic fish, to put pressure on Iceland to abandon whaling. A list of the brands they suggested should be boycotted is given below.

If Iceland is still actively whaling when you read this, contact Greenpeace for the latest information on the brands to boycott. Remember, though, it is important to tell stores that you are boycotting particular products — and why. Otherwise your protest may go unnoticed in the blizzard of everyone else's purchases.

BRAND NAMES

Birds Eye Wall's	John West
Billy Boy	Maconochies
Bluecrest	Marr
Brekkles	Norsea
Diamond B	Regal
Dolphin	Ross
Findus	Samband
Icelandic	Seafro
Iceland Waters	Young's
Island	

OWN BRANDS

Asda	Iceland
Bejam	International
Carrefour	Lipton
Cordon Bleu	Locost
Finefare	Marks & Spencer
Galbraith	Mojo
Hintons	Presto

Safeway   Templeton
Sainsbury   Tesco
Selfridge   Waitrose
Snow King   William Low

Salmon

Once, salmon was so common that London apprentices complained that they were being forced to eat it every day. More recently, however, it has been an expensive commodity available only to the well-heeled. All that is changing with the introduction of salmon farming in Scotland and Norway.

Carp and trout were among the first, but now a growing range of species are being farmed. Longer term candidates include halibut and turbot. The pace of development in the Scottish salmon farming industry, in particular, has been very rapid. Around 60 per cent of the farmed fish is turned into smoked salmon.

Like other farmers, fish farmers view natural predators as competitors — which often brings them into conflict with conservation interests. According to the Marine Conservation Society, more than 1,000 seals, 2,000 cormorants and 200 herons are shot every year by Scottish salmon farmers alone.

The RSPB has estimated that each year between 3,600 and 5,600 herons (a protected bird) are shot at Britain's fish farms. Scarecrows, lights and other scaring devices have no effect: the birds are intelligent enough to get used to them.

As salmon farms proliferate, their intrusion into valued landscapes (including, it has been proposed, Loch Ness) grows, as does the threat of local pollution, caused by food, fish wastes, fish viruses and the antibiotics used to control infections. It takes 100 tonnes of food pellets to produce 50 tonnes of salmon, and 20 per cent of the food falls through the bottom of the cages, along with fish faeces and other wastes. The local pollution effect is rather like that of a sewage outfall. Norway's experience also shows that farmed salmon can escape and interbreed with wild fish, resulting in fish which are less well adapted to survival in the wild.

Another possible concern: farmed salmon is not rosy pink like the wild varieties, because it doesn't get the same nutrients. One

American company, Igene Biotechnology, has developed a reddish pigment which it hopes — when incorporated in their rations — will give farmed salmon a suitable pinkness. Canthaxanthin is already used for this purpose by salmon farmers. This is clearly an area which needs close scrutiny.

At this stage it is probably better that you eat farmed salmon than fish caught in the wild, where many salmon are in decline. But the environmental impact of the salmon farming industry may well make it a target for boycotts in the future.

Trout

This is the most extensively farmed fish in Britain — with the growing number of trout farms (over 300 throughout the UK) implicated in water pollution and pressure on local heronries. Properly handled, however, trout are an excellent way of producing protein from feed: 1.5 tonnes of feed can produce 1 tonne of fish.

At the same time, however, there is evidence that our native brown trout is under threat from pollution, from East Anglia to the River Tweed in Scotland. Scientists blame a mix of acid rain, caused by sulphurous emissions from power stations, and agricultural pollution — produced by intensive piggeries, silage heaps and fertilizers.

Tinned sardines and tuna

We know of no particular reasons to avoid tinned sardines or pilchards, but tuna is another matter. People who eat a great deal of tuna in the United States have been warned that tuna may contain high levels of mercury. Some of this mercury comes from natural sources, such as undersea volcanoes, but some enters the sea as air pollution or effluents.

Another issue related to tuna is the incidental killing of dolphins by tuna fishermen. The air-breathing dolphins are caught — and drowned — in their nets. If sufficient care is taken, the dolphin can be released before the tuna are hauled in, but few fishermen bother. Sainsbury, however, points out that its own-brand tuna is caught by line, which avoids the dolphin problem.

Caviare

Made from the roe of the sturgeon (especially the beluga) and other large fish, obtained from the lakes and rivers of Eastern Europe, caviare has caused the over-fishing of sturgeon populations in the Caspian Sea. Its scarcity makes it enormously expensive — and increases the pressure on the slow-breeding fish. Most supermarkets offer lumpfish roe, which is an ecologically preferable substitute.

'Real fish'

After the Campaign for Real Ale and Campaign for Real Bread, there has been talk of a campaign for 'Real Fish'. Farmed fish, says Egon Ronay, 'has a distinctly muddy taste, whereas wild salmon really tastes like salmon. It is much the same as comparing frozen chicken with fresh chicken.' Wild fish are lean and healthy, whereas farmed fish have much higher levels of fat. (But see also page 192.)

Herbs, Oils, Salt and Colours

Herbs

The increasing use of herbs in British cooking has been one of the most interesting trends in recent years. We spend a total of some £35 million on herbs each year, with UK production accounting for around 10 per cent of that figure. They contribute significantly to a healthy diet — and are now offered, in both dried and fresh forms, by most supermarkets. Organic herbs are available from **Hambleden Herbs** and **Suffolk Herbs** (see *The Garden Centre*).

Salt

All the medical evidence suggests that we would do well to cut down on the amount of salt we eat. Among the alternatives for those who can't give up altogether: **Boots'** low sodium table salt,

Kinge's *LoSalt* and **Prewett**'s new formula low sodium salt substitute. *LoSalt* contains more potassium chloride than ordinary salt, and less sodium chloride. Remember, though, that many processed foods also contain a great deal of salt.

Oils

There has been considerable growth in demand for healthier cooking and salad oils, including those produced from the olive, safflower and sunflower. Avoid unbranded oils when on holiday, unless you know exactly where they have come from. There have been a number of serious mass-poisoning incidents in Europe caused by contaminated, unbranded oils.

Colours

In general, artificial colours should be avoided in food and drink. Check individual colours in Maurice Hanssen's *E for Additives* (Thorsons, 1987). If you do use colours, however, check out the *Zohar* range of food colours (red, blue, yellow and green) and flavours (almond, rum and vanilla), guaranteed to be free of animal products and cruelty-free and available from **Broom Lane Enterprises**.

The Bread and Cereals Counter

Farmers who use inorganic fertilizers often increase water pollution and boost their yield of crops at the expense of the soil's long term productivity. US evidence also suggests that modern intensive arable farms lose four times more topsoil each year than do organic farms, which use traditional low-chemical or no-chemical methods. Our survey highlights the wide variation in the extent to which different supermarkets offer organic bread and cereals.

Bread

Britons eat 65 loaves of bread per head per year. The

traditional high-street bakers have been able to fight off the challenge from supermarkets because of their willingness to meet the demand from health-conscious customers for rougher, darker, fresh bread.

The **Campaign for Real Bread and Flour** (CAMREB) has helped to reinforce the interest in wholesome breads which surfaced in the 1960s. CAMREB has been aiming to persuade pubs selling Real Ale to sell Ploughman's Lunches with Real Bread as well. There is still a need to clarify the confusion among shoppers and sales people over the various labels used, however. These include 'brown' (can mean anything, including dyed with food colourings), 'granary' (has added whole grain), 'wheatgerm' (added wheatgerm) and 'wholemeal' (contains 100 per cent of the grain). Wherever possible, ask for granary or wholemeal, which provide useful dietary fibre.

Cereals

One of the pioneering companies in the transition to healthier cereal products has been **Jordans**. It switched to wholemeal flour in the early 1970s, well ahead of most of its competitors. It then came up with its own version of American granola, Jordans' *Original Crunchy*. To start with, the product was only available through health food shops, but then **Waitrose** began stocking the product — and it is now widely available in supermarkets. Jordans also offers muesli and porridge oats, and three varieties of its Crunchy granola.

Jordans was a founding member of the **Organic Food Manufacturers Federation**. Although some criticize the Federation's standards as too lax, the Federation itself says that the 'conservation grade' it has adopted is an intermediate step to full organic status. The company bans over 200 agrochemicals, allowing only those that leave no toxic residue.

Cakes and biscuits

Watch out for over-packaging on the cake and biscuit shelves. Again, Jordans' Crunchy Bars provide a good substitute for chocolate. If you have children, try weaning them onto these healthier snacks.

Pasta

The range of organic wholemeal pastas on sale here is constantly growing, with **Euvita**, **Lima**, **Ugo** and **Waymill** among the labels to watch out for.

Jams, Honeys and Sweeteners

Sugar

Astoundingly, the average Briton eats an estimated 30–40 kg (66–86 lb) of sugar a year, most of it in manufactured foods. Apart from obviously sweet foods like confectionery, cakes, biscuits and ice creams, many other foods also contain sugar, including canned vegetables and meat. Among the health problems in which sugar is implicated are tooth decay (particularly in children), obesity, coronary heart disease, and cancer of the breast, colon and rectum. If you eat a lot, you should cut down.

Sugar is an important cash crop in the Third World, although too often sugar is grown at the expense of crops local people actually need. Ironically, too, the misuse there of pesticides which have been banned in the developed countries has led to concern that there might be a 'boomerang' effect, with pesticides banned in Europe and the US finding their way back into our diet through imported food.

The sugar industry can also pollute the environment. 15,000 fish on a 12-mile stretch of the River Lark, near Bury St Edmunds, were killed when concentrated sugar syrup from **British Sugar** spilled into the public drains. This was a freak accident, but it illustrates the environmental problems which can be created in the manufacture of any chemical product, including sweeteners.

Honey

Apart from the fact that honey is a healthier food than most sugars, the honey bee plays an important role in plant fertilization. Bee keepers are also worth supporting, since they are often in the front line of the battle against the over-use and misuse of pesticides by farmers and gardeners.

Maple syrup

Maple syrup prices have risen, partly as a result of environmental factors. A combination of warm weather and maple tree die-off because of acid rain dented North American maple syrup production for the second year running in 1987. If you eat maple syrup, you encourage Americans and Canadians to plant more maple trees — and to protect the ones they already have.

Peanut butter

In the US, the peanut is generally carefully rotated with other crops, like cotton, to protect sandy soils in which they grow against erosion. But in many developing countries — and in Australia — peanut production has led to widespread soil erosion problems. As with many other products, the less we pay in our local supermarket the less money the farmers get and the greater the incentive for them to cut corners — resulting in major, often irreversible damage to the environment.

Snacks and Fast Food

Fast food is often unhealthy — and it is a major contributor to litter problems. But some leading fast-food chains are now casting around for ways of making their product range at least look a little healthier.

Hamburgers

If you eat fast-food hamburgers regularly, there are a number of points to ponder. Hamburger chains like **McDonald's** and **Burger King** have been implicated in tropical deforestation, for example, with cattle ranching in some parts of Latin America helping to turn virgin rainforest into worn-out semi-desert. And the cartons used to pack many take-away foods often contain CFCs — although McDonald's planned to have switched away from CFCs in the UK by the end of 1988.

With the growing interest in healthier foods, McDonald's have been thinking of introducing salads, but have found it hard to fit such healthier food into their fast-food format. Salad bars work against the fast food image and slow down the processing of customers. The compromise may be to offer pre-packed salads. **Wimpy**, meanwhile, has introduced the *Beanburger*.

If you frequent fast-food chains, insist on healthier food. It may be a small step for mankind, but it could be a larger one for Big Mac. Alternatively, try a vegetarian pizza or switch to **Spud-U-Like**, which has built a fast-food business around that highly nutritious vegetable, the potato. It may not be an organic potato as yet, but you won't be biting into the world's rainforests with every mouthful.

Children's food

It's widely known that a diet of fizzy drinks, crisps, biscuits and sliced white bread may be convenient, but is highly unlikely to be healthy. Finding acceptable alternatives isn't always easy. Many children enjoy a diet which includes too much salt, fat and refined sugar, and too little fibre and fresh fruit and vegetables. They are often attracted by bright, artificial food colours and over-packaging. But health food stores have long sold healthier snacks aimed at children and the supermarkets are now beginning to catch up. Parents should help keep up the pressure, both on their children and on the supermarkets!

Crisps

Hedgehog brand crisps, which are widely available, contain no additives, are made from potatoes grown using organically based fertilizers and contain only natural flavours. If you save and send in 20 tokens, **Hedgehog Foods** will make a donation in your name to British hedgehog conservation.

Frozen wholefoods

Interestingly, the wholefood movement now recognizes that it must make healthier foods more convenient. Companies like **Whole Earth Foods** are selling frozen vegetables and convenience wholefood in cellophane wrappers, and you can now get vegetarian meals packed for your freezer. **Mange Tout Foods**, to take another example, uses free-range eggs and vegetarian cheeses in its frozen foods.

Lunch packs

Safeway, meanwhile, has introduced a line of organic lunch packs, *Cheese'n'Crunch*. In your plastic(!) box you find four wholemeal biscuits, two radishes, a tomato, a stick of celery, carrot slices, cauliflower florets, a sprig of parsley and either 3 oz (84 g) of hard organic Cardigan cheese or 3 oz (84 g) of soft Pencarreg organic cheese.

Pasta

Whole Earth Foods, which now has a multi-million pound turnover, is offering a new organic *Pasta Pots* line, including 'Napoli', made with dried tomato, oregano, garlic and onions; and 'Pesto', which contains dried tofu, basil, parsley and garlic.

Household Cleaners and Detergents

The British housewife spends an average of 31 days a year cleaning her home, or two hours a day. The cleaning tasks carried out most frequently are dusting, vacuuming the lounge and cleaning the loo and bath.

The household cleaning market is dominated by a small number of major companies. They include **Lever Brothers** (*Domestos, Frish, Jif, Handy Andy, Vim*), **Reckitt & Colman** (*Airwick, Clean-o-pine, Harpic, Windolene*), **Colgate-Palmolive** (*Ajax*), **Procter & Gamble** (*Flash, Vortex*) and **Johnson Wax** (see

CHEMICALS IN THE HOME

Product	Hazardous Ingredients	Nature of risk	Alternatives
Silver polish	acidified thiorea, sulphuric acid	corrosive toxic	Soak in boiling water with baking soda, salt and a piece of aluminium foil
Oven cleaner	potassium hydroxide, sodium hydroxide, ammonia	corrosive toxic	baking soda and water
Lavatory cleaner	muriatic (hydrochloric) or oxalic acid, paradichlorobenzene, calcium hypochlorite	corrosive irritant toxic	Loo brush and baking soda, mild detergent
Disinfectants	diethylene or methylene glycol, sodium hypochlorite, phenols	corrosive toxic	½ cup of borax in 4.5 litres (1 gallon) of water
Drain cleaner	sodium or potassium hydroxide, sodium hypochlorite, hydrochloric acid, petroleum distillates	corrosive toxic	Plunger; flush with boiling water, ¼ cup baking soda and 50 ml (2 oz) vinegar

Rug and upholstery cleaners	naphthalene, perchloroethylene, oxalic acid, diethylene glycol	corrosive toxic irritant	Cornflour sprinkled on rug and then vacuumed up
Floor and furniture polish	diethylene glycol, petroleum distillates, nitrobenzene	flammable toxic	Beeswax or 1 part lemon juice, 2 parts olive or vegetable oil
Bleach cleaners	sodium or potassium hydroxide, hydrogen peroxide sodium or calcium hypochlorite	corrosive	For laundry, use ½ cup of sodium hexametaphosphate per 22.5 litres (5 gallons) of water
Mothballs	naphthalene, paradichlorobenzene	toxic	Cedar chips, newspapers, lavender flowers, herbs
Ammonia-based cleaners	ammonia, ethanol	corrosive toxic irritant	Vinegar, salt and water mixture for surfaces, baking soda and water for the bathroom
Powder or abrasive cleaners	trisodiumphosphate, ammonia, ethanol	corrosive toxic irritant	Rub area with ½ lemon dipped in borax-rinse dry

Source: Environmental Hazards Management Institute, 10 Newmarket Road, PO Box 932, Durham, NH 03824, USA/authors' own data

below). Smaller companies include **Jeyes** (*Brobat, Parozone, Sanilav*) and **McBrides** (*Formula 77*). Such products are obviously a tremendous boon for those of us who have to clean houses or offices — but they should always be used as sparingly as possible.

Environmental pressures elsewhere in Europe are making industry think much harder about the cleansing products it develops. Unusually, **Johnson Wax**, an American company, has had a published environmental policy for many years. Since 1976, the company, whose products include *Brillo* pads, *Goddards* silver and metal polishes and *Pledge* furniture polish, has promised 'to develop and market products which are environmentally sound, and which do not endanger the health and safety of consumers'.

The company was among the very first to pull out of CFCs, also in 1976. It subsequently broke ranks with its competitors, announcing that it would label its products: 'Contains No Propellant Alleged To Damage Ozone'. This was a key factor in pushing the rest of industry into accepting a ban on the most damaging CFCs.

As far as detergents and washing powders are concerned, you should beware of products containing phosphates, bleaches, optical whiteners and — particularly if members of your family have allergies — enzymes.

Phosphates have been a particular environmental concern for many years. The Great Lakes of America suffered an ecological disaster in the 1960s and 1970s, for example, when excess phosphates caused algae to 'bloom', locking up the oxygen in the water and suffocating fish and most other species.

In Britain, manufacturers switched from 'hard', non-biodegradable detergents to 'soft', biodegradable detergents following widespread water pollution in the 1950s and early 1960s. The hard detergents tended to pass straight through sewage works, producing enormous heads of foam on the rivers into which the sewage effluents were discharged.

Typical modern detergents contain enzymes, to remove biological stains; cellulose ethers, to make polyester fabrics water-attracting rather than water-repellent; fluorescers, to make the eye believe that whites are whiter and colours brighter; and perfumes, to make the washing smell fresher. Manufacturers tend to be very secretive about the ingredients (and quantities) involved. Most supermarkets have not yet recognized that, if offered a choice, many consumers would prefer to buy environmentally acceptable cleansing products, such as those offered by **Ecover**. (See also pages 210 – 11.)

Some points to consider when buying cleaning products:

Bathroom cleaners

Ecover's *Cream Cleaner*, which is non-abrasive and free from phosphates, is suitable for all areas in kitchens and bathrooms. Ecover also offers a *Toilet Cleaner*, which does not contain the phosphoric or hydrochloric acids found in many loo cleaners. Instead, it contains milder acetic acid (vinegar). It does not affect the microbes which ensure the breakdown of sewage in septic tanks.

Oz Bathroom Cleaner, which is made by **DDD** and is available from most supermarkets, removes limescale from baths, taps, sinks and tiles. It is non-toxic, non-caustic, biodegradable and not harmful to animals. Unusually, too, its pack talks about bio-degradability, although the pack itself is still made of non-biodegradable plastic.

Bleach

Around 80 per cent of UK households buy bleach. **Lever Brothers** has dominated the market with its *Domestos* brand for some years. In 1984, **Procter & Gamble** entered the fray with *Vortex*, a thick bleach packaged in a directional bottle. As with many other cleansing products, use bleaches sparingly if you want to cut back on your contribution to water pollution.

Dishwasher detergents

Don't overdo the detergent in your dishwasher. Test out different quantities to see which work best in particular circumstances. For hard-to-clean items, such as pans with burnt-on stains, use *Zohar* steel wool soap pads, offered by cruelty-free suppliers like **Broom Lane Enterprises**.

Floor cleaners

Ecover's *Floor Soap* is suitable for all floors.

Furniture polishes

If you are using an aerosol product, check through the list to make sure that it is a CFC-free brand.

CFC-FREE AEROSOLS

Amway	Buff-up Furniture Polish
Applied Chemicals	1-23
Asda	Wax Polish (Natural, Lemon, Lavender)
Boots	Beeswax Polish
Bowmar	Hail Furniture Polish
Briggs	Anti-Quax Wax
British Products	Sanmex Polish (Lavender, Lemon and Natural)
British Products	Charm
British Products	Charm Spray Shine
Co-op	All-Purpose Polish
Co-op	Beeswax Polish
Co-op	Clean & Shine Polish
Co-op	Furniture Polish
Co-op	Furniture Polish with Bouquet Air Freshener
Co-op	Silky Furniture Polish
Diversey	Handipak Furniture Polish
Domestic Fillers	Big D Polish
Domestic Fillers	Big D Furniture Polish
Fine Fare	Yellow Pack Wax Polish
Fine Fare	Yellow Pack Clean & Shine
Gateway	Furniture Polish
Gateway	Multi Purpose Polish
Haventrail	Provence Furniture Polish
Haventrail	Provence Original Old English Furniture Polish
Haventrail	Provence New Pine Furniture Polish
E. R. Howard	Topps Teak Oil Spray
E. R. Howard	Topps Original English (Lemon, Lavender, Traditional)
Jeyes	Jeybrite Wood Polish

John Lewis	Jonelle Furniture Polish
Johnson Wax	Pledge
Johnson Wax	Teak Wood Care
Keen	Glowman
Medicare	Beeswax Polish
Mrs Mop	Beeswax Polish
New Hygiene	Scentinel Silicone Wax Spray Polish
NIB	Really Nice
Nichol	Deep Glow Polish
Nichol	Nichol Supershine
Odex	Spray Polish
Safeway	Fine Wood Beeswax Polish
Safeway	Furniture Polish
Safeway	Shine
Sainsbury	Clean & Shine
Sainsbury	Beeswax Polish
Sainsbury	Lavender Spray Furniture Polish
Spar	Beeswax Polish
Spar	Spar Household Cleaner
Spar	Spar Furniture Polish
Spar	Supershine Polish
Tesco	Tesco Furniture Polish
Thomas	Queen Bee Polish
VG	Beeswax Polish
VG	Furniture Polish
Waitrose	Furniture Polish (Lemon and Lavender)
Wellcome	HiFi Polish

Hand cleaners

Whether for use in the home or when working on the car, **Ecover**'s *Heavy Duty Hand Cleaner* will remove oils, grease, dirt.

Kettle descaler

If your kettle gets furred up, its energy efficiency will fall sharply. Use *Oz Safe Kettle Descaler*, recommended for use on metal and plastic kettles and jugs, coffee machines and tea makers.

Lavatory cleaners

The products available range from specialist cleaners (liquids and powders designed for cleaning the loo), through in-cistern devices (designed to be put in the cistern and colour and/or clean the water flushed into the pan) to pan blocks or 'in-the-bowl' devices. Some of the disinfectants used are ecologically undesirable. We would advise using such cleaners as sparingly as possible, which is more difficult if you buy in-cistern or in-the-bowl devices.

Oven cleaners

If you are using an aerosol, ensure that it is one of the CFC-free brands listed below.

CFC-FREE AEROSOLS

Bristol-Myers	Mr Muscle
British Products	Sanmex Oven Cleaner
Domestic Fillers	Oven Cleaner
E. R. Howard	Easy Off
Kleenoff	Oven Cleaner
Keen	Keen Oven Cleaner
Mrs Mop	Mrs Mop Oven Cleaner
Safeway	Safeway Oven Cleaner

Room fresheners

Wherever possible open a window or door, rather than using an aerosol or other chemical product. And put out a bowl or two of pot pourri. If you do use an aerosol, pick a CFC-free brand, some of which are listed below.

CFC-FREE AEROSOLS

Amway	Green Meadows
Asda	Dry Air Fresh
Bayer	Bayfresh
Betterward	Country Garden
Boots	Air Freshener
Boots	Boots Air Freshener
Bowmar	Riviera Airfresh
Bowmar	Lords Airfresh

BP Detergents	BP Air Freshener
British Products	Charm Air Freshener
British Products	Sanmex Air Freshener
Cromessol	Air Freshener
Co-op	Dry Air Freshener
Co-op	Original Air Freshener
Co-op	Silky Dry Air Freshener
Cooper	Freshaire (all fragrances)
Domestic Fillers	Big D Air Freshener
Domestic Fillers	Big D Air Freshener Dry
Domestic Fillers	Carpet Freshener (Bouquet and Lavender)
Fine Fare	Yellow Pack Airfresh
Gateway	Air Freshener
Haventrail	Provence Air Freshener
E. R. Holloway	Gnome Air Freshener
E. R. Howard	Wizard Spring Bouquet
E. R. Howard	Wizard English Rose
E. R. Howard	Wizard Lavender
E. R. Howard	Wizard Bathroom
E. R. Howard	Wizard Carnation
E. R. Howard	Wizard Freesia
Jeyes	Airzone
Johnson Wax	Glade
Johnson Wax	Glade Dry
Keen	Deodorising Air Freshener
Keen	Keen Fragrant Air Freshener
Keen	Keen Jasmine Air
Keen	Lemon
Keen	Zeste
Kleeneze	Citrus Mist
Medicare	Air Fresh
Mrs Mop	Dry Air Fresh
Napa	Brocade Air Freshener
NIB	Really Nice Air Fresh
Nichol	Nichol Air Fresh
Odex	Air & Fabric Freshener
Odex	Odex Fresh Air
Permaflex	Perma
Safeway	Room Fragrance
Sainsbury	Dry Air Freshener range
Spar	Dry Air Freshener
Temana	Cooper Freshaire
Tesco	Dry Air Fresh
Tesco	Premium Air Freshener
Tip Top	Dry Air Fresh
Wellcome	Freshaire

Shower jet cleaner

As we explain in *The DIY and Hardware Store*, showers are more energy- and water-efficient than baths, but they can scale up in hard water areas if you are not careful. **Oz**'s *Shower Jet Cleaner* safely cleans and unblocks shower jets and heads.

Starches

If using an aerosol, pick one of the CFC-free brands listed below.

CFC-FREE AEROSOLS

Boots	Spray Starch
Bowmar	Hail Starch
British Products	Sanmex Starch
Co-op	Silky Starch
Co-op	Spray Starch
Domestic Fillers	Big D Starch
Haventrail	Provence
E. R. Howard	Easy On
John Lewis	Jonelle Spray Starch
Keen	Keen Spray Starch
Medicare	Spray Starch
Nichol	Spray Starch
Safeway	Safeway Spray Starch
Sainsbury	Spray Starch
Share Drug	Spray Starch
Waitrose	Spray Starch

Steam iron cleaner

In hard water areas, steam irons can clog up, cutting their energy efficiency. Use **Oz**'s *Steam Iron Cleaner*, which cleans steam irons and allows the use of tap water.

Washing machine liquid detergents

The detergents stocked in the average supermarket are all pretty much of a muchness, at least ecologically speaking. If you are looking for an environment-friendly liquid detergent, try **Faith Products'** *Clear Spring* (see page 265), which you will have to get from the manufacturer or specialist stockists. *Clear Spring* is advertised as 'gentle on clothes, on the skin and on the environment'. It is fully biodegradable and free of phosphates, enzymes and 'all the harmful chemicals which sully commercial products'.

Washing machine powders

Ecover's *Washing Powder* contains no phosphates or enzymes and can be used either in a washing machine or for handwashing. Ecover also offer a *Wool Wash Liquid*, which can be used for both machine washes on the wool setting or in hand washes, and *Fabric Conditioner* based on processed natural fatty acids, lemon oil and water. This last product does not contain imidazoline, which is found in most conditioners. As a result, it is approximately 85 per cent biodegradable in 20 days, compared with 15 per cent in the case of many other conditioners. None of Ecover's products is tested on animals, nor do they contain optical or chemical bleaches.

Washing up liquids

Ecover's *Washing Up Liquid* cleans effectively without producing a mass of foam. It contains milk whey, which keeps your hands in good condition.

Window cleaners

These come in three basic forms — emulsions, trigger packs and aerosols. If you are using an aerosol, pick a CFC-free brand from among those listed below. Some products, like Windolene, come in all three forms. Trigger packs have grown rapidly and are an effective alternative to aerosols.

CFC-FREE AEROSOLS

Amway	See Spray
Briggs	Antiquax Chandelier and Glass Cleaner
British Products	Sanmex Window Cleaner
Cleenol	Window Cleaner
Deb	Debby Glass Cleaner

Domestic Fillers	Big D Window Cleaner
Domestic Fillers	Pink Window Cleaner Liquid
Mrs Mop	Window Cleaner

Ecover: Cleaner Cleaners

The **Ecover** range of household cleaning products, which has been progressively expanding over the last 10 years, is designed to clean your home with the minimum impact on the environment. The products are designed to be fully biodegradable in a maximum of three days — or, in the case of Ecover's Washing Powder, five days. But they are also formulated with a number of other guidelines in mind.

- No petroleum based detergents, which are slower to biodegrade and may contain toxic impurities. Instead, Ecover uses natural vegetable oil based cleaners, which break down rapidly and safely.

- No phosphates, which can over-fertilize algae in rivers and lakes, causing them to lock up oxygen and suffocate other organisms — particularly fish. In many areas, your local sewage works should be able to remove phosphates from the incoming water, but in areas like the Norfolk Broads a switch to products like Ecover could help significantly.

- No foam-building chemicals like NTA or EDTA, once considered the alternatives to phosphates. Recent research suggests that both substances can help remobilize toxic materials, such as lead and mercury, which would otherwise remain 'safely' locked up in river muds.

- No optical bleaches, which are added to washing powders to give an illusion of whiteness. They can irritate the skin and tend to biodegrade slowly.

- No chlorine bleaches, which can produce toxic and cancer-causing chemicals as they break down in the sewage system or environment.

- No enzymes, which can produce severe allergic reactions in some sensitive people.

- No synthetic colourings or perfumes, which are often based on petroleum products, are slow to biodegrade and either toxic or irritant — or both. Instead, Ecover uses natural plant extracts for perfumes and no colourings at all.

The range of products includes Washing Powder, Washing Up Liquid, Cream Cleaner, Fabric Conditioner, Toilet Cleaner, Floor Soap, Wool Wash Liquid and Heavy Duty Hand Cleaner. These products are not stocked by the main supermarkets yet, but are available in a growing number of smaller outlets. Details from **Full Moon**.

Having dismissed the challenge from such 'green' products, a number of the major detergents manufacturers are now beginning to edge towards this market — which they fear could develop rapidly and blow the froth off their own sales.

Other Household Products

Aluminium foil and pans

Making aluminium consumes a great deal of energy: 4 – 6 tonnes of oil for every tonne of aluminium. So use aluminium foil sparingly, if at all. An equally pressing concern is that acid foods and liquids cooked in aluminium pots, pans or pressure cookers can become contaminated with the metal. Aluminium, whether we eat it or drink it in tap-water, may help cause premature senility — in the form of Alzheimer's disease. So if you are considering buying aluminium pans don't, and if you have old ones, consider sending them off for recycling.

Clingfilm

First we had greaseproof paper, then kitchen foil, then clingfilm. Most clingfilms use plasticizers to make them clingy. High doses of one plasticizer, DEHA, produce an increase in liver tumours in mice — and affect the sperm of male mice. Such plasticizers can migrate into foods, particularly fatty foods such as salami, cheese and halved avocados. Remember, too, that cooking food in clingfilm-covered dishes in microwave ovens can cause high levels of plasticizer migration.

A number of safer alternatives are now available. **Bejam** says that its non-PVC *Food Wrap* 'contains no plasticizer'. **Waitrose**'s two new products are *Non-PVC Polythene Film Food Wrap*, which comes in sheets, and *Microwave and Freezer Food Wrap*, which comes in a roll, 'for use in microwaves and freezers'. These products are less clingy, but safer. Look for labels saying 'non-PVC' or 'plasticizer free'.

Loo paper

Enormous quantities of paper are flushed down the drain every day. There has been concern for a number of years that coloured loo paper is less biodegradable — and therefore more of a pollution problem — than uncoloured paper. The best way to reduce the impact of the loo paper you use is to buy brands containing a certain amount of recycled fibre. Suppliers include **Traidcraft** (mail order) and, in the High Street, **Safeway**'s own-brand product.

Beers, Wines and Spirits

Beers

The average Briton drank 190 pints (108 litres) of beer in 1986, down from 204 pints (116 litres) in 1980. As with cheeses, there has been an enormous growth in demand for 'real ale' products in Britain. But many British brews would still provoke derision in countries like West Germany where all beers are already additive-free.

West Germany's 'purity' laws allow only malt, hops and water in beers. The Germans complain that elsewhere in Europe brewers 'pollute' their brews with gum arabic, sulphur dioxide and hydrogen sulphate. With the Bavarians consuming 235 litres (412 pints) of beer a year per head, the Germans argue that they have to be much more careful about what goes into their beers. Various supermarkets offer additive-free beers and lagers, including *Lowenbrau*, *Brown Master Pils*, *Edelhau Export* and *Berliner Export*.

An essential reference for the serious beer drinker is the *Good Beer Guide*, published by the Campaign for Real Ale (CAMRA). This lists over 5,000 pubs throughout Great Britain and the beers they serve.

Cider

Believe it or not, the average Briton drinks 109 pints (62 litres) of cider each year. If you are looking for an organic cider, check through the *Good Cider Guide*, published by CAMRA, which has around 2,500 entries. One good candidate is **Aspall Cyder**, all of whose products sport the Soil Association's symbol of organic quality. The orchards are entirely free of artificial fertilizers and pesticides, and the (delicious) end product is free of any preservatives. Unfortunately, you can't yet buy most of the products listed in the *Guide* in supermarkets.

'It is not as easy to define an honest pint of cider as it is real ale', says CAMRA. 'In theory it should be made strictly from the juice of cider apples, fermented in their own yeasts with sweetness controlled by racking off, without any filtration, artificial colour, or pasteurization, for serving without the use of extraneous carbon dioxide and it should be matured only in oak casks.'

But, CAMRA notes, 'If we were to stick rigidly to this definition the *Guide* would be a thin pamphlet, for few cider makers adhere to every point.' Some do, and are listed in the *Guide*, while most turn out something approaching the original article, 'good, old fashioned, and natural'.

Wine

Consumption of wine in the UK went up to 16 bottles per head per annum in 1986, compared to 10 bottles in 1980. Even so, Europe still produces more wine than it needs and a great deal of wine is converted at ridiculous expense into alcohol for industrial use.

Of more concern to the consumer, however, is the adulteration of wine. Austria, for example, ended up using millions of litres of wine as an antifreeze additive, after revelations that many dealers had been sweetening and smoothing their wines with diethylene glycol, a component of some antifreeze products.

Even when done properly, however, conventional wine-making uses enzymes, sorbic acid to slow the yeasts down, diammonium phosphate to feed them, kaolin and bentonite to fine the wine, citric acid to stabilize it, and tartaric acid and carbonates to alter the acid balance.

Among the phrases you should look for on French organic wines and champagnes are *culture biologique, sans produits chimiques, sans engrais chimique, ni herbicide, ni insecticide de synthèse* or simply *made from unsprayed grapes,* and a certifying symbol. Many organic wines are not identified as such on the label, however, partly because the wine producers are unaware that it might be a marketing advantage. An excellent source of information is the *Organic Wine Guide* (Mainstream Publishing, 1987). Importers specializing in organic wines include **West Heath Wine** and **Wholefood**.

Vegetarians might like to discover first whether the wine or champagne they are drinking has been treated with gelatine, egg white, dried blood, powder or sturgeons' air bladders.

We asked Charlotte Mitchell, co-author of *The Organic Wine Guide* with Iain Wright, to review some of the best organic wines and champagnes for us. The range of fine wines available is large and growing. She also mentions an organic apple wine and a range of organic fruit juices, which she suggests as a wine alternative. Ask your local off-licence or supermarket and if they cannot supply you go to **Real Wines** or **Vinceremos**. They will send mixed cases by mail order.

A TASTE OF ORGANIC WINE

FRANCE

Champagne and Méthode champenoise

Carte d'Or Champagne José Ardinat   A fine, characteristically dry champagne, fresh and light with a biscuity gooseberry flavour, well balanced and rounded.

Saumur Méthode Champenoise Brut Gérard Leroux   A good yeast nose and gorgeous straw colour with tiny bubbles. This is dry, toasty and strong with a lovely slightly bitter finish.

Red Wines

MIDI, PROVENCE AND SOUTH

Domaine de Clairac Jougla Vin de Table   With a fruity nose, this is a well-balanced dry red in a one-litre bottle.

Domaine de l'Ile, Vin de Pays de l'Aude   A southern wine from the midi region, this is a good red, from Carignan and Cinsault grapes, with a pleasant, fruity, dry flavour.

BORDEAUX

Château du Moulin de Peyronin AC 1986   A youthful purply colour, with a variety of smells — fig, blackcurrant, nutmeg. A good fruity flavour.

Château Renaissance AC 1986   A medium red with a light nose and a hint of smokiness. A supple, balanced wine, full of warmth, with enough tannin to improve for many years.

Château de Prade Bordeaux Supérieur AC 1985   A lovely mature orangey colour with a concentrated ripe nose and superb texture, this is a particularly fine example of a Castillon.

Château Méric Graves AC 1985   Pierre Barron, who makes this wine, advises 'Drink little but drink well, drink natural wine in order to drink for a long time', and this wine has an enticing raspberry and blackcurrant bouquet with a touch of cloves in the finish.

Château Barrail des Graves St Emilion AC 1986   Matured in oak casks, this wine has a lovely woody flavour; it is fruity and delicious. Made from Cabernet Sauvignon and Merlot grapes.

Domaine St Anne Entre-deux-mers AC 1986   (sold at Safeway) Slightly flat but yeasty smell led to a spritely, full-flavoured white wine with a good finish.

RHONE

Cave la Vigneronne Villedieu AC 1986   The light, bright citrus flavours of this wine belie the 14% alcohol. Fruity, attractive and strong, good tannin.

Vignoble de la Jasse AC 1985 A full bouquet with an attractive hint of oak. A well-balanced flavour and tannin make this a really excellent smooth rich wine.

Domaine St Apollinaire AC Côtes du Rhône 1985 (sold at Sainsbury's) One of the most disappointing of all organic wines available in the UK. An almost rubbery medicinal taste.

BURGUNDY

Mâcon Alain Guillot AC 1986 This family claims to be one of the oldest organic wine producers — since 1954. There is no sulphur used during vinification. A full dry wine from the Gamay grape, dark purple with lots of character.

Bourgogne Alain Guillot AC 1986 A classic wine made from the Pinot Noir grape (the red wine grape of Burgundy). No sulphur used during vinification. This is a lovely complex and full-flavoured wine with a fragrant bouquet.

BEAUJOLAIS

Château de Boisfranc Beaujolais Supérieur AC 1987 M. Doat does not use any sulphur in his vineyard or during vinification, and adds only 1 – 2 grammes per hectolitre when bottling, which is very low. The wine is very fruity and well rounded. Top quality Beaujolais.

White Wines

LOIRE

Blanc de Blancs Guy Bossard An excellent value wine, dry and refreshing but with a fullness of flavour that goes well with everything. Best-selling white organic wine in the UK.

Gros Plant du Pays Nantais sur Lie Guy Bossard VDQS 1986 (Médaille d'Or) Extra dry, superbly crisp, similar to a genuine Vinho Verde. Balances beautifully with strong-flavoured food, particularly fish.

Muscadet de Sèvre et Maine sur Lie Guy Bossard AC 1986 Pale yellow with a decided *pétillance*, a dry grapey wine, with balanced fruit, clean lemons predominating. Truly outstanding.

Sancerre Christian et Nicole Dauny AC 1986 Dry, elegant and exquisitely balanced with a lime and lychees bouquet and a good Sauvignon grapey flavour.

SOUTH OF FRANCE

Mauzac Vin de Pays de l'Aude 1986 Made from the lesser-known Mauzac grape (which forms the base of the famous sparkling wine,

Blanquette de Limoux). This southern white is fresh and dry with a good fruity acidity and a pale greenish colour.

Limoux, Domaine de Clairac AC 1986   Lovely fresh grapes in the bouquet lead to a mellow, well-balanced and not over-dry flavour.

Chardonnay Vin de Pays de l'Aude 1986   Excellently balanced, elegant, full and buttery on the palate, with a good long finish. A classic grape variety, currently very fashionable.

Pétillant de Raisin   A medium white with only 2 per cent alcohol, very fruity, good for staying sober!

BORDEAUX

Château Ballue Mondon Sec AC 1986 (Médaille Bronze)   A full-flavoured Bordeaux white, a real classic of a wine, dry with a distinct gooseberry taste — very popular.

Château Ballue Mondon Moelleux AC 1985   From the same producer as the dry white (Guy Ballue) this is a light sweet dessert wine, delicious with fruits — pungent and aromatic.

Château Méric Graves Supérieur AC 1986   Crisp and fresh, good acidity, a wine with finesse, carefully blended from 50 per cent Sémillon, 40 per cent Sauvignon and 10 per cent Muscadelle grapes. Superior in every way.

Château le Barradis Monbazillac AC 1985   A beautiful golden-coloured wine with a strong Muscadelle flavour, made from Sauvignon Blanc, Sémillon and Muscadelle grapes. This is top quality sweet Sauternes-type wine — rich and irresistible.

BURGUNDY

Bourgogne Rouge Alain Guillot AC 1986   100 per cent Chardonnay, superb almost bronze colour bursting with character and individuality. No sulphur is used during the vinification, and the cork is dipped in wax to seal the wine from the air and prevent oxidization.

ALSACE

Sylvaner Pierre Frick AC 1986   Fragrant and fruity, yet still clean and dry, this wine is easy drinking, suitable for all occasions.

Klevner Cuvée Spéciale Pierre Frick AC 1985   A top quality, reserve wine made without *chapitalisation* (ie adding sugar to increase alcohol), it displays an excellent honeyed, fruity, fresh and alive flavour with a long finish.

Gewurztraminer Pierre Frick AC 1986   A classic and distinctive grape, the Gewurztraminer is the best known wine of Alsace, spicy and aromatic on the nose, full and tangy on the palate with a powerful finish.

Rosé Wines

Rosé d'Anjou Gérard Leroux AC 1986   A beautiful straw pink colour made from the Gros Lot grape, which is particular to the Loire valley. This wine has a medium dry nose with a fresh and surprisingly fruity flavour.

Domaine de Clairac Jubio Rosé   A youthful wine, dry and light with a delicate fruit.

SPAIN
Red Wines

Biovin Valdepenas DOC 1986   A light dry red, very fruity and all too quaffable.

ITALY
Red Wines

Chianti DOCG Roberto Drighi 1986   A bright, clear ruby red colour, medium body, fresh and fruity with zest, this is an excellent blend of San Giovese, Canaiolo, Trebbiano and Malvasia grapes.

Valpolicella DOC Classico Superiore 1985   A pale red with an almost nutty nose, it is smooth but fresh with a typical bitter almond finish.

White Wines

San Vito Verdiglio Roberto Drighi 1986   Made from 100 per cent Verdicchio grapes, this wine has a light straw colour, is dry but soft and harmoniously balanced — delicious.

San Vito Bianco Toscano Roberto Drighi 1986   A subtle yet fresh bouquet leads to a wine that is vivid and clean with a good flavour. Made from Trebbiano and Malvasia grapes, it is a beautiful colour with golden hints.

Soave DOC Classico 1986 Guerrieri-Rizzardi   A clean light nose, delicate depth and lots of flavour with a good acidity and fruit.

ENGLAND

Organic Apple Wine — Avalon Vineyard   Made from dessert apples and Bramleys, this is crisp and refreshing, amazingly reminiscent of grape wine, strong but light and delicious.

ALCOHOL-FREE ORGANIC FRUIT JUICES

French Organic Grape Juice, White, Guy Bossard   A very fruity, grapey flavour, the same as Guy Bossard's Blanc de Blancs but sweeter as not fermented to produce alcohol. Excellent wine alternative.

Spirits

On average each Briton downs nearly 6 bottles of spirits each year. The fermentation processes involved in producing spirits like gin and whisky have traditionally produced very strong effluents, which caused recurrent water pollution problems. In recent years, however, the industry has invested heavily in effluent treatment facilities — and much of the organic material in the effluent streams emerging from distilleries is now reclaimed for use in animal feed.

That doesn't mean that your tot has no impact on the environment, however. The whisky industry's need for peat has led to conflicts with conservationists on the Scottish island of Islay, with peat extraction threatening to destroy an important feeding ground for migrating geese.

THE PACKAGING ISSUE UNWRAPPED

If you unwrapped your weekly shop all at once, you would be surrounded by a mountain of paper, plastics, metals and glass which would have seemed a treasure trove at any other period of human history.

Packaging is important, protecting products from damage, ensuring hygiene, permitting information to be provided for users and enormously adding to consumer convenience. But the production, use and disposal of packaging materials can also contribute to many environmental problems, from litter to acid rain.

As a result, more and more of us worry about the wasteful use of packaging. Indeed, in a survey carried out by *Good Housekeeping* in 1987, people rated bottle banks second only to lavatories in the list of facilities they wanted supermarkets to provide.

But most supermarkets refuse to stock returnable containers and are not among the most active promoters of bottle banks or other recycling facilities. They need to be pushed. As a first step, write to your local supermarket and ask the manager to contact the local authority and arrange for a bottle bank to be installed.

Overall, the Green Consumer would be well advised to act according to the advice offered by Richmond Borough Council in its recycling campaign: *Don't Choose What You Can't Re-use.* Other broad guidelines would include the following:

- Don't litter.

- Return refillable glass bottles for re-use.

- Put non-returnable bottles in your nearest bottle bank.

- If there is no bottle bank nearby, ask your local authority to provide one. But remember that it may not make environmental sense to collect glass for recycling where transport distances are too long — or, the other side of the coin, the population is too scattered.

- Put cans in a Save-a-Can skip, where available.

- Support separate aluminium can collections.

- Collect your newspapers and either take them to a paper recycling collection point — or have them collected. Recycling schemes are run by local authorities, community associations, political parties, scout groups and other organizations. If no one is doing this in your area, consider organizing one.

- Cut down on the amount of plastics you buy.

- Ask for paper bags, rather than plastic ones. Buy beverages in returnable bottles or recycle single-trip glass containers.

- Don't discard plastics in the environment — apart from the litter problem, they can kill wildlife. Plastic wrappers and six-pack plastic rings suffocate or strangle fish and birds alike.

- Ask your local authority if a future waste disposal plan has been prepared — and whether recycling, or incineration with heat recovery, have been properly considered.

● And, very importantly, buy recycled paper products. Increased consumer demand will encourage manufacturers to use more recycled raw materials. Specifically ask for recycled products. At the moment, some suppliers are nervous about mentioning the fact that their products (some brands of loo paper, for example) contain recycled paper, whereas in different circumstances they could be promoting the fact.

Clearly, the designer has an important role to play in making sure that more products are safely and attractively packaged with less materials and less energy used — and less pollution produced — as a result. But, as the facts below show, there is no ideal packaging material for all purposes.

Paper and cardboard

Issues: Despite the computer industry's claims that we are moving towards the 'paperless society', we use ever-growing amounts of paper and cardboard. Each year, every one of us consumes paper and board equivalent to an average of at least two trees. And it is not simply a matter of trees. Apart from the 2.2 tonnes of wood needed to make a tonne of paper, considerable quantities of energy, water and chemicals are also used. Indeed, pulp and paper production are generally highly polluting and energy-intensive activities.

Paper is an excellent material for many types of packaging. The Tetrapak, for example, is a close-packing carton used for liquid products. Because Tetrapaks are so light, and are designed to fit together with no gaps, they save space — and therefore help economize on fuel in transport.

Re-use: Today's newspaper may be tomorrow's fish and chip wrapper, but generally re-use is not an option with paper products. But it *is* often worth re-using cardboard boxes.

Recycling: About 30 per cent of the paper products we buy are made from recycled paper. Recycled paper products are now often of high quality, and range from stationery, paper towels and loo paper to newspapers and egg boxes.

Forty per cent less energy is needed to make paper from recycled fibre than to make it from virgin pulp. Unfortunately, too few local authorities operate waste paper collection programmes. At the same time, many companies do not yet mention the fact that their products (particularly hygienic products) contain recycled materials — because they feel it may dent their image. But the recycled paper industry is rapidly improving the quality of its products and, increasingly, targeting the Green Consumer in its marketing. Green Consumers, it hardly needs saying, like recycled products.

Biodegradability: Although paper packaging is a major contributor to litter, at least paper and paper products generally break down rapidly in the environment.

Glass

Issues: Glass making is an energy-intensive business, and it can also have a considerable environmental impact. It takes a total of 1.1 tonnes of sand, limestone and soda ash to make 1 tonne of glass, as well as a great deal of energy and water. Some 6 billion glass bottles and jars are used every year in Britain, and over 1.5 million tonnes of waste glass are produced.

Re-use: The returnable bottle is a highly environment-friendly form of packaging, as long as the bottle is returned. Milk bottles are re-used an average of 20 times, although some may be re-used as many as 40 or 50 times. Supermarkets and off-licences generally hate returnable bottles, however, because they take up valuable space.

Recycling: Unlike materials such as paper, glass can effectively be recycled forever. Every tonne of crushed waste glass (or 'cullet') used saves the equivalent of 30 gallons (135 litres) of oil and replaces 1.2 tonnes of raw materials. In 1987 there were 3,100 bottle banks, all of them profitable, with an industry target of 5,000 by 1991. This would represent one bottle bank for every

10,000 people. Even so, experience elsewhere in the EEC suggests that the optimum ratio would be five times higher.

Biodegradability: To all intents and purposes, glass doesn't biodegrade. It's also dangerous to children, pets and wildlife if left in the open environment.

Cans

Issues: Over 10 billion cans are used in Britain every year. Cans make up about 6 – 9 per cent of the rubbish in your dustbin. The main materials in cans are steel, aluminium and tin. It takes about 4 tonnes of bauxite to make 1 tonne of aluminium, a highly energy-intensive business. In fact, metal smelting is always an environment-intensive business.

Re-use: Not really an option.

Recycling: Recycling an aluminium can saves 95 per cent of the energy used to make aluminium from scratch — and cuts the air pollution by 95 per cent. Put another way, the energy needed to make 1 tonne of virgin aluminium could be used to recycle 20 tonnes of aluminium from scrap. The Aluminium Recycling Can-paign are active in the area covered by Central TV and are planning to expand nationally.

The benefits of recycling tinplate are somewhat less exciting, but still well worth pursuing. The Can Makers have set up Save-A-Can skips at selected sites around the country. If there is one near you, use it. They take food and drink cans, pet food cans and even biscuit tins.

Biodegradability: Metals are not biodegradable to any great extent. Some alloys, and metals such as aluminium, are very long-lived, but many metals do rust. That does not mean that metal cans should be thrown away in the open environment, however. They will take a very long time to rust away, if they ever do. And in environmental resource terms rust represents a problem, rather than an asset. When we lose metals (which are themselves in increasingly short supply) to rust, we also lose all the energy that went into making them. So, wherever possible, they should be reclaimed and recycled.

Plastics

Issues: There are over 50 types of plastic, made from such raw materials as oil, natural gas, coal and salt. They make up about 5 – 7 per cent of the rubbish in your dustbin. They take a fair amount of energy to produce, although much less than metals, and do not biodegrade readily once out in the environment. Some plastics, like PVC, may contribute to air pollution problems if burned in poorly designed — or operated — waste incinerators.

Re-use: Plastic's long life is totally inappropriate for most of the throwaway products made from it, although some plastic products can be re-used.

Recycling: There are no plastics recycling schemes aimed at the consumer. The problem is the sheer number of plastics in use. Where they can be separated out easily, as in the factory where they are being used, recycling often makes sense. If, instead, you have to sort them out of the domestic waste, you have problems. Even so, around 10 per cent of polyethylene film is recycled (that's what black plastic refuse sacks are made from) and 7 per cent of polypropylene (used to make drainage pipes, for example).

Biodegradability: Most plastics do not biodegrade readily, although biodegradable plastics have been developed. To date, however, they tend to be costlier and more difficult to store and distribute, while their degradation is still slow and unpredictable. The industry feels that, while plastics recycling is difficult, it is probably the way to go in the longer term.

To find out more about recycling you can contact the **Aluminium Recycling Can-paign**, **British Plastics Federation**, **Glass Manufacturers' Federation**, **Incpen**, **Recycling Advisory Unit**, **Save-A-Can** and **Wastewatch**. (Addresses are given on pages 236 – 8.)

WHICH IS THE GREENEST SUPERMARKET?

Our telephone surveys in April and May 1988 have shown that the major supermarkets are rapidly waking up to the threat posed by the Green Consumer — and to some of the emerging opportunities. **Safeway** and **Sainsbury** are vying for the top slot. Our rating ranges from ★ ★ ★ ★ ★ for a supermarket which seems to have everything the Green Consumer is likely to need (there isn't one yet) to ★ for supermarkets which are being very slow to catch on to the potential of the Green Consumer.

Two supermarkets — **Bejam** and **Spar** — do not merit a star within the terms of our survey. **Tesco** and **Asda**, which both rate ★ ★ ★, have been involved in a race to demonstrate their environment-friendliness. Not only are they offering 'ozone-friendly' products, but Tesco are introducing lead-free petrol at all their service stations. They are also only buying company cars which can run on unleaded fuel. Tesco has not yet started stocking organic produce, however.

★ ★ ★ ★ ★	None
★ ★ ★ ★	Safeway Sainsbury
★ ★ ★	Asda Tesco
★ ★	Gateway Waitrose
★	Marks & Spencer

★ ★ ★ ASDA

120 stores nationwide, with another 16 due to open soon. The information requested did not seem to be easily to hand.

Organic range in store   Stock organic produce in 31 of their 120 stores. Range varies seasonally but includes: oranges, apples, cooking apples, pears, chinese leaves, tomatoes, iceberg lettuces, capsicums, cucumbers, courgettes, broccoli, white cabbage, swedes, carrots, parsnips,

	red cabbage, onions, potatoes, mushrooms and cherries.
Organic standards	Have their own symbol and claim their produce is grown to internationally accepted standards. No hormones in beef, pork or lamb.
Beverages	No organic wine
Meat	Withdrawal periods for antibiotic residues in meat must be adhered to and are spot checked.
Eggs	Free-range eggs are available in all Asda stores.
Detergents	No biodegradable detergents.
Food irradiation	No policy towards food irradiation.
Vegetarian	Asda are in the process of introducing specifically labelled vegetarian food to their frozen and chilled range of products.
CFC issue	Say they aim to have removed CFCs from all their own brand products by the end of June 1988. These products will be clearly labelled 'ozone-friendly'. They stressed that they cannot dictate to manufacturers on this subject, but will encourage them wherever possible. CFCs are currently used in meat and vegetable trays but Asda are in the early stages of investigating alternatives.
Packaging	Customer convenience is their yardstick. Egg boxes are made from either PVC or pulp board. Only plastic bags at the check-out.
Recycling facilities	66 stores have bottle banks near by.
Additives	Claim not to use any unnecessary additives.
Information	Provide leaflet on organic food, but like to include as much information as possible on the packet itself.

BEJAM

265 stores nationwide, specialize in frozen foods. Helpful, but as a company not very progressive in this area.

Organic range in store	Do not sell any fresh produce. Most of their products are frozen. Sell Jordans Conservation Grade products.
Beverages	No organic drinks.

Meat	Said the label would inform the consumer if additives were used to tenderize a particular meat product. They thought that their pork could well contain limited quantities of antibiotics and hormones, but they do not permit Carbadox, a growth promoter. Do not sell free-range chickens. They believe that it would be too costly.
Eggs	No free-range eggs.
Detergents	No biodegradable detergents.
Food irradiation	Not applicable, as only applies to fresh produce.
Vegetarian	No specifically vegetarian dishes, although some are suitable for vegetarians.
CFC issue	Do not produce own-brand aerosols. Said that the manufacturers' brands they sell do not contain CFCs, although this is coincidental rather than a matter of policy. Their foam packaging could well contain CFCs.
Additives	Have removed them in new products, and say they do not use them unless 100 per cent necessary. 95 per cent of their products are free from artificial colours.
Information	They supply a Healthy Eating leaflet with nutritional information on 300 own-label products. Over 75 per cent of their products have nutritional information on the pack.

CO-OP

We have not covered the Co-op in our survey because they have 90 different head offices, each with a number of stores with different names operating under them. Therefore there is no overall company policy.

★ ★ GATEWAY

An important chain, with 830 stores. They were quite helpful, although it seemed as if they had not thought much about this as an area of interest.

Organic range in store	In most of their stores, depending on availability. During one week in April 1988 they had stocked onions, white cabbage, garlic, mushrooms, lemons, tomatoes and broccoli. So far, they had rejected organic oranges and potatoes.

Organic standards	Soil Association standards — symbol is being put on packaging for their organic range.
Beverages	No organic drinks.
Meat	Tried introducing free-range chickens two years ago but they did not sell. However, are currently actively considering re-introducing them.
Eggs	Free-range eggs in all stores.
Detergents	No biodegradable detergents.
Food irradiation	Would not stock irradiated food, because of consumer resistance.
Vegetarian	Special health food sections in their larger stores with products such as tofu, soya milk and cheeses approved by the Vegetarian Society.
CFC issue	Household products are CFC-free. Said they were actively working on their health and beauty ranges and hoped to have them CFC-free by mid-1988. Ask them whether they have succeeded — and congratulate them if they have!
Packaging	Supply cardboard egg boxes, but only have plastic bags at their check-outs.
Recycling facilities	Bottle banks at a number of stores but not centrally organized. Say they always co-operate with local schemes. Also involved in a 'Cash for Trash' scheme in the Midlands.
Additives	Their own-label people have been investigating ways of removing additives. Meanwhile they are including additives on their labels. They have not considered including environmental issues on their labels.
Information	Do not provide information leaflets. Publish an in-store magazine, but were unable to say whether subjects of interest to the Green Consumer were covered.

★ MARKS AND SPENCER

263 stores, all with food departments and sell all own-brand goods. Helpful, but have not really woken up to the potential of the Green Consumer. Said they had loyal customers who tend to have shopped with them for a long time and whose priority is convenience.

Organic range in store	No organic foods.

Beverages No organic drinks.

Meat Their policy is to 'abide by legal requirements'. They do sell free-range chickens. (See also p. 184.)

Eggs Free-range eggs in all stores, in cardboard boxes.

Detergents Nothing particularly suitable for the Green Consumer.

Food irradiation See no need for the irradiation of food.

Vegetarian They offer a large range of vegetable-based meals suitable for vegetarians. Vegetarian Society recommend the range and M & S use their guidelines, although not their symbol.

CFC issue Aiming to remove CFCs from the bulk of their aerosols by end of 1988. CFCs currently used in egg box packaging but all CFCs will be removed from all packaging by end of 1988.

Packaging Plastic bags only.

Recycling facilities They do not have many car parks and have no plans to offer recycling facilities.

Additives Cutting back on additives, but still use them for appearance. Do not permit tartrazine and their marzipan contains no artificial colour.

Information Lists of suitable products are supplied for those on special (eg gluten-free) diets.

★ ★ ★ ★ SAFEWAY

Were very helpful, aware of all the issues and were actively looking into ways of addressing them. They have a total of 165 stores and are opening 1 – 2 a month. Appear to be the supermarket group which is doing most to appeal to the Green Consumer.

Organic range in store Stock the best organic range of any supermarket chain, with organic fruit and vegetables in every store. Their organic selection includes: lemons, grapefruit, oranges, rhubarb, dates, celery, swede, new potatoes, red potatoes, white potatoes, french carrots, baby carrots, purple broccoli spears, red broccoli, red cabbage, white cabbage, green cabbage, parsley, artichokes, mushrooms, garlic, small onions, Dutch onions, pre-packed beetroot, avocados, tomatoes, American cress, five different salad packs and a cheese crunch pack (includes hard or soft cheese, salad selection and digestive biscuits — all organic). They also stock organic yoghurt (*Busses Farm* brand) and organic frozen corn and frozen cobs.

Organic standards   Conform to Soil Association standards. Also label suitable products as 'Organically Grown'.

Beverages   Sold one brand of organic wine, produced by a single supplier, but demand was so great they ran out. This was Safeway's *Domaine St Anne Bordeaux*, in red and white. Said it would be in stock again shortly. They are also looking into the possibility of following Sainsbury's lead with an additive-free cider.

Meat   Do not sell additive-free meat because there are no reliable standards or guarantees of quality yet. They sell free-range chickens in most of their stores.

Eggs   Free-range eggs in all stores.

Detergents   No biodegradable detergents.

Food irradiation   Not yet an issue, as far as they were concerned, since no supermarket stocks irradiated food. Said it was too early to make a definite policy decision and that they would wait until the law is changed, if it is. But they would first gauge customer demand and if they stocked irradiated food they would label it.

Vegetarian   The Vegetarian Society told us that Safeway's labelling on vegetarian food was either non-existent or bad.

CFC issue   The first supermarket group to go entirely CFC-free in their own-label range. In response to consumer pressure, branded products will have an ozone-friendly sticker if they are CFC-free. Production of a CFC-containing hair mousse had been stopped. Also developing a hand pump hairspray. They had not yet considered the problem of CFCs in egg boxes and meat trays.

Packaging   Offer brown recycled paper bags as an alternative to plastic bags at the check-out. Also sell recycled loo paper (own label). Use both cardboard and plastic egg boxes.

Recycling facilities   Some of their car parks have bottle banks.

Additives   Claim to be the first supermarket chain to implement a policy of removing where possible and practical all unnecessary ingredients and contentious food additives from own-label products. A range of leaflets and booklets on additives is available.

Information They have information booklets on diet, nutrition, additives and organic produce.

★ ★ ★ ★ SAINSBURY

279 stores, nationwide but not in Scotland. Were aware of the issues we raised and in most cases were trying to address them.

Organic range in store At the time of the survey, 50 Sainsbury stores stocked organic produce. Their current products range included: mixed vegetable pack, potatoes and new potatoes, swede, white and red cabbage, carrots, cauliflower florettes, onions, mushrooms, mixed salad, tomatoes, apples, oranges, avocados and lemons.

Organic standards Have adopted the Soil Association's standards.

Beverages At the time, they were selling one organic wine in a single store, in the Cromwell Road, London. This was *Domaine Saint Apollinaire* (Côtes du Rhône 1985), which will be going into more stores and into their Vintage Selection. This venture had apparently been successful, but there are no immediate plans to sell any further organic wines. Also sell *Medium Dry Cider*, which contains no artificial preservatives and they say is the only cider of its kind on supermarket shelves.

Meat and poultry Say they are closely involved in the production of pork right through from rearing to processing. In conjunction with the Ministry of Agriculture, Fisheries and Food, they regularly test the residue levels in pigs slaughtered in their abattoirs. They are satisfied that there are no residues in the meat. Sainsbury's process 5 per cent of the pigs killed in the UK. They sell free-range chickens and, at Christmas, turkeys in 60 of their stores.

Eggs Free-range eggs sold in all stores.

Detergents No biodegradable detergents.

Food irradiation　If the government were to decide in favour of food irradiation, Sainsbury's would support any labelling programme that was adopted.

Vegetarian　Own-label range of vegetarian 'ready meals', sold in their chilled (not frozen) cabinet section; only supermarket range officially approved by the Vegetarian Society. A full list of this range is available from Sainsbury's.

CFC issue　In February 1988, launched labelling scheme for all their own-label CFC-free aerosols. Anticipated that by end 1988 all Sainsbury's own-label toiletry and household aerosol products would be CFC-free. Currently 85 per cent of expanded polystyrene foam (EPS) trays they sell contain CFCs. Said they planned to change the formula in these trays to a less damaging CFC by end of 1988. Looking at ways to reduce their dependence on these trays.

Packaging　Egg boxes either PVC or *papier maché* based. No policy on use of biodegradable materials.

Recycling facilities　No policy on supporting recycling facilities near their stores.

Additives　Where an additive is necessary, will try to use an effective and safe natural compound rather than a synthetic one. Colours gradually being phased out. Tartrazine has been removed from all soft drinks and crumb-coated foods. Have produced a booklet called *Facts about Food Additives*.

Information　Wide range of information leaflets on diet, nutrition and additives, but not available in all stores. No leaflet on organic produce, but offer to answer customer inquiries.

Comments　Sainsbury's won the Beta Award for Energy Efficiency, in 1987. Heat lost from the back of their refrigeration units is being recycled to heat one-sixth of the group's 280 stores.

SPAR

2,450 stores nationwide. The central office has a policy only towards Spar's own-brand produce. Stores are individually owned and therefore supplies are ordered locally. Individual stores may be greener than the centre.

Organic range in store No organic range is supplied centrally.

Beverages No organic drinks or additive-free brands.

Meat Supply tinned meat only, with no particular attention paid to hormones or other additives. Some stores do carry fresh meat, but buy it locally — and are unlikely to be looking for 'real meat'.

Eggs Free-range eggs in some stores, but customer demand is limited.

Detergents No particularly suitable products.

Vegetarian Sell products that do not contain meat, but nothing specifically catering for the vegetarian sector. Vegetarian Society have said that Spar do not respond to their requests for information.

CFC issue Said they took CFCs out of all aerosols last year. Also said that they would shortly start to label aerosols as CFC-free when they get the next batch of labels or cans printed. They did not know about CFCs in packaging, and mentioned that they possibly used them in fish fillet trays.

Packaging They offer the option of biodegradable plastic bags at the check-out, and have done since the 1970s. They are the only group in our survey to do this.

Recycling facilities Thought that they had one or two bottle banks, but are generally very squeezed for space — and do not have large car parks.

Additives Anything about additives, they said, is likely to be on the pack.

Information Do not provide information sheets.

★ ★ ★ TESCO

380 stores nationwide, including 120 superstores.

Organic range in store No organic produce in any of their stores.

Beverages No organic drinks.

Meat Packaged meats are free of growth-promoting residuals of any description, including hormones and antibiotics — or indeed any contaminant injected, ingested or specially applied. Evidence of any breach of legislation regarding the use of residual presence of contaminants will automatically place producers and suppliers on a blacklist. Free range chickens are available in selected stores.

Eggs   Free range eggs in all their stores.

Detergents   No biodegradable detergents.

Food irradiation   Had carried out a lot of research in this area, but would not introduce irradiated produce into their stores until more research has been carried out — even if it was legalized by the Government.

Vegetarian   Selection of vegetarian foods — chilled ready meals, frozen dishes and vegeburgers. Also sell pre-packed mild and full-flavoured vegetarian cheddars.

CFC issue   Planned to get CFCs out of all its own-label aerosols by September 1988. Had 16 CFC-containing products. When reformulated, these will all have a Tesco's label identifying them as CFC-free. Branded products will only be labelled if the manufacturer labels them. Had not yet thought about CFCs in packaging of egg boxes and meat trays.

Packaging   Offer a choice of plastic or cardboard egg boxes.

Recycling facilities   Are encouraging recycling facilities near — or in - their stores. Under a new policy, if local councils are agreeable, bottle banks will be introduced into all new stores.

Additives   In their own-label range of products, they have replaced over 600 additives with natural alternatives — or have taken them out altogether. Moving towards removing unnecessary additives from all their own-label products.

Information   Claim to have been the first supermarket to complete nutritional labelling, moving well beyond the legal requirements. In 6 supermarkets have Consumer Advisory Kitchens, with trained Home Economists advising on diet and nutrition. In all stores they have a Nutrition Centre with information leaflets on fibre, fat, sugar and other problem foods.

★ ★ WAITROSE

Have 84 stores in the Midlands and Southern England. Helpful and clearly recognize this is an area they cannot ignore, but gave the impression they do not aim to be frontrunners in this area.

Organic range in store Organic produce was available in 48 of the group's 84 stores. Have been working with their suppliers to reduce the use of chemicals in the growing of all fruit and vegetables. In addition, they have been working for some time to develop a range of organic fruit and vegetables. When we called, 10 kinds of green and root vegetables and 5 kinds of fruit (including oranges, lemons, grapefruit and avocados) were being sold.

Organic standards They observe guidelines laid down by IFOAM, labelling appropriate products as 'organically grown'.

Beverages No organic wines or juices.

Meat The use of hormones is banned in beef produced specifically for Waitrose. Mutton is fine, since no hormones are used in sheep. For pigs, Waitrose specify that growth promoters should not be used, though they impose no restrictions on veterinary treatment. They mentioned that they imposed restrictions on additives in pig feed. They expect suppliers to guarantee the quality of the meat: they do not themselves test the meat for additives. They sell free-range chickens. Customers have apparently asked why they do not offer free-range for other meats, but they say that as yet there are no standards for other animals.

Eggs Free-range eggs in all Waitrose stores.

Detergents Sell own-label washing powders which do not contain optical whiteners. To date insufficient customer demand for and limited supply of suitable alternative products. Offer Jonelle's Colour Care, a low-suds automatic washing powder with no optical brightener.

Food irradiation Said they would not sell irradiated food unless and until they were satisfied that it was safe, wholesome and tasty, and met with their standards. They would insist that material was clearly labelled in this case.

Vegetarian   A number of vegetarian dishes but few are labelled as such. Vegetarian cheeses include cheddar, gouda and edam. Sell soya milk in all their stores.

CFC issue   Clearly aware of the problems associated with CFCs and were in discussion with suppliers about safe alternatives. Said their own-label products would all be CFC-free by end 1988. The label will say: 'This product does not contain CFCs'. All other brands are expected to be CFC-free by the end of 1989. Said they were aware of the problem of CFCs in polystyrene trays and said they would use safer alternatives, when they are available. Were not sure if they used this type of packaging for their egg boxes and have not looked into this.

Packaging   Had not done anything special in the packaging field — and do not offer recycled paper bags.

Recycling facilities   No company policy on this.

Additives   Provide information and booklets on additives and on their policy, which is updated regularly.

Information   When asked if they provided any information on organic produce for their customers, a spokesman replied: 'We don't consider it our responsibility to educate the public'. However, information on additives and nutrition is available through most stores.

This table is based on a telephone survey conducted by SustainAbility during April/May 1988. The information was provided through the press office of each chain. SustainAbility also telephoned the Vegetarian Society and asked for their assessment of the individual supermarkets' vegetarian range.

USEFUL ADDRESSES

Aluminium Recycling Can-paign, PO Box 57, Newport, Gwent MP1 9XS. Tel: 0633 892 722

Aspall Cyder, Cyder House, Aspall Hall, Debenham, Suffolk IP14 6PD. Tel: 0728 860510

British Plastics Federation, 5 Belgrave Square, London SW1X 8PH. Tel: 01-235 9483

Broom Lane Enterprises, 23 Leicester Road, Salford M7 0AS.
Tel: 061-792 7311

Campaign for Real Ale (CAMRA) and **Campaign for Real Bread
(CAMREB)**, 34 Alma Road, St Albans, Herts AL1 3BW.
Tel: 0727 67201

Chickens' Lib, PO Box 2, Holmfirth, Huddersfield HD7 1QT.
Tel: 0484 861814

Ecover see **Full Moon**

Faith Products, 52-56 Albion Road, Edinburgh EH7 5QZ

Full Moon (Ecover), Charlton Court Farm, Mouse Lane, Steyning, West
Sussex BN4 3DF

Glass Manufacturers' Confederation, Northumberland Road, Sheffield
S10 2UA. Tel: 0742 686201

Incpen, College House, Great Peter Street, London SW1P 3NQ.
Tel: 01-222 9434

Janco Sales, 11 Seymour Road, Hampton Hill, Middlesex TW12 1DD

Little Green Shop, 8 St George's Place, Brighton, Sussex BN1 4GB.
Tel: 0273 571221

Mange Tout Foods, 18 Clanwilliam Road, Deal, Kent. Tel: 0304 363862

Natural Farms, Cockham Farm, Ewhurst Green, Robertsbridge, East
Sussex TN32 5RD. Tel: 058083 855

Neal's Yard Dairy, Neal's Yard, London WC2. Tel: 01-379 7222

Pure Meat Company, Coombe Court Farm, Moretonhampstead, Devon
TQ13 8QD. Tel: 0647 40944

Real Cheese Shop, 96A High Street, Wimbledon, London SW19.
Tel: 01-878 6676. Also at 62 High Street, Barnes, London SW13.
Tel: 01-878 6676

Realeat, 2 Trevelyan Gardens, London NW10 3JY. Tel: 01-459 7354

Real Foods, 14 Ashley Place, Edinburgh EH6 5PX. Tel: 031-554 4321

Real Meat Company, East Hill Farm, Heytesbury, Warminster,
Wiltshire BA12 0HR. Tel: 0985 40436

Real Wines, 14 Ashley Place, Edinburgh EH6 5PX. Tel: 031-554 4321

Recycling Advisory Unit, Warren Spring Laboratory, Department of
Trade and Industry, Gunnels Wood Road, Stevenage, Herts SG1 2BX

Save-A-Can, Queen's House, Forbury Road, Reading, Berks RG1 3JH.
Tel: 0734 581177

Selfridges, Oxford Street, London W1. Tel: 01-629 1234

Vegan Society, 33-35 George Street, Oxford OX1 2AY.
Tel: 0865 722166

Vegetarian Centre and Bookshop, 53 Marloes Road, Kensington, London W8 6LA. Tel: 01-937 7739

Vegetarian Society, Parkdale, Dunham Road, Altrincham, Cheshire WA14 4QG. Tel: 061-928 0793

Vessen Ltd, Hazel Grove, Cheshire SK7 4RF. Tel: 061-483 1235

Vinceremos, Beechwood Centre, Elmere Lane, Leeds LS8 2LQ. Tel: 0532 734056

Wastewatch, NCVO, 26 Bedford Square, London WC1B 3HU. Tel: 01-636 4066

WaterAid, 1 Queen Anne's Gate, London SW1H 9BT. Tel: 01-222 8111

West Heath Wine, West Heath, Purbright, Surrey

Wells Stores, Reading Road, Streatley, Berkshire RG8 9HY. Tel: 0491 872367

Wholefood, 24 Paddington Street, London W1. Tel: 01-486 1390

THE CHEMIST

Walk into a High Street chemist like Boots or Underwoods and it is clear that the environmental pressures of the 1970s and 1980s *have* had an impact. For one thing, although you can still find glaring examples of over-packaging, there is less of it about — for good economic reasons. There still remain many environmental problems to be faced and positive choices to be made by the Green Consumer.

Cosmetics and Toiletries

There has been growing concern about the use of animals in the safety testing of all types of products, but cosmetics have been particularly controversial because they are seen as non-essential. It is worth noting that just about every ingredient which goes into a perfume or cosmetic has had to be tested on animals. Three main types of test are carried out:

- For **toxicity**: the most common test is the LD50 procedure, which aims to find the lethal dose (LD) of any given substance. A group of animals, normally small mammals like mice or rats, are force-fed with the substance (be it a bleach or a lipstick) until 50 per cent die.

- For **eye irritation**: the Draize eye test is the most notorious test among animal rights campaigners.

Products such as shampoos or hairsprays are dripped or sprayed into the eyes of conscious rabbits. Their tear ducts are structured in such a way that they cannot flush such substances away. This can continue for some days, to see whether the eye is damaged.

- For **skin irritation**: substances, such as deodorants and face cream, are applied to the shaved skin of animals, usually guinea pigs or rabbits. They are held in place for some time with sticky tape, to see whether there is an adverse reaction. Symptoms may include inflammation and swelling.

The pressure from lobbying groups and consumers to abandon the use of animals has meant that there is growing industrial interest in alternative testing methods. 'Were there any validated tests other than animal testing for cosmetics,' said Marion Kelly, Director of the Cosmetic Toiletry and Perfumery Association, 'my members would fall over backwards to use them.' In fact FRAME (Fund for the Replacement of Animals in Medical Experiments) has been working on cell culture tests as an alternative to animal testing. FRAME has been funded by such companies as **Avon Cosmetics**, **Bristol Myers** and **Rimmel**.

We asked the best-known high street chemists, **Boots,** what their policy was. 'Boots have not used laboratory animals in the testing of cosmetic and toiletry products for the last few years,' the company replied. 'Our products are based on established ingredients where the safety record is known to us,' the company continued. 'None of our manufactured cosmetics or toiletries are marketed unless our medical advisers are satisfied about their safety. In assessing our products they do, of course, take into account any background work, including any work on animals either carried out by ourselves in the past, or by others, such as our suppliers.'

The British Union for the Abolition of Vivisection (BUAV) has supplied us with a list of some major cosmetic companies which they do not consider to be cruelty-free. Their assessment is based on the fact that the companies use animal ingredients in all or some of their products and that some products or ingredients have been tested on animals in the last five years. (The fact that a company does not appear in the list does not necessarily mean that it is cruelty-free. It may be that information is incomplete in these cases.)

MAJOR COMPANIES NOT CONSIDERED BY BUAV TO BE CRUELTY-FREE

Company	Products include
Avon	*Avon* brand name products
Beecham	*Silvrikin* hair products
Bristol Myers	*Clairol* *Nice & Easy* *Fresh & Dry* *Mum* deodorants *Glints* hair lighteners
Chanel	*No.* 5 and *No.* 19 perfumes
Chesebrough-Ponds	*Vaseline* products *Ponds* Cold Cream *Cutex* nail products *Cachet* perfume *Rave* perms and hairspray
Colgate-Palmolive	*Soft & Gentle* anti-perspirant *Fresh* soap *Colgate* toothpaste *Blue Minty Gel* toothpaste
Cussons	*Imperial Leather* products
Gillette	*Right Guard* deodorant *Soft & Dry* deodorant *Silkience* hair care *Toni* home perms
Johnson & Johnson	Baby products
L'Oreal	*Frequence* shampoo *Free Style* hair preparations *Elnett* hairspray *Ambre Solaire* products
Marks & Spencer	Cosmetics and toiletries
Max Factor	Make-up range
Procter & Gamble	*Zest* soap *Crest* toothpaste *Camay* soap

Reckitt & Colman	*Loxene* shampoo
	Veeto depilatory cream
Revlon	Cosmetics range
Unilever	*Sunsilk* shampoo and hairspray
	Pears shampoo and skin cream
	Sure deodorant
	Elida Gibbs range
Wella	*Wella* hair care range
	Colour Confidence hair colour

BUAV also mention several companies which are fairly borderline and which they do not class as major animal experimenters:

Oxfam
Rimmel
Simple

Do not test on animals, but do use some animal derived ingredients in some products.

Sainsbury's 'J'
range

Do not carry out or commission animal tests. They are typical of all the major supermarket chains with regard to their testing policy in that they do not ensure that their suppliers use cruelty-free ingredients.

Going cruelty-free is not an easy step for companies — product innovation may be severely stunted, production costs can be higher, reformulation can be more difficult if an ingredient becomes unavailable, and it is much harder to develop an exclusive substance. The RSPCA has been examining the claims of companies which are marketing products as 'cruelty-free'.

'There is no natural or synthetic ingredient that can be guaranteed "never" to have been tested on animals,' says Bryony Cobby, Scientific Administrator at the Society. 'Regretfully, some fringe cosmetic companies and some well-meaning but ill-informed animal welfare campaigners have made claims that certain products contain ingredients never tested on animals. These companies should be very precise on claims, clearly stating that their ingredients would have been likely to have been tested on animals by third parties at some time in the past.'

The *Choose Cruelty-Free* campaign run by the British Union

The Body Shop

Named 'Company of the Year' at the 1987 Business Enterprise Awards, The Body Shop reported a turnover of more than £28.48 million, had almost 300 branches in 31 countries around the world, and was predicting an expansion rate of 20 new outlets a year in the UK alone.

The Body Shop, though not the green equivalent of the ordinary High Street chemist, sells environmentally acceptable alternatives for many of the products sold there. Among the company's main attractions for Green Consumers are its:

- formulation of products from natural ingredients

- refusal to sell products whose ingredients have been tested on animals during the last five years

- use of minimum packaging, including biodegradable plastics, and provision of a bottle refill service

- support for individuals, and joint projects with groups such as Friends of the Earth and Greenpeace, campaigning on inner city, Third World and environmental issues (from whales to acid rain)

The Body Shop listens carefully to its customers. 'Can you imagine,' asks Anita Roddick, 'that we are the only high street retailer which has suggestion boxes in its shops? Why spend billions of pounds on market research when you can do it yourself?' But she also sees customer education as a key role for the company. 'We reckon that about 25 million people must pass our shops at one time or another,' she says. 'So we use our windows to promote environmental or community issues. Every one of our shops is like a major poster site.'

for the Abolition of Vivisection (BUAV) has emphasized the need for careful cross-checking of the claims made by manufacturers. Different companies selling cruelty-free goods have different cut-off points as far as animal testing is concerned: **The Body Shop** and **Body Reform** refuse to use a substance if it has been tested on animals in the past five years, while **Beauty Without Cruelty** insists on ten years.

A growing number of suppliers try to avoid products which contain any animal ingredients, whether or not they come from rare or endangered species. Animal products used in cosmetics include tallow, made from animal fat and used in some soaps and lipsticks; stearic acid, a solid fat found in soaps, shaving creams and some foundation creams; and collagen and gelatin, produced by boiling down bones, skin, tendons and connective tissue.

A fair number of cosmetic manufacturers still use products derived from rare species. Now that whale products like spermaceti (a white waxy substance from the head of the sperm whale, traditionally used in cosmetics) are banned in Britain, the attention of lobbying organizations such as the Marine Conservation Society has switched to creatures like the harmless, filter-feeding basking shark.

The livers of harpooned basking sharks taken in British waters are used to produce a refined oil, squalene, that has a low freezing point. A single six-tonne basking shark can produce 1,000 litres (220 gallons) of oil. It is used for a range of consumer products, including cosmetic face creams (as well as in high altitude aircraft).

Companies using basking shark oil, including **Estée Lauder**, admit that other oils from fish and seeds could be used. But Estée Lauder, based in New York, has claimed that such oils do not have the proven safety or efficacy of squalene.

ALONG THE SHELVES

Anti-perspirants and deodorants

These are designed to stop you sweating or to make you smell

Check the Label

Chemists like Underwoods now stock *E for Additives* and the range of on-pack information on additives has exploded in recent years. But don't expect — at least at this stage of the game — to be told whether the product has been tested on animals or is likely to damage the environment. There are the occasional honourable exceptions, of course, including **Vidal Sassoon**'s entire hair care range (labelled as ozone-friendly), but the green label is conspicuous by its absence in the High Street chemist. Look for the 'ozone friendly' label on aerosols (details from Friends of the Earth).

Boots did try a cruelty-free labelling scheme on some products, but found that consumers tended to become suspicious of all non-labelled products, whether or not they were tested on animals. Unfortunately, Boots abandoned the scheme.

sweeter if you do sweat. Apart from the fact that washing with soap and water tackles most of the problems anti-perspirants are used for, anti-perspirants and deodorants often come in aerosols. If you buy such products, use a roll-on.

If you have to use an aerosol, check that you are buying a CFC-free brand.

CFC-FREE AEROSOLS

Family

Amway	Deter Anti-Perspirant Spray
Amway	Tonga Spray Deodorant
Bellair	Cool 'n' Dry (anti-p.)
Bellair	Fresh 'n' Cool (deo.)
Sainsbury	Family Antiperspirant (deo.)
Spar	Spar Antiperspirant (deo.)
Tip Top	Tip Top Antiperspirant

Women's

British Products	Charm (anti-p.)
Chesebrough-Ponds	Cachet Deodorant Aerosol
Sainsbury	Antiperspirant Deodorant
Tip Top	Tip Top Antiperspirant Blue Mist (deo.)
Tip Top	Tip Top Antiperspirant Pink Mist (deo.)

Men's

British Products	Blue Ridge (anti-p.)
British Products	Blue Ridge (deo.)
Fabergé	Brut 33 Deodorant
Fabergé	Brut 33 Antiperspirant
Fabergé	Brut 33 Musk Deodorant (anti-p.)
Fabergé	Brut 33 Musk Antiperspirant (deo.)
Fabergé	Turbo (deo.)
Haventrail	Clubman Antiperspirant (deo.)
Playboy	Playboy Antiperspirant
Playboy	Playboy Deo-cologne (deo. anti-p.)
Sainsbury	Antiperspirant Deodorant For Men

As explained on page 3, eight companies producing 65 per cent of the aerosols used for toiletries have agreed to switch by late 1989 to propellants which do not damage the ozone layer. They are: **Beecham**, **Carter Wallace**, **Colgate-Palmolive**, **Cussons**, **Elida Gibbs**, **Gillette**, **L'Oreal**, and **Reckitt and Colman**. The Green Consumer should note, however, that most aerosols, whether or not they contain CFC propellants, are tested on animals. Also, the containers are not recyclable.

Remember that anti-perspirants and deodorants are tested on animals. Try to use a cruelty-free supplier such as **Beauty Without Cruelty**, **Body Care**, **Creighton Products**, **Martha Hill** or **Pure Plant Products**.

An 11 per cent rise in demand in the anti-perspirant and deodorant sector during the mid-'80s resulted from the success of **all-over deodorant sprays** (see over for CFC-free aerosols).

CFC-FREE AEROSOLS
Family

Keen	Zest Fragrant

Women's

British Products	Charm
Co-op	Sheer Silk Body Spray
Coty-Goya	Body Sprays (all fragrances)
Elida Gibbs	Vivas
Haventrail	Exposé Body Spray
Haventrail	Exposé
Napa	It Perfume Body Sprays
Statestrong	Shelley
Statestrong	Voodoo

Men's

Cache d'Or	Cache d'Or
Coty-Goya	Cedar Wood Body Spray
Fabergé	Brut 33 Body Spray
Medicare	Medicare Body Sprays for Men
Playboy	Playboy Body Spray
Share Drug	Share Drug Body Spray (Bali, Capri, L.A., Rio)
Statestrong	Shelley

WC deodorants, which you place in the cistern or basin of your WC should be avoided altogether. They are not just unnecessary: many contain paradichlorobenzene (PDCB), a potential water pollutant.

Baby care

A range of baby-care products tested with the Assissi Test (based on the use of human volunteers), rather than animal tests, is available from **Cosmetics To Go**.

Heinz have taken a lead in banning the use of certain pesticides in the production of raw materials used in their foods.

The question of whether to use disposable nappies represents the ultimate trade-off between convenience and wasted natural resources. But don't kill yourself boiling nappies to avoid using disposable ones. There are more important environmental problems that need your time and energy!

Bath products

Many bath foaming products contain formaldehyde, which you should try to avoid. It can cause allergies. To find cruelty-free bath products, try the **Body Shop** or contact such suppliers as **Creighton Products**, **Honesty Cosmetics**, **Pecksniffs Bespoke Perfumery** and **Pure Plant Products**.

Contraceptives

It is often forgotten that the first oral contraceptives derived from substances found in wild yams — many of which are now locally extinct. Central American Indians knew of their contraceptive effect long before Western scientists recognized that they might become a mainstay of family planning, the number one priority world-wide for population control.

Contraception can bring its own problems, however. Apart from the possible health side-effects of the Pill, the *Sunday Times* reported that the increased use of condoms due to the spread of AIDS was causing problems in the countryside. Apparently, farmers were worried that discarded condoms could choke their grazing bulls! If you engage in such rural pursuits, follow the Countryside Code.

Depilatories

Watch out for products in aerosols, which may contain CFCs.

CFC-FREE BRANDS

Carter Wallace	Nair
International Chemicals	Immac Regular
International Chemicals	Immac Lemo
Richards & Appleby	Legs in Action
Scholl	Smooth Touch Moisturising Legshave Mousse

Hairsprays

When the British Aerosol Manufacturers' Association (BAMA) celebrated its twenty-fifth anniversary in 1985, changing fashions meant that it was able to announce record sales in the previous year. Output of aerosols had climbed 11 per cent to 697 million units. More than half of that rise was attributed to heavy demand for hair mousses and other sprays demanded by young post-Punk consumers.

Follow Prince Charles's lead, ban all non-essential aerosols from your home. But if you feel you must use them, look out for CFC-free aerosols.

CFC-FREE AEROSOLS
Women's Hairsprays

Alberto-Culver	Get Set Normal Hold
Alberto-Culver	Get Set Dry
Alberto-Culver	Get Set Super
Alberto-Culver	VO5 Normal
Alberto-Culver	VO5 Hard Hold
Alberto-Culver	VO5 Extra Hard Hold
Alberto-Culver	TCB Reversion Resistant
Alverto-Culver	Tresemme
Alberto-Culver	Tresemme pH natural
Alberto-Culver	Salon Hairspray
Bellair	Bellair Hairspray
Bellair	Estolan
British Products	Charm
Co-op	Hairspray Normal
Co-op	Hair Spray Firm
Co-op	Hair Spray Extra Firm
Elida Gibbs	Shine (spray-on conditioner)
Fabergé	Organics Hair Spray
Haventrail	Acquiesce Hair Spray
Keen	Keen Firm Hold
Napa	It Hair Spray
Nichol	Hair Spray
Safeway	Safeway Hairspray Normal
Safeway	Safeway Hairspray Hard Hold
Safeway	Safeway Hairspray Extra Hard Hold
Share	Hair Works
Spar	Normal Hair Spray
Spar	Firm Hair Spray

Spar	Extra Firm Hair Spray
Statestrong	Minuet (Normal and Firm Hold)
Statestrong	Professional Touch (Normal and Extra Hold)
Statestrong	Shelley (Normal and Firm Hold)
VG	Hair Spray Normal
VG	Hair Spray Firm

Men's Hairsprays

Fabergé	Brut 33
Statestrong	Shelley

Styling Mousses and Sprays

Alberto-Culver	Quickset Normal (spray)
Alberto-Culver	Quickset Dry (spray)
Alberto-Culver	Quickset Flyaway (spray)
Alberto-Culver	Body & Shine Frequent
Alberto-Culver	Body & Shine Volume Plus
Alberto-Culver	Body & Shine Dry & Damaged
Amway	Satinique
Amway	Satinique Hair Mousse
Beecham	Brylcreem Styling Mousse
Beecham	Silvrikin Styling Mousse
Bellair	Estolan Styling Mousse
British Products	Charm
Gateway	Normal Mousse
Gateway	Firm Mousse
Napa	Continental Styling Mousse
Napa	It Styling Mousse
Sainsbury	Hair Mousse (Normal and Extra Hold)
Spar	Styling Mousse Normal Hold
Spar	Styling Mousse Firm Hold
Spar	Styling Mousse Extra Firm Hold
Statestrong	Shelley (for men)
Statestrong	Shelley (for women)
Statestrong	Minuet
Statestrong	Professional Touch
Tip Top	Normal Mousse
Tip Top	Firm Mousse
Tip Top	Super Mousse
Tip Top	Silk Mousse — normal
Tip Top	Silk Mousse — firm
Waitrose	Styling Mousse (Normal and Firm Hold)

Some firms are also offering hairsprays in non-aerosol packs. **Estée Lauder** produces *Azurée Natural Hair Spray*, which contains conditioning elements extracted from seaweed for additional shine. **Clinique**'s non-aerosol hairspray is allergy-tested and fragrance-free. **Vidal Sassoon**, which pioneered non-CFC hairspray aerosols in the UK, also offers a Non-Aerosol Hair Spray (regular and extra hold) and Hair Mist.

Aerosols are not particularly efficient. **Clairol** point out that the average aerosol can contains one third hairspray and two-thirds propellant. Clairol took a full-page advertisement in national newspapers following Prince Charles's speech in European Year of the Environment which announced his ban on aerosols in Kensington Palace. The advertisement showed the company's non-aerosol *Finale* hairspray, under the headline: *One hairspray one would prefer one's wife to use.*

Nail varnish

Go for cruelty-free brands, which you can get through **Barry M**, **Beauty Without Cruelty** and **Natural Beauty Products**.

Perfumes and toilet waters

Perfume production depends on animals in at least two main ways: for fixatives used to retain the scent, and, secondly, for safety testing.

Among the animal products used as fixatives are musk (taken from the musk deer), castoreum or civet (extracted from the anal sex glands of beavers or civet cats, respectively), and ambergris (from the intestines of the sperm whale). Both the musk deer and the sperm whale are endangered species.

Unfortunately, because full product labelling is not required by the EEC, it is generally impossible to find out what is in such products, unless you ask the manufacturers (and then, of course, only if they reply fully and honestly). And, if there is a potential problem, it is hardly in their interest to tell you.

The French perfume houses, which depend on many long-established recipes, are most likely to use rare, high-priced animal ingredients. Many other parfumiers have replaced such animal products, usually because of their scarcity and price, rather than for humanitarian reasons. Many parfumiers have not used musk for over 20 years, having switched to synthetics or vegetable materials.

Shampoos and conditioners

In most areas of the country, your local sewage works should be able to cope with the pollution load produced by the shampoos and conditioners you use. But do try to use cruelty-free products, such as those supplied by **Bodyline Cosmetics**, **Caurnie Soap**, **Creighton Products**, **Crimpers Pure Products**, **Culpeper**, **Faith Products**, **Honesty Cosmetics**, **Martha Hill**, **Natural Beauty Products**, **Pecksniffs**, **Pure Plant Products**, **Tiki Cosmetics** or **Weleda**.

Shaving aids

If you want to take things to extremes, the greenest approach to facial hair is probably to grow a beard. For the shavers among us, however, and 93 per cent of British men shave daily, spending 3,350 hours during an average lifetime in front of the mirror, here are the options.

If you wet-shave, beware of: CFCs in shaving foam aerosols; disposable razors and excessive packaging. (Particularly undesirable products include packs of disposable razors, such as **Bic**'s *Razor* and *Lady Shaver* and **Wilkinson Sword**'s *Retractor*.) Also avoid shaving brushes using badger bristles and ivory. On the other hand, there are the acid rain and radiation problems associated with electric shaving. On balance, however, the electric shaver seems to come out on top.

But for a range of wet shaving products, including *Carters Shaving Cream* (based on Egyptian quince seed, raisins, juniper and eucalyptus) and a pyramid razor-blade sharpener, get in touch with **Cosmetics to Go**.

CFC-FREE AEROSOLS

Asda	Asda Shave Foam Regular
Asda	Asda Shave Foam Cologne
Asda	Asda Shave Foam Sensitive Skin
Beecham	Brylcreem Shave Foam
Boots	Boots for Men Shave Foam
Boots	Flint Shave Foam
British Products	Blue Ridge
Colgate-Palmolive	Palmolive Rapid Shave Regular
Colgate-Palmolive	Palmolive Rapid Shave Alpine Fresh
Colgate-Palmolive	Palmolive Rapid Shave Spice Fragrance
Colgate-Palmolive	Palmolive Rapid Shave Cologne Cool
Co-op	Original Shave Foam
Co-op	Lemon Shave Foam
Elida Gibbs	Erasmic Superfoam
Elida Gibbs	Denim
Fabergé	Brut 33 Creme Shave
Fabergé	Turbo
Gateway	Gateway Shave Foam Citrus
Gateway	Gateway Shave Foam Cologne
Gateway	Gateway Shave Foam Sensitive Skins
Gillette	Foamy
Gillette	Special
Gillette	Contour
Goya	Cedar Wood Foam Shave
Goya	Matchroom Foam Shave
Haventrail	Clubman Shaving Foam
Playboy	Playboy Shave Foam
Sainsbury	Shaving Foam (Regular and Sensitive Skin)
Shulton	Old Spice Smooth Shave
Shulton	Blue Stratos Smooth Shave
Shulton	Insignia
Tesco	Tesco Shaving Foam (Regular and Citrus)
Waitrose	Shaving Foam

Most brands of aftershave will have been tested on animals. Suppliers of cruelty-free aftershave include **Honesty Cosmetics** and **Natural Beauty Products**.

Soaps and skin care

Most of the firms listed in the cruelty-free table offer soaps and other skin care products. Try the oatmeal cleansing bars offered by the **Green Farm Nutrition Centre**.

Sun tan preparations

Again, avoid CFC-containing aerosols. Friends of the Earth suggest *Ritz Bronze Self* by **Charles of the Ritz** and *Shelley Legs 'n' Body* by **Statestrong**.

Thermometers

Most thermometers contain mercury, which is highly poisonous. Order a mercury-free thermometer from the **Green Farm Nutrition Centre**.

Toothpaste

Toothpaste may be the last product to come to mind when you are thinking of environmental pollution, but the acid effluents produced during the manufacture of the titanium dioxide pigments used to make toothpaste white are worth thinking about. Discharged by companies like **Bayer**, **Laporte** and **Tioxide**, they have helped to make some of Europe's rivers and seas more acid.

This is not a simple story of good and evil, however. Used in a wide range of paints, paper, plastics, inks and man-made fibres, titanium dioxide has revolutionized some parts of the paint industry, where it has replaced materials like zinc oxide and lead (see *The Hardware and DIY Store*). Unlike lead, it is completely non-toxic, and therefore a distinct improvement both in health and in environmental terms. At this stage there is no obvious substitute, so the main option for the Green Consumer is to join lobbying organizations dedicated to clean rivers and clean seas.

Apart from titanium dioxide, toothpaste generally contains the same sort of detergents that are used in washing powders. The **Green Farm Nutrition Centre** offers a pure fennel toothpaste, using such natural materials as glycerine, water, chalk, gum tragacanth, sodium laurel sulphate (from the coconut) and oil of fennel. Other suppliers of more natural toothpastes include **Mandala Ayurvedic Imports**, **Sarakan** and **Weleda**.

One plus-point: plastic containers have replaced lead-based tubes. The plastic dispensers used for such toothpastes as **Colgate**'s *Dentifrice* are masterpieces of convenience, but the plastics used are neither recyclable nor biodegradable.

Health Care

Given the growing alarm in recent years about additives in our food and drink, it is peculiar — to say the least — that people are still happy to swallow considerable numbers of pills, tablets and other medicines with hardly a second thought. For, as Maurice Hanssen put it in *E for Additives*:

> A licensed medicine has only to state the details of the active ingredient or ingredients. All the other components of the product are exempt from labelling requirements. It is not at all uncommon for the good effects of the medicine to be entirely negated by the adverse effects of the other ingredients being used. This is especially true of colours and preservatives.

But the picture is changing rapidly. Europeans are spending around £800 million a year on alternative therapies such as acupuncture, homeopathy, and herbal and natural medicines. Indeed, this market sector has been growing so fast that it could pose a real threat to the pharmaceutical industries of Germany, France, Switzerland and the UK.

Just a few years back, the idea of using a herbal medicine based on mistletoe to treat circulatory problems instead of a conventional anti-hypertensive drug, or of using a camphor-based homeopathic remedy instead of analgesics to fight colds, would have seemed cranky in the extreme. No longer. Alternative medicine is moving strongly into the mainstream.

In contrast to its European counterparts, however, the National

Health Service has been extremely conservative in adopting
alternative therapies. Even so, homeopathic and other natural
remedies are increasingly popular and are now widely available
in High Street chemists and health food stores.

Britain's Royal Family are well known as supporters of alternative medicine. Prince Charles has also spoken out strongly in
favour of what he and others now dub 'complementary
medicine', in that it operates alongside conventional medicine.
The **Institute for Complementary Medicine** sums the picture up:
'no single therapy has all the answers to sickness. The Institute
believes that everyone should have the means to begin to understand their problems and come to terms with the cause. This can
take time and effort, and an ideal situation is when a number of
therapies can be made available at the appropriate time.'

Complementary Therapies

- **Acupuncture** is founded on the principle that health
  is dependent upon a proper balance of vital energy
  forces (Chi) within the body. Chi can be modified by
  the insertion of fine needles, finger pressure or heat
  (moxibustion). These are the most common methods
  of acupuncture treatment.

  British Medical Acupuncture Society, 67-69 Chancery
  Lane, London WC2A 1AF

  The Council for Acupuncture, Suite 1, 19a Cavendish
  Square, London W1M 9AD

  British Academy of Western Acupuncture, 12 Rodney
  Street, Liverpool L1 2TE. Tel: 051 709 0479

- **Homeopathy** is a system of medicine based on the
  principles that agents which produce certain
  symptoms in health can be used to cure such
  symptoms in disease. This can be available on the
  National Health Service. Doctors must be qualified
  in orthodox medicine before training in
  homeopathy.

  British Homeopathic Association, 27a Devonshire Street,
  London W1N 1RJ. Tel: 01-935 2163

  Society of Homeopaths, 2a Bedford Place, Southampton
  S01 2BY

- **Herbalism** aims to restore the body's own self-healing abilities by using plants and their extracts in order to prevent and heal disease.

  British Herbal Medicine Association, 1 Wickham Road, Boscombe, Bournemouth, Dorset BH7 6JX. Tel: 0202 431901

  National Institute of Medical Herbalists, c/o 41 Hatherley Road, Winchester, Hants

- **Osteopathy** is a form of joint manipulation. Osteopaths believe that many illnesses stem from misaligned bones and joints. The forms of treatment are mostly manipulative in character.

  General Council and Register of Osteopaths, 21 Suffolk Street, London SW1Y 4HG

- **Chiropractic** specializes in treating mechanical disorders of the joints, particularly the spine and disorders of the nervous system.

  British Chiropractors' Association, Premiere House, 10 Greycoat Place, London SW1P 1SB

- If you would like further information on alternative medicine you should contact **The Institute of Complementary Medicine**, 21 Portland Place, London W1N 3AS. Tel: 01-636 9543. They are very helpful and have information on all alternative medicine practices. They can also give you a local contact for information about practitioners in your area.

- When writing to any of these organizations for information, please enclose a stamped, self-addressed envelope.

Becoming — and staying — informed about all complementary therapies is a tall order for the ordinary, hard-pressed general practitioner. But many patients are now voting with their feet — and, where necessary, with their wallets. When *Which?* surveyed 28,000 of its members in 1986, one in seven reported that they had used complementary medicine. Of those who had, 31 per cent said that they had been cured by complementary treatments — while another 51 per cent felt that their condition had been improved. 74 per cent said that they would definitely try this form of treatment again and 69 per cent said that they would certainly recommend this form of medicine to someone else with a similar complaint.

For those interested in herbalism, a number of suppliers are now offering organically grown herbs, including **Hambleden Herbs** and **Suffolk Herbs**. Hambleden Herbs mainly offer dried herbal medicines, sold through the **Neal's Yard Apothecary**.

It is worth noting, however, that the mere fact that a product is natural does not mean that it is automatically safe in all circumstances. Popular herbal remedies such as comfrey or sassafras herbal teas could cause cancer, while broom and devil's claw can trigger miscarriages. Most of the 5,000 herbal preparations on sale to the British public are perfectly safe, but it is worth taking proper advice — particularly if you are already taking conventional drugs which might react with the herbal treatments.

Low-chemical lifestyles

Life without chemicals would be unthinkable. Ever since we learned to collect salt from evaporation ponds or began to use herbal cures, we have come to depend on a growing range of chemicals, from pharmaceuticals to pesticides. The positive impact of industrial chemistry on our diet, health and lifestyles has been tremendous, but many of these chemicals have also turned out to have highly undesirable health or ecological side-effects. Even relatively innocuous chemicals can be dangerous if over-used.

Clearly, the best approach in these circumstances is moderation — coupled with a willingness to seek out accurate, up-to-date information on the products you buy. Remember that a low-chemical lifestyle is likely to be not only healthier but cheaper, too.

The more stressful our lives, however, the greater our 'need' for chemical crutches. By contrast, complementary medicine aims to boost the body's natural abilities to fight disease and cope with stress. Don't be afraid of trying some of the complementary therapies. Ask your doctor for advice, but don't be put off if he or she is dismissive. Find out if any of your friends or colleagues have tried complementary medicine. Contact the Institute of Complementary Medicine (see above) and ask for further information.

Remember: even medical insurance companies are now beginning to recognize the value of a veritable A-to-Z of 'holistic' therapies (which aim to treat the whole person), including acupuncture, biofeedback and chiropractic. Partly this is because holistic therapies are often much cheaper than high technology medicine, but partly, too, it is because holistic medicine can produce results where conventional therapies have failed.

Natural answers

We shall need many more chemicals and chemical products in the future. Happily, the natural world around us is full of extraordinarily sophisticated biochemicals which have evolved over thousands of years to perform complex, life-sustaining tasks. Indeed, one of the strongest arguments for halting the destruction of the tropical rain forests is that the plant, insect and animal species they harbour represent an almost totally unexplored source of potential pharmaceuticals and other products.

The natural world, in short, is a living pharmacy. At least twenty per cent of all prescriptions filled in the USA get their active ingredients from plants, and there are many extraordinary drugs still waiting to be discovered. One thing which we can almost guarantee is that there is a cure waiting to be discovered in the natural world for most forms of cancer — and many other diseases which currently plague us — if only we knew how and where to look. The worry is that by the time we discover where we should have been looking, the pharmacy may have been destroyed.

ACTION CHECKLIST

1. **Cut down on the quantities of chemicals you use**, particularly for less important applications.

2. **Search out products with natural — rather than synthetic — ingredients.**

3. **Pick simple, additive-free products which are not over-packaged.**

4. **Avoid products which are likely to have been recently tested on animals.** Be wary of brands advertised as 'new' or 'improved'. These will almost certainly have required a recent batch of animal tests. Buy cruelty-free products.

5. **Avoid aerosols** wherever possible. If you must use them, make sure that you buy CFC-free brands.

6. Remember, **a healthy diet** goes a long way towards ensuring that you do not spend all your time picking up prescriptions from your doctor's surgery.

7. **Avoid cigarettes**, which cause a variety of specific health problems and depress the immune system. Cut down on other stimulants and depressants, including coffee, tea and alcohol.

8. **Look after your body.** Take regular exercise. Don't drive: walk or cycle. Exercise improves the circulatory system, keeping your blood pressure down, countering osteoporosis, and cutting the likelihood that you will suffer from circulatory disease or diabetes.

9. **Exercise also helps you sleep. And relaxation is one key to low-chemical lifestyles.** Make sure you get plenty of sleep: Greek doctors estimate that the afternoon siesta taken in Mediterranean countries may cut the risk of coronary heart disease by as much as 30 per cent.

SUPPLIERS OF CRUELTY-FREE PRODUCTS

Company	Product range	Vegetarian? (Exclude all animal ingredients except lanolin, honey or beeswax)	Cruelty-free? (No animal testing)	Vegan?¹	Retail outlets	Mail order
Barry M Unit 1 Bittacy Business Centre Mill Hill East London NW7 1BA Tel: 01-349 2992	Skin and hair care Bath products Make-up Nail polish Glitter dust Men's range	✗	✓	✗	Primarily through fashion shops and boutiques. Also healthfood shops and chemists. Retail outlets include Holland & Barrett, The Body & Face Place, Hennes (Oxford Circus, London; Newcastle; Birmingham), Selfridges (London), Fenwicks (Newcastle) and Top Shop (Liverpool; Southampton). Barry M shops are planned to open late 1988	✓
Beauty Without Cruelty Avebury Avenue Tonbridge Kent TN9 1TL Tel: 0732 365291	Skin and hair care Make-up Nail polish Perfumes Deodorants and talc Sun preparations Aftershave	✓	✓	✗	Chemists and healthfood shops including Holland & Barrett and Food for Thought	✓

Company	Products			Availability	
Body Shop International Hawthorn Road Wick Littlehampton West Sussex BN17 7LR Tel: 0903 717107	Make-up Skin and hair care Soaps and perfumes Bath products Men's range	✓* *except that Colourings make-up range includes silk; bath beads and fruit soap should be vegetarian by Summer 1988	×	Nationwide Body Shops	✓
Body Care 50 High Street Ide Exeter Devon EX2 9RW Tel: 0392 217628	Skin care Soaps Deodorants Body oil (Ranges = *Mellow Soap, Coconut Grove* and *Kobashi*)	✓	×	Healthfood shops and chemists throughout the South-east	✓
Bodyline Cosmetics Ltd Unit 5, Alders Way Yalberton Industrial Estate Paignton Devon TQ4 7QL Tel: 0803 555582	Skin and hair care Hand and body cream Shampoos Perfumes and oils Men's range Bath products	✓	× (products unsuitable for vegans clearly identified)	Outlets nationwide especially through chemists, healthfood shops and hair salons	✓
Camilla Hepper Ltd 15 Exebridge Park Dulverton Somerset TA22 9BL Tel: 0398 23618	Skin and hair care Hand and body cream Soaps Perfumes and oils Bath products Men's range Sun preparations	✓	× (products that include lanolin or beeswax are identified)	Own shops in Norwich, Manchester, London (Knightsbridge and Docklands), St Albans, Farnham, Sutton, Staines, Stratford-upon-Avon (also a shop in Texas, USA). Also available through some 'concessions'	✓

CRUELTY-FREE SUPPLIERS (continued)

Company	Product range	Vegetarian?	Cruelty-free? (No animal testing)	Vegan?[1]	Retail outlets	Mail order
Caurnie Soap Company The Soaperie Canal Street Kirkintilloch Scotland G66 1QZ Tel: 041 776 1218	Shampoos Soaps Hand and body lotion (Also produce household products: washing-up liquid, household soap, disinfectant)	✓	✓	✓	Healthfood shops in the North but hoping to expand to outlets in the South soon	✓
Chandoré Perfume 2 Ashtree Avenue Mitcham Surrey CR4 3DR Tel: 01-648 5129	Perfumes	✓	✓	✓	Own shop in Leeds. Available mainly through mail order but also through selected health stores and beauty salons	✓
Cosmetics To Go 29 High Street Poole Dorset BH15 1AB Tel: 0800 373366 [FREE]	Sun creams Shampoos Baby products Perfumes and soaps Skin care Make-up Men's range	✓	✓	✗	Own shop in Poole. Otherwise exclusively mail order	✓

Company	Products				Notes	
Creighton Products Water Lane Storrington Pulborough Sussex RH20 3DP Tel: 09066 5611	Hair and skin care Bath products Deodorants Sun creams Soaps	✓	✓	×	'Own-label' products available in healthfood stores	✓
Crimpers Pure Products 63 – 67 Heath Street London NW3 6UG Tel: 01-794 2949	Hair care	✓	✓	✓	Available at their two London salons. Also in London's department stores – Selfridges, Dickins & Jones and D. H. Evans. Healthfood stores, including Holland & Barrett, stock their products	✓
Culpeper Ltd Hadstock Road Linton Cambridge CB1 6NJ Tel: 0223 891196	Soaps Shampoos Range of herbal products	×	✓	×	Culpeper shops nationwide	✓
Faith Products 52 – 56 Albion Road Edinburgh EH7 5QZ Tel: 031-661 0900	Skin and hair care Soaps (Also produce Clearspring laundry liquid and washing-up liquid which are biodegradable)	✓	✓	×	Faith in Nature products mainly available at healthfood shops including Holland & Barrett and Food for Thought	✓

CRUELTY-FREE SUPPLIERS (continued)

Company	Product range	Vegetarian?	Cruelty-free? (No animal testing)	Vegan?[1]	Retail outlets	Mail order
Honesty Cosmetics 33 Markham Road Chesterfield Derbyshire S40 1TA Tel: 0246 211269	Skin and hair care Bath products Perfumes Aftershave Sun creams *Pacific Isle* soaps	✓	✓	✗	'Own-label' products through healthfood shops. Suppliers of some perfumes in Oxfam shops. (Currently planning a range of biodegradable household items eg washing-up liquid and cleaning products)	✓
Innoxa (England) Ltd (also **Leichner**) Beauty House Hawthorne Road Eastbourne East Sussex BN23 6QX Tel: 0323 641244	Make-up (day and stage make-up) Skin care Perfume	✓	✓	✗ (products unsuitable for vegans clearly identified)	Widely available through beauty salons and chemists	✗
Jeunique 64a Peascod Street Windsor Berkshire SL4 1DE Tel: 0753 869022	Skin and hair care Cosmetics (Ranges = *Jeunique*, *Puressence* and *Body Farm Shop*)	✓	✓	✓	'Own-label' products sold in their shops in Windsor and Barnet. Also available at healthfood shops and beauty salons	✓

Company / Address	Products				Notes	
Kay's Britannia Works Ramsbottom Bury Lancashire BL0 0AE Tel: 070682 2216	Soaps (perfumed and unperfumed)	✓	✓	✓	Available in most supermarkets	✗
Mandala Ayurvedic Imports 7 Zetland Road Redland, Bristol Tel: 0272 427124	VICCO toothpaste	✓	✓	✓	Health shops — products imported direct from India to cater for Asian communities	✓
Martha Hill The Old Vicarage Laxton, Nr Corby Northants NN17 3BR Tel: 078085 259	Skin and hair care Make-up Men's range Perfumes Bath products	✓	✓	✗	Mainly mail order. Available at Fenwicks (Bond Street, London) and selected health shops stores	✓
Natural Beauty Products Ltd Western Avenue Bridgend Industrial Estate Mid Glamorgan CF31 3RT Tel: 0656 766566	Make-up Body and skin care Hair care Perfume Sun preparations Aftershave Nail polish	✓	✓	✗	Over 30 Body Reform shops nationwide	✓
Next plc Desford Road Enderby Leicester LE9 5AT Tel: 0533 866411	Skin care Cosmetics Perfumes	✓	✓	✗	Available through the Next retail chain	✗

CRUELTY-FREE SUPPLIERS (continued)

Company	Product range	Vegetarian?	Cruelty-free? (No animal testing)	Vegan?¹	Retail outlets	Mail order
Pecksniffs Bespoke Perfumery 45 – 46 Meeting House Lane Brighton Sussex Tel: 0273 28904	Perfumes Bath and shower products Soaps and shampoos Skin care	✓	✓	✓	Own shop in Brighton	✓
Pure Plant Products Grosvenor Road Hoylake Wirral Merseyside L47 3BS Tel: 051 632 5998	Skin care Shampoos Bath products Perfume Deodorant and talc Sun preparations	✓	✓	✗	Own shop in Hoylake. Available at chemists and healthfood shops	✓
Sarakan Ltd 106 High Street Beckenham Kent BR3 1EB Tel: 01-650 3476	Toothpaste Breath freshener	✓	✓	✗	Healthfood shops	✓
Simply Herbal Kingsway Wilton Salisbury SP2 0AW Tel: 0722 743012	Hand and body lotion Eye cream Skin and hair care	✓	✓	✗	Healthfood shops and salons including Natural Life Health Foods	✓

Tiki Cosmetics Sisson Road Gloucester GL1 3QB Tel: 0452 24012	Hair care Soaps Skin care	✓	✗	'Own-label' products widely available at healthfood shops including Holland & Barrett and Lifecycle	✓
Weleda Heanor Road Ilkeston Derbyshire Tel: 0602 303151	Skin and hair care Bath products Toothpaste	✓	✗	Own-label products available at healthfood shops and chemists	✓
Yin Yang Beauty Care Abbey Chase Bridge Road Chertsey Surrey Tel: 09328 60672	Skin care	✓	✓	Branches of Holland & Barrett	✓

1. This means the entire range is vegan ie no animal products or by-products.

Source: BUAV and SustainAbility May 1988

OTHER USEFUL ADDRESSES

Green Farm Nutrition Centre, Burwash Common, East Sussex
TN19 7LX. Tel: 0435 882482

Hambleden Herbs, Henley-on-Thames, Oxfordshire. Tel: 0491 571598

Institute of Complementary Medicine, 21 Portland Place, London
W1N 3AF. Tel: 01-636 9543

Neal's Yard Apothecary, 2 Neal's Yard, London WC2.
Tel: 01-379 7222

Suffolk Herbs, Sawyers Farm, Little Cornyards, Sudbury, Suffolk
CO10 0NY. Tel: 0787 227247

THE TRAVEL
AGENT

Mr Green

PASSPORT

THE GREEN
·CONSUMER GUIDE·

083620

The Green Tourist

Wildlife tours: from bird-watching to whale-watching

Good, bad and ugly beaches

Hiking and biking

Photography: shooting not to kill

Tourism now ranks as the world's third largest industry — and its impact on the environment is causing increasing concern. Unlike many other industries, tourism always wants to locate in the choicest landscapes and, in doing so, changes them. These changes are rarely for the better.

In too many areas of the world the picture is one of 'battery tourism'. Highly fragmented, with intense pricing battles the rule in most sectors, the industry tends to 'quarry' environmental quality, with little or no interest in re-investing a proportion of its profits in the areas which it exploits. If one Shangri-La is wrecked, the industry's boom-town mentality suggests that another can always be found.

Some tour operators do co-operate with conservation interests to protect wildlife. When WWF and the Greek Sea Turtle Protection Society became worried about the devastating impact tourism was having on the loggerhead turtles of the island of Zakynthos, they managed to win the support of such tour operators as **Grecian Holidays**, **Sun Med Holidays** and **Thomson Holidays** (see page 299). These companies aided in distributing a leaflet explaining to visitors how they could help to protect the turtles. But increasingly, mass tourism and environmental protection interests find themselves in conflict and a growing number of countries — from Portugal to Barbados — are beginning to realize that package tours are not the key to a prosperous future.

At the other end of the spectrum there are the specialist operators, many of whom recognize that a growing number of consumers are becoming more discerning. Some of these belong to the Association of Independent Tour Operators. But, inevitably, some of the specialist tour operators are also helping to destroy fragile environments, simply by introducing people into unsuitable areas. Hardly anywhere in the world remains sacrosanct from the tour operator's desire to open up new markets. As a result, Sir Edmund Hillary complained recently that Mount Everest is 'in danger of becoming a rubbish dump'.

The growing interest in wildlife is itself imposing increasing pressure on some of the world's most treasured ecosystems. Take the Galapagos Islands, where Darwin uncovered many of the basic rules of evolution. Although a limit of 12,000 visitors had been set, this was quickly breached and a new limit of 25,000 was imposed. Yet in 1986, the numbers were in excess of 30,000.

While small tour operators like **Exodus Expeditions** offer low-impact holidays, many visitors arrive in the Galapagos Islands in large boats, all disgorged onto the islands at the same time. The problem for a country like Ecuador, which has to set the conditions for the use of the Galapagos, is that while the smaller, low-impact operators tend to bring lower returns, the big boats tend to bring the big profits.

A small number of travel firms have begun to plough a proportion of their earnings back into conservation, however. **Twickers World**, for example, offers a number of holidays where a proportion of the purchase price is paid to WWF. The firm celebrated its 21st anniversary in 1987. 'Our original enthusiasm for the preservation of the world's wildlife and wild places, and our efforts to help the plight of some endangered species, has not diminished,' reported Managing Director Nedda Lyons. 'In fact, whereas in our early days we were one of a small band of brothers, we are now delighted to be among an increasingly large group of those who care about our planet and its creatures.'

But usually the amounts contributed to conservation are relatively small. **Turkish Delight**, which specializes in holidays in Turkey, has advertised the fact that a proportion of the money you pay goes to the Conservation Foundation. This is obviously a step in the right direction, although at the time of writing the proportion that was being recycled for conservation purposes was less than one per cent.

So, as holidays take an increasing bite out of our budgets, how can we ensure that the money is spent in a way which helps conserve the environment, rather than wrecking it? Whether you want a day trip or a once-in-a-lifetime holiday, the list below should give you some ideas. Useful addresses are provided at the end of the chapter.

Adventure holidays

If you want to get back to nature, one possibility is to try an adventure holiday. Among the market leaders are: **Encounter Overland**, **John Ridgway School of Adventure**, the **Outward Bound Trust**, and **Wilderness Expedition & Survival Training (WEST)**.

At WEST the aim is to help you to 'live with nature, rather than against it'. But remember that adventure holidays are by no means guaranteed to appeal to the Green Tourist. The *macho* culture sometimes encouraged can lead to unnecessary environmental damage.

Alternative technology

See alternative technology in action at the **National Centre for Alternative Technology (NCAT)**. NCAT offers short courses on renewable energy, low energy building, organic gardening, healing herbs and woodland skills. An independent voluntary co-operative, **ARA Study Tours**, also offers a range of short courses covering aspects of alternative technology.

Angling

By all means go fishing, but if you do, make sure you use non-lead weights, see page 303, and try not to leave any tackle in the river or on the banks.

Beaches

If you are looking for an attractive, clean British beach, track down a copy of the *Good Beach Guide* (Ebury Press and Heinz, Guardians of the Countryside, 1988), compiled by the Marine Conservation Society. This provides detailed information on over 180 beaches in England, Scotland, Wales and Northern Ireland.

Following the enactment of an EEC Directive in 1976, Britain dragged its heels and finally listed a miserly 27 beaches as European bathing beaches, compared to the 1,498 listed by France and 3,308 listed by Italy!

As the Marine Conservation Society points out, the Government's thinking was clearly that if it only designated 27 then it would only have to clean up 27 to suitable standards. Following enormous pressure, however, the Government increased the number of designated beaches to 392 in 1987 — of which an astounding 40 per cent subsequently failed to meet the European standard.

In 1987 the only British beaches which qualified for the European Blue Flag, awarded to beaches with clean water, free from visible litter, and with good provisions for safety and environmental education, were: **Bridlington North** and **Bridlington South**, **Carnoustie**, **Crinnis**, **Fraserburgh**, **Pembrey**, **Portenon**, St Ives – **Porthmore**, **Southsea**, **Swanage**, 5 beaches at Torbay, (**Broadsands**, **Goodrington**, **Oddiscombe**, **Paignton**, **Redgate**) and **Weymouth**.

We list below the designated beaches which failed to meet the standard. Some of these beaches will have improved by the time you read this section; if you want to check the latest state of play, contact the Marine Conservation Society.

- **South West England**
  Bembridge, Bude, Burnham-on-Sea, Charmouth, Clevedon, Colwell Bay, Combe Martin, Cowes, Dunster, Exmouth, Gurnard, Ilfracombe, Instow, Lyme Regis, Lynmouth, Marazion, Mawgan Porth, Minehead, Mullion, Pentewan, Plymouth Hoe, Porthallow, Portleven, Readymoney Cove, Rock, Ryde, St Ives – Porthgwidden, Salcombe, Shaldon, Thurlestone, Totland, Trevaunance Cove, Trevose Bay, Ventnor and Weston-super-Mare.

- **South East England**
  Broadstairs, Deal Castle, Dymchurch, Felixstowe
  South Beach, Folkestone, Great Yarmouth, Hove,
  Hythe, Joss Bay, Kingsgate Bay, Lancing,
  Leysdown-on-Sea, Littlestone-on-Sea, Lowestoft
  North Beach, St Mary's Bay, Sandgate, Sandwich
  Bay, Seaford, Sheringham, Thorpe Bay, Wells-next-
  the-Sea, Westcliffe and Worthing.

- **The East Coast**
  Cleethorpes, Crimdon Park, Flamborough,
  Newbiggin-by-the-Sea, Redcar, Roker, Saltburn-by-
  the-Sea, Seaburn, Seaham, Seaton Carew, South
  Beach Scarborough, Seaton Sluice, South Landing,
  Spittal, Sutton on Sea, Whitburn, Whitley Bay, and
  Withernsea.

- **North West England**
  Ainsdale, Allonby, Askam-in-Furness, Bardsea,
  Blackpool, Cleveleys, Fleetwood, Haverigg,
  Heysham, Lytham, Moels, Morecambe, New
  Brighton, Roa Island, St Bees, Seascale, Silecroft,
  Silloth and Southport.

- **Scotland**
  Belhaven, Gailes, Montrose, Nairn, North Berwick
  and Saltcoats.

- **Wales**
  Aberavon, Abersoch, Amroth, Barmouth, Broad
  Haven, Cold Knap, Colwyn Bay, Jackson's Bay,
  Kinmel Bay, Langland Bay, Limeslade Bay,
  Llandudno West Shore, Morfa Bychan, Newgale,
  Prestatyn, Rest Bay, Rhosili Bay, Rhyl, Sandy Bay,
  Saundersfoot, Southerndown, Swansea Bay, Tenby,
  Trearddur Bay, Trecco Bay, Tywyn and Whitmore
  Bay.

- **Northern Ireland**
  Newcastle.

Bird-watching

When we carried out a survey of firms specializing in environmental and wildlife holidays, bird-watching dominated the scene. Firms active in this area include: **Barn Owl Travel**, **Birdquest**, **Branta Travel**, **Caledonian Wildlife**, **Cambrian Bird Holidays**, **Cygnus Wildlife**, **Hosking Tours**, **Ornitholidays**, **RSPB Holidays**, **Sunbird** and **Twickers World**. Other key contacts are the **Royal Society for the Protection of Birds** and the **Wildfowl Trust**. Although an excess of bird-watchers can sometimes disturb the very birds they come to see, most bird-watchers are strongly committed to conservation.

Boating and yachting

If you are repainting a boat or yacht with an anti-fouling coating, avoid paints containing tributyl tin (TBT) (see page 44). TBT paints have been shown to cause extraordinary disruption of the sexual organs of the dog whelk, indicating that they could be having a profound effect on marine and freshwater life near marinas and other mooring areas.

Be careful when fuelling boat engines not to spill fuel or oil into the water. Oil is still a major pollutant of rivers, lakes and coastal waters. Make sure, too, that your boat's sewage does not go straight into the sea: install a cistern if you don't already have one. Once under way, don't dump rubbish into rivers, lakes or the sea. If you must dump waste overboard, make sure it is biodegradable and save any plastics for onshore disposal. Don't chase sea mammals in power-boats. And do respect protected areas.

Butterfly farms

If butterfly farms breed their own butterflies, well and good. But if they import them, they help to encourage an international trade which the WWF estimates is worth $100m. Be particularly wary of buying tourist trinkets made from butterflies when travelling overseas. By all means visit butterfly farms, like **Butterfly World**, set in 8 acres of farm land in the heart of Shropshire. But ask the owners if they support conservation. If they don't, suggest they begin to.

Canoeing and kayaking

One excellent way to see wildlife is to travel in a two-seater, 18-foot Canadian-style canoe. You are at the same level as most forms of wildlife and your passage is much less likely to disturb the worlds you pass through.

In the UK, you can book a canoe holiday through firms like **Roger Drummond Outdoor Services** or **Tops Holidays**. If you are interested in canoeing in France, **PGL Sunsports** organizes trips through the Ardèche gorge to the natural rock bridge at Vallon-Pont d'Arc.

Further afield, you can canoe through Canada with a holiday from **All-Canada Travel**. More exotically, try **Canoeing Safaris of Zimbabwe**, who offer a one-week guided paddle down the Zambezi, from the Kariba Dam to the game lodge at Mana Pools (available through **Abercrombie and Kent**). For something even more invigorating, consider sea kayaking with **Wilderness Expedition & Survival Training (WEST)**.

Chimpanzees

When on holiday in countries like Spain, don't be hoodwinked into having your picture taken with the chimps used by beach photographers. WWF points out that you run the risk of contracting hepatitis, herpes and rabies from such animals. For every one chimp you see, at least 10 died during capture or transport. And the animals you see will almost certainly be killed after a couple of years, once they have outgrown their purpose. WWF's campaign against the use of chimps has been a model of how to engage the consumer in conservation. Reports from concerned tourists provided indisputable evidence that conservation laws were being widely flouted.

City farms

Many urban children grow up with no experience of animals

other than household pets, and little idea of where eggs, milk and other animal foods come from. Now, with the spread of the city farm movement, they have less of an excuse. Make a day trip to one: the growing number of city farms are co-ordinated through the **National Federation of City Farms and Community Gardens**.

Conservation

If you are interested in seeing what conservation is like on the ground, check through the 'working holidays' offered by the **British Trust for Conservation Volunteers (BTCV)**. BTCV's 'Natural Break' conservation working holidays cost very little — and can also be an excellent start if you are thinking in terms of a 'green career'.

Other organizations, including the **Marine Conservation Society**, **RSPB** and **WWF**, also need volunteers. The **Nature Conservancy Council**, for example, needs volunteers to survey 5,000 miles of coastline. Interested? If so, contact the NCC's Coastwatch Co-ordinator. The **British Trust for Ornithology** needs volunteer bird counters for the largest ever survey of British breeding birds.

Cruises

If money is no object, there are a number of cruises on offer. **P&O Cruises**, for example, has offered ornithological tours aboard the *Canberra*, while Galapagos cruises are available from **Swan Hellenic Natural History Tours**, **Speedbird** and **Twickers World**. In general, though, cruises tend to distort local economies in holiday areas. One honourable exception is the *Lindblad Explorer*, which goes to the Falklands (contact **Salen Lindblad Cruising**).

Cycling

A thoroughly green leisure option. A holiday on two wheels can be an eye-opener, with holidays being peddled from the Channel Islands to China. For holidays in Britain, the possibilities include: **Adventure Cycles**, **Bicycle Beano**, **Bike Events**,

Cyclecraft, **Rydene Holidays** and **Wessex Cycling Holidays**. Other useful sources of information and advice include the **Cycle Touring Club**, and the **Youth Hostels Association**.

For *overseas* cycling, key contacts include: **Anglo-Dutch Sports**, **Bike Events**, **Bottom Bracket**, **Cycling for Softies**, and **Triskell Tours**.

Development

What marks **North-South Travel** out from the herd is the fact that the firm invests all its profits in Third World development projects, through the North-South Charitable Trust. The projects it funds generally relate to travel and tourism, and aim to meet the needs of local people and the environment.

Energy

Probably the most publicized energy tour is that offered by **British Nuclear Fuels** at Sellafield, where you can go and see nuclear power in action. **Mountain Goat Holidays** have built a weekend break around a tour of the nuclear plant. For a totally different perspective on the energy prospect, visit NCAT (see Alternative Technology).

Farm holidays

If you want to get first-hand experience of what it is like to work on an organic farm, try **Working Weekends on Organic Farms**. Expect to work long and hard! Irish organic farmers and growers also offer a range of family and self-catering holidays. Details from **Gillies Macbain**.

Field studies

Don't just read about nature in books, see it — and study it — in the field. A wide selection of courses designed to increase environmental understanding are available through the **Field Studies Council**. Two small firms operating in Scotland are **Aigas Field Centre Holidays** and **Albannach Insight Holidays**.

Many of the holidays offered by the wildlife tour operators listed in the table also contain a field study component.

Food

Alan Gear's *The Organic Food Guide* (Dent, 1987) lists over 600 suppliers, from wholefood shops to supermarkets, throughout Britain and Ireland. Two useful guides for vegetarian travellers are the *International Vegetarian Handbook*, produced annually by the Vegetarian Society of the UK and published by Thorsons, and Lynne Alexander's *Staying Vegetarian*, subtitled 'A Guide to Guesthouses and Hotels for Vegetarians, Vegans and Wholefooders' (Fontana/Collins, 1987). Egon Ronay also publishes the *Bird's Eye Guide to Healthy Eating Out*, which lists over 500 restaurants, cafés, wine bars and pubs offering wholefood and vegetarian dishes.

Gardens

Apart from the obvious choices, like the gardens run by the **National Trust**, you can visit the **National Centre for Organic Gardening** and learn about the organic approach to gardening. This 22-acre showpiece of organic gardening methods is open all year round and you can see such techniques as 'no-dig' gardening, composting and biological pest control in action. The **National Centre for Alternative Technology** offers courses, in organic gardening. See Alternative Technology.

Kayaking   See Canoeing and kayaking.

National Parks

Our National Parks are not truly 'national', because they are not wholly government owned. Nor are they really 'parks', given that much of the land is used for farming rather than conservation and recreation. But they can offer an interesting range of holidays in some of Britain's most spectacular environments. In fact, there are so many options that the best first step is to contact the

National Park in the area you want to visit for a free information sheet.

There are 10 National Parks: **Brecon Beacons**, **Dartmoor**, **Exmoor**, **Lake District**, **North Yorks Moors**, **Northumberland**, **Peak District**, **Pembrokeshire Coast**, **Snowdonia**, and the **Yorkshire Dales**.

As an example of the sort of holidays on offer, the North Yorks Moors National Park organizes four-day breaks, focusing on marine life in Robin Hood's Bay, woodland management in the Forge Valley, the creation of wildflower areas, and industrial archaeology in Rosedale.

One specialist firm in this area is **HF Holidays**, a non-profit organization founded over 70 years ago. It offers a range of wild-life and environmental special interest holidays, mainly set in Areas of Outstanding Natural Beauty or National Parks.

National Trust

Apart from its holdings of coastline, open country and gardens, the **National Trust** has 57 nature reserves and over 400 designated Sites of Special Scientific Interest. Indeed, it claims to protect more countryside especially suited to wildlife than any other landowner in Britain.

Ornithology   See Bird-watching.

Otters

If you want to see these delightful animals in near-natural settings, visit the **Otter Trust**.

Photography

Shoot wildlife with a camera, not a gun. Photography is an important element of most holidays, but a special feature offered by some specialists. They include **Alfred Gregory Photo Holidays**, which can help you take the photographs of a lifetime in locations from the Himalayas to the Galapagos Islands.

Plants

If you are interested in plants and in botany, Britain is richly endowed with gardens and herbariums. Apart from the **Royal Botanic Gardens** at Kew, which has strong links with conservation and endangered species projects around the world, there are an increasing number of interesting specialist gardens.

Firms specializing in botanical and garden-related holidays include **Cox & Kings Travel**, **David Sayers Travel** and **Fairways & Swinford Travel**. The Cox & King guides include professionals who work with such organizations as the Nature Conservancy Council and the Royal Society for the Protection of Birds.

Rare breeds

It is as important to preserve old species of farm animal and agricultural plants as it is to protect most forms of wildlife. Help fund this activity by visiting some of the rare breed survival centres around the country. Details can be had from the **Rare Breeds Survival Trust**. See feather-legged Salmon Faverolles and Pied turkeys at the **Domestic Fowl Trust**. For wild birds, try the seven centres around the country run by the **Wildfowl Trust,** founded by Sir Peter Scott.

Safaris and expeditions

As the table on pages 288–95 shows, many companies offer expeditions, safaris and other forms of wildlife holidays. Such holidays need to be carefully managed and supervised if they are not to cause damage to the environment. Before booking, check whether the operator of your choice ploughs back any of its profits into conservation.

Skiing

One of the fastest growing sports, but one which has shown a growing tendency to compete with conservation interests. In Scotland, for example, proposed ski slopes have threatened the habitats of birds like the golden plover and dotterel.

The Alps, meanwhile, have been described as the 'most threatened mountain system in the world'. One contributory factor has been the explosive growth of skiing developments. Deforestation, some of it caused by the clearance of trees for skiing pistes, is turning the Alps into a region of devastating landslides. In many places, the trees have had to be replaced, at considerable cost, by barriers of concrete and steel.

If you ski off-piste remember that you are not only risking your own life but also intruding on wilderness: you can alarm wildlife and damage the flora. As with any other sport, the key is to understand and respect the environment you are enjoying. Leave it as you found it.

'Smokestack' tourism

The city and urban fringe greening projects now blossoming around the country are often worth a visit. Organizations like the **Groundwork Foundation** may not be in the business of building new hotels or fun fairs, but they are steadily improving key areas of the local environment and opening them up both to local people and to visitors. Several of the Groundwork Trusts have produced attractive, well-researched guides to their areas for visitors — including walkers, cyclists, the elderly, the disabled and people with small children. The Garden Festivals which have begun to appear around the country are also well worth supporting. Much of the planting survives the festival, so the greening effect can be permanent.

Vegetarian holidays

Among the firms specializing in vegetarian holidays is **Canterbury Travel**. It offers holidays in countries like Austria, West Germany, Portugal and Cyprus. See under Food.

Walking

Too many walkers can wear out the environment just as surely as a platoon of tanks. The Green Tourist recognizes that going on foot is almost always the best way of getting inside a landscape, but steers clear of the most heavily beaten paths and areas.

The **British Tourist Authority** and the **Sports Council** publish lists of firms offering walking holidays. Nature walks are featured by the **National Trust**. Other people to talk to include: **Countrywide Holidays Association**, **Footpath Holidays**, **Headwater Holidays**, **HF Walking Holidays**, **High Places**, **Mountain Goat Holidays**, **North-West Frontiers**, **Peak Walks**, **Ramblers Holidays**, **Sherpa Expeditions**, **Waymark Holidays**, **The Wayfarers**, and the **Youth Hostels Association**.

Walking holidays are available worldwide. **Ramblers Holidays**, for example, offers holidays in many different countries — including, for the more adventurous, Papua New Guinea.

Whales

Now that commercial whaling has all but stopped, many countries are discovering that their whale stocks can be key tourism assets. Indeed, so great is the interest that the grey whales of California have already had to be protected from over-eager sightseers. Whales can be seen during visits to Canada, the East and West Coasts of the United States, and Mexico. Contact **Twickers World**.

Wildlife

The table on pages 288 – 95 lists a range of firms offering holidays of interest to the Green Tourist. A growing number of mainstream companies also offer holidays with a substantial wildlife flavour. The Green Tourist can play an important role in conservation and 'sustainable development'. The conservation of Rwanda's mountain gorillas for example, has benefited enormously from the money injected by visitors.

Yachting   See Boating and yachting.

Young people's holidays

You can volunteer to help in many forms of conservation activity.

Key contacts include the **British Trust for Conservation Volunteers** (see Conservation) and the **National Trust**, which offers Acorn Camps and Young National Trust Groups for those of 16 and over. Expect to contribute to the cost of food and accommodation. Another option is the **Youth Hostels Association**, which offers a number of special interest weekends focusing on natural history.

If you are interested in fieldwork and expeditions, try the **Brathay Exploration Group**. The basic approach involves building up young people's skills and confidence, and introducing them to the natural world. In BEG's Trans-Snowdonia Trek, for example, you can try your hand at assessing the environmental impact of hill farming, tourism and hydroelectric schemes, as well as past mining and quarrying activities.

Zoos

There are good zoos, bad zoos and ugly zoos. The Green Tourist is unlikely to spend much time at the zoo, but properly financed, intelligently designed and well-run zoos have a vital role to play in international conservation work. They are few and far between, however.

As far as most zoos are concerned, the Green Tourist might as well give them a miss — and spend the money saved on membership of: **Zoo Check**, which campaigns for the closure of most zoos; the **Royal Society for the Protection of Animals (RSPCA)**, which inspects zoos to ensure that conditions are adequate; or **WWF**, which campaigns to protect animals in the wild.

The RSPCA carried out a recent survey of British zoos, and was none too complimentary. There are honourable exceptions, however. **Drusilla's Zoo Park** in East Sussex, for example, won the first Universities' Federation for Animal Welfare (UFAW) award for its new beaver enclosure. As a general rule, though, zoos have surprisingly weak links with wildlife conservation. If you visit a zoo, make a point of asking what they are doing for the conservation of plants and animals in the wild.

Dolphinaria, which show dolphins and killer whales, have been particularly controversial in Britain. Despite the protestations of **Windsor Safari Park** that there is 'no scientific data or evidence to suggest that there is any basic reason why killer whales and dolphins need to be in water deeper than 10 metres', groups like Greenpeace and the RSPCA are right to call for much improved facilities — or, if such improvements are not made, to insist on the liberation of the animals.

People go to zoos and aquaria to have fun, but they can also learn, if they are given the chance. Some of the new American aquaria — like **Sea World** — have extraordinary facilities and go to great lengths to get across the conservation message. The killer whale pool at the Florida Sea World, in Orlando, is 40 metres deep. And over a million teachers and students have studied marine sciences at the various Sea World parks, with courses on whales, sharks, coral reef ecosystems, tropical fish, marine ecology and animal behaviour.

Few British zoos can yet afford the levels of investment needed to bring their facilities up to American standards — but our best zoo directors and designers need to raise their sights. They need to think of zoos as learning environments, where people are brought together with animals in a way which promotes respect — and interest. Designed and operated in the right way, zoos could become extraordinarily powerful promoters of the conservation cause, spreading the word and carrying out pioneering research.

Back in the USA, visitors to Washington State's **Seattle Aquaria** are encouraged to get involved in the cleaning up of nearby Puget Sound. Is it too much to hope that leading British zoos might follow suit? A truly green zoo would be well worth the entry ticket.

THE GREEN TOURIST GUIDE

Tour operator	Type of holiday	Destinations	Policy on conservation
Abercrombie & Kent Sloane Square House Holbein Place London SW1W 8NS Tel: 01-730 9600	Luxury holidays	Africa Egypt India China	**Overall Policy** Consistent policy of donation on behalf of clients taking the more luxurious holidays. Would not specify exact amount donated. **Membership or Support** Actively support WWF, Friends of Kenya's National Parks, Rhino Rescue
Arctic Experience 29 Nork Way Banstead Surrey SM7 1PB Tel: 07373 62321	From adventure holidays to luxury hotels	Iceland Greenland Canada Spitsbergen Islands	**Overall Policy** Not yet contributing anything, but attracted to the idea in the future.
Bales Tours Bales House Barrington Road Dorking Surrey RH4 3EJ Tel: 0306 885991	Luxury holidays Tours Safaris	Africa India	**Overall Policy** They make no contributions, are not affiliated in any way and apparently would not consider it.
Birding Lattendenz's Farm Ashburnham nr Battle East Sussex TN33 9PB Tel: 0323 833245	Exclusively bird-watching	Worldwide	**Overall Policy** They do not plough money back into conservation projects. However, each trip is limited to 16 people and a tour manager and bird expert accompany all tours.

★ Birdquest Two Jays Kemple End Birdybrow Stonyhurst Lancs BB6 9QY Tel: 025 486 317	Bird-watching tours	South America Australia China Siberia Africa India Lapland	**Overall Policy** Very actively involved in financially supporting projects worldwide. **Membership or Support** Members of RSPB, ICPB (International Council for Preservation of Birds) and Flora & Fauna Preservation Society. Donations to Mauritius Wildlife Appeal **Projects** The Gurneys Pitta Project in Thailand — financial support to promote bird preservation.
Branta Travel 11 Uxbridge Street London W8 7TQ Tel: 01-229 7231	Specialist bird-watching tours	Europe North Africa	**Overall Policy** No overall company policy, although a responsible attitude is encouraged by all tours being accompanied by a tour leader. **Membership or Support** Corporate member of the RSPB.
David Sayers Travel 10 Barley Mow Passage London W4 4PH Tel: 01-994 6477	Specialist in garden and botanical holidays	Far East Siberia	**Overall Policy** No sponsorship activities.
★ EcoSafaris 146 Gloucester Road London SW7 4SZ Tel: 01-370 5032	Safaris Also offer a panda tour, special tiger watching tours and whale and polar bear watching tours	Worldwide	**Overall Policy** They organize a number of special tours which are associated with appeals, conservation trusts and charities and pay between 2 ½% and 5% of monies received towards the particular cause. They say that they are very keen on conservation and support organizations that are inclined to protect endangered species. **Membership or Support** Corporate members of the RSPB and the Wildlife Conservation Society of Zambia. Support the work of WWF, the RSNC and its associated trusts through the British Wildlife Appeal. **Projects** This year they have a tour for Zoo Check's Save the Rhino Appeal.

THE GREEN TOURIST GUIDE (continued)

Encounter Overland 267 Old Brompton Road London SW5 Tel: 01-370 6951	Adventure holidays	Asia Africa South America	**Overall Policy** They do give their clients fundamental guidelines regarding litter and waste but say they are not an 'ecological company'. **Membership or Support** Affiliated with the Flora and Fauna Preservation Society and claim to be the first tour operator to promote tourism in Rwanda to help fund game wardens to protect the gorillas.
Erskine Expeditions 14 Inverleith Place Edinburgh EH3 5PZ Tel: 031-552 2673	Expeditions and tours	Arctic Antarctic Falklands Africa	**Overall Policy** This company says it is not large enough for a consistent sponsorship policy, although they do give token donations where possible and encourage holidays drawing attention to endangered species.
Exodus Expeditions All Saints Passage 100 Wandsworth High Street London SW18 4LE Tel: 01-870 0151	Safaris Bird-watching holidays	Africa South America Himalayas	**Overall Policy** They have no consistent policy of sponsorship, but do give token donations where budget allows.
★ **Field Studies Council** Flatford Mill Field Centre East Bergholt Colchester Essex CO7 6UL Tel: 0206 298283/252	460 courses at nine residential centres in the UK and expeditions abroad. For students or holiday makers with a serious interest in environment.	UK Africa China Spain	**Overall Policy** They are a self-supporting charity aiming to bring environmental understanding to everyone. They are concerned with all aspects and aim to provide the facilities to allow environmental studies on site. They also carry out research on oil pollution, acid rain and other subjects.

Guerba Expeditions 101 Eden Vale Road, Westbury Wiltshire BA13 3QX Tel: 0373 826611	Safari specialists, not hotel based.	Africa	**Overall Policy** No direct sponsorship or corporate membership.
Hann Overland 268 Vauxhall Bridge Road London SW1V 1EJ Tel: 01-834 7337	Wildlife excursions Trekking Rail tours Adventure holidays	Worldwide	**Overall Policy** They offer cheapish holidays with wildlife interest, but are not members of any conservation organization — nor do they sponsor.
Hoskings Tours Hunworth Melton Constable Norfolk NR24 2AA Tel: 0263 713969	Small operation offering special-interest holidays accompanied by photographer or ornithologist.	N. Yemen Africa Falklands Rwanda Canada	**Overall Policy** They do not yet financially contribute to conservation, but do intend to and they like to stimulate discussion around these issues in the countries they visit. **Membership or Support** Involved with Middle East Bird Club.
Journey Latin America 16 Devonshire Road London W4 2HD Tel: 01-747 3108	Independent travel Adventure travel	Latin America	**Overall Policy** They have no definite policy on the environment, although are interested in finding out what they could do.
Kuoni Travel Kuoni House Dorking Surrey RH5 4AZ Tel: 0306 885044	Luxury, hotel-based holidays including safaris	Worldwide	**Overall Policy** Occasional donations to WWF.

THE GREEN TOURIST GUIDE (continued)

Ornitholidays
1 – 3 Victoria Drive
Bognor Regis
Sussex PO21 2PW
Tel: 0243 821230

Bird watching and natural history holidays

Worldwide

Overall Policy They donate money periodically.
Membership or Support Corporate member of RSPB

★ **Papyrus Tours**
4 Howden Close
Doncaster DN4 7JW
Tel: 0302 530778

Specialist wildlife holidays, hotel-based

East Africa and Kenya

Company Policy Not really a commercial concern and they plough back surplus into 'particular projects of conservation interest'
Membership or Support Director of Papyrus is Chairman of Yorkshire Wildlife. Everyone going on a tour automatically becomes a member of the East Africa Wildlife Society
Projects Papyrus are lending financial support to a joint project between Leicester University and the Kenyan Government who are conducting a large scale ecological survey of Kenya. Also contributes to Elsamere Conservation Centre, where people stay on some Papyrus tours, and to the Daphne Sheldrick Wildlife Appeal which is geared to the rehabilitation of injured animals to the wild.

★ **Peregrine Holidays**
40 – 41 South Parade
Summertown
Oxford OX2 7JP
Tel: 0865 511642

Special interest tours including bird-watching and wildlife

Greece
Crete
Africa

Overall Policy They are extremely active in promoting environmental conservation and are involved in specific projects with a wide range of organizations. They would like to encourage all operators to 'contribute to the conservation of the environment which is vital to their operation'. Clients can contribute to conservation through them and they will add a further contribution from the company.
Membership or Support Raised money for RSPB 'Stop the Massacre' campaign. Supported Friends of the Earth in

Cyprus. UK representative of Hellenic Society for the Protection of Nature.
Projects They have raised money for a wide range of projects, including recent York Seal Project and the gorilla conservation in Rwanda.

Company	Region	Details	Policy
			Membership or Support Corporate Members of WWF and RSPB.
Premier Faraway Holidays 10 Rose Crescent Cambridge CB2 3LL Tel: 0223 311103	Africa China	From Wildlife Bus in Kenya for students to luxury tours Safaris Trekking Special interest holidays	
Raoul Moxley Travel 76 Elmbourne Road London SW11 8JJ Tel: 01-672 2437	Worldwide	Upmarket holidays	**Company Policy** They do not have a consistent policy of sponsorship, but on some holidays they donate £5.00 per head to WWF. **Membership or Support** Occasional donations to WWF.
★ RSPB Holidays The Lodge Sandy Beds SG19 2DL Tel: 0767 80551	Worldwide	Bird-watching holidays (Programmes differ yearly) Holidays for the disabled	**Company Policy** They have charity status, so all money is ploughed back into conservation projects. No restrictions for non-members going on these holidays.
Safari Consultants 83 Gloucester Place London W1H 3PG Tel: 01-486 4774	Africa	Safaris Specialist company with no standard package Personal service and itinerary	**Company Policy** They specifically cater for individual requirements eg vegetarianism. Also they encourage clients to donate to conservation projects like Rhino Rescue.

THE GREEN TOURIST GUIDE (continued)

Sherpa Expeditions 131a Heston Road Hounslow Middlesex TW5 0RD Tel: 01-577 2717	Mountain walking holidays Long haul holidays	Himalayas	**Overall policy** They operate a mountain code which includes keeping trails clean by burning or burying all litter and recently started advising travellers to use kerosene instead of dead wood, because of deforestation pressures. The guidelines include not encouraging children to beg and suggestions about how to approach the local people.
Sunbird PO Box 76 Sandy Beds SG19 1DF Tel: 0767 82969	Bird-watching holidays	Australia Morocco Kenya India Trinidad Europe	**Overall Policy** All the tours are led by a representative who would observe country codes. **Membership or Support** They operate a couple of tours for the RSPB.
Swan Hellenic 77 New Oxford Street London WC1A 1PP Tel: 01-831 1234	Cruises Natural history tours Luxury holidays and package tours	Worldwide	**Overall Policy** They have no environmental policy, connections or guidelines.
Thomson Holidays Greater London House Hampstead Road London NW1 7SD Tel: 01-387 9321	Major package tour operator Standard tours for 'adventure lovers', but not appropriate for wildlife enthusiasts	Worldwide	**Company Policy** They have no affiliations with or sponsorship links with conservation organizations.

★ Turkish Delight 164b Heath Road Twickenham Middlesex TW1 4BN Tel: 01-891 5901	Hotel-based holidays in Turkey	Turkey	**Company Policy** They are actively involved in conservation projects in Turkey, recognizing the problems with over development in this area and ploughing back a percentage of their revenue into conservation. They discriminate against using hotels which do not fit into the environment and have invested in research into the loggerhead turtle. **Membership or Support** They have links with Turkish environmental organizations and are affiliated with the Conservation Foundation in this country.
★ Twickers World 22 Church Street Twickenham TW1 3NW Tel: 01-892 81	Adventure holidays Wildlife holidays Cultural holidays	South, Central and North America Iceland Greenland	**Overall Policy** On certain holidays they allocate a small percentage to particular conservation organizations. **Membership or Support** Corporate members of RSPB, FFPS, WWF. **Projects** In the Galapagos and Madagascar, where WWF are encouraging responsible attitudes to tourism, they have tours which plough back approximately 1% to WWF.
Wildlife Explorer 25 Carpalla Road Foxhole St Austell Cornwall Tel: 0726 824132	Upmarket personalized safari consultants. Modify itineraries according to clients' needs and interests	Tanzania	**Company Policy** They are a small company and have no set policy for financial support, but do take an active interest.

★ These tour operators are recommended for the green tourist.

This table is based on a telephone survey of tour operators conducted by SustainAbility Ltd in April 1988. Comments on policy were given by representatives of the companies.

OTHER USEFUL ADDRESSES

Adventure Cycles, 2 Snow Cottages, Mamhead, Kenton, Exeter, Devon. Tel: 0626 864786

Aigas Field Centre Holidays, Beauly, Inverness-shire IV4 7AD. Tel: 0463 782443

Albannach Insight Holidays, Hamilton House, Strathpeffer, Ross & Cromarty IV14 9AD. Tel: 0997 21577

Alfred Gregory Photo Holidays, Westgate, Elton, Nr Matlock, Derbyshire DE4 2BZ. Tel: 0629 88451

All-Canada Travel, 90 High Street, Lowestoft NR32 1XN. Tel: 0502 85825

Anglo-Dutch Sports, 30a Foxgrove Road, Beckenham, Kent. Tel: 01-650 2347

ARA Study Tours, 10 Highfield Close, Wokingham, Berks RG11 1DG. Tel: 0734 783204

Association of Independent Tour Operators, Knoll House, Pursers Lane, Peaslake, Nr Guildford GU5 9SJ.

Barn Owl Travel, 27 Seaview Road, Gillingham, Kent ME7 4NL. Tel: 0634 56759

Bicycle Beano, Erwood, Builth Wells, Powys, Wales. Tel: 09823 676

Bike Events, PO Box 75, Bath, Avon. Tel: 0225 310859

Bottom Bracket, J & N Spurr, 13 Killerton Road, Bude, Cornwall. Tel: 0288 3618

Brecon Beacons National Park, 7 Glamorgan Street, Brecon, Powys LD3 7DP. Tel: 0874 4437

British Tourist Authority, Thames Tower, Black's Road, London W6 9EL. Tel: 01-846 9000

British Trust for Conservation Volunteers (BTCV), 36 St Mary's Street, Wallingford, Oxon OX10 0EU. Tel: 0491 39766

British Trust for Ornithology (BTO), Beech Grove, Tring, Herts HP23 5NR. Tel: 044 282 3461

Butterfly World, Yockleton, Nr Shrewsbury SY5 9PU. Tel: 0743 84217

Caledonian Wildlife, 30 Culduthel Road, Inverness IV2 4AP, Scotland. Tel: 0463 233130

Cambrian Bird Holidays, Henllan, Llandysul, Dyfed, Wales. Tel: 0559 370240

Canoeing Safaris of Zimbabwe (contact **Abercrombie & Kent**).

Canterbury Travel, 248 Streatfield Road, Kenton, Harrow, Middx
HA3 9BY. Tel: 01-204 4111

Countrywide Holidays Association, Birch Heys, Cromwell Range,
Manchester M14 6HU. Tel: 061 225 1000

Cox & Kings Ltd, St James Court, 45 Brunswick Court, London
SW1E 6AF. Tel: 01-931 9106

Cyclecraft, 12 Morningside, Lancaster, Lancashire. Tel: 0524 62742

Cycle Touring Club, Cotterell House, 69 Meadrow, Godalming, Surrey
GU7 3HS. Tel: 048 68 7217

Cycling for Softies, Susie Madron's Cycling Holidays, Lloyds House,
22 Lloyd Street, Manchester. Tel: 061 834 6800

Cygnus Wildlife, 96 Fore Street, Kingsbridge, Devon TQ7 1PY.
Tel: 0548 6178

Dartmoor National Park, Haytor Road, Bovey Tracey, Devon
TQ13 9JQ. Tel: 0626 832093

Domestic Fowl Trust, Honeybourne Pastures, Honeybourne, Evesham,
Worcestershire. Tel: 0386 833083

Drusilla's Zoo Park, Alfriston, East Sussex BN26 5QS.
Tel: 0323 870234

Exmoor National Park, Exmoor House, Dulverton, Somerset
TA22 9HL. Tel: 0398 23665

Fairways & Swinford Travel Ltd, 20 Upper Ground, London SE1 9PF.
Tel: 01-261 1744

Footpath Holidays, 4 Holly Walk, Andover, Hampshire SP10 3PJ.
Tel: 0264 542689

Gillies Macbain, Cranagh Castle, Templemore, Co. Tipperary, Ireland.
Tel: 0504 53104

Groundwork Foundation, Bennett's Court, 6 Bennett's Hill,
Birmingham B2 5ST. Tel: 021 236 8565

Headwater Holidays, 62a Beach Road, Hartford, Cheshire CW8 3AB.
Tel: 0606 782011

HF Holidays and **HF Walking Holidays**, 142-144 Great North Way,
London NW4 1EG. Tel: 01-203 0433

High Places, Bob Lancaster & Associates, 15 Spring Hill, Sheffield
S10 1ET. Tel: 0742 682553

International Association of Zoo Educators, Devon Zoology Centre,
Penwill Way, Paignton, Devon TQ4 5JS. Tel: 0803 559674

John Ridgway School of Adventure, Ardmore, Rhiconich, By Lairg,
Sutherland, Scotland IV27 4RB. Tel: 097 182 229

Lake District National Park, National Parks Visitor Services, Brockhole, Windermere LA23 1LJ. Tel: 096 62 6601

Mountain Goat Holidays, Victoria Street, Windermere, Cumbria LA23 1AD. Tel: 096 62 5161

National Centre for Alternative Technology, Machynlleth, Powys, Wales SY20 9AZ. Tel: 0654 2400

National Centre for Organic Gardening, Ryton-on-Dunsmore, Coventry CV8 3LG. Tel: 0203 303517

National Federation of City Farms and Community Gardens, The Old Vicarage, 66 Fraser Street, Windmill Hill, Bedminster, Bristol BS3 4LY. Tel: 0272 660663

North Yorks Moors National Park, The Old Vicarage, Bondgate, Helmsley, York YO6 5BP. Tel: 0439 70657

North-South Travel, The Moulsham Mill Centre, Parkway, Chelmsford, Essex CM2 7PX. Tel: 0245 492882

Northumberland National Park, Eastburn South Park, Hexham, Northumberland NE46 1BS. Tel: 0434 605555

North-West Frontiers, 19 West Terrace, Ullapool, Ross-shire IV26 2UU. Tel: 0854 2571

Otter Trust, Earsham, Nr Bungay, Suffolk NR35 2AF. Tel: 0986 3470

Outward Bound Trust, Chestnut Field, Regent Place, Rugby CV21 2PJ. Tel: 0788 60423

Peak District National Park, Aldern House, Baslow Road, Bakewell, Derbyshire DE4 1AE. Tel: 062 981 4321

Peak Walks, Ash Lea, 10 Rainbow Road, Macclesfield SK10 2PF. Tel: 0625 612291

Pembrokeshire Coast National Park, County Offices, Haverfordwest, Dyfed SA61 1QZ. Tel: 0437 4591

PGL Sunsports, Station Street, Ross-on-Wye HR9 7AH. Tel: 0989 65556

Ramblers Holidays, 13 Longcroft House, Fretherne Road, Welwyn Garden City, Herts AL8 6PQ. Tel: 0707 331133

Rare Breeds Survival Trust, 4th Street, National Agricultural Centre, Stoneleigh, Kenilworth, Warwickshire CV8 2LG. Tel: 0203 696551

Roger Drummond Outdoor Services, 8 Severn Bank, Shrewsbury SY1 2JD. Tel: 0743 65022

Rydene Holidays, Unit 8B, Lower Sunny Bank Mills, Meltham, West Yorkshire. Tel: 0484 850074

Salen Lindblad Cruising, 6 Shepherd Street, London W1. Tel: 01-499 7522

Sherpa Expeditions, 131a Heston Road, Hounslow, Middx TW3 0RD. Tel: 01-577 2717

Snowdonia National Park, Penrhyndeudraeth, Gwynedd LL48 6LS. Tel: 0766 770274

Sports Council, 16 Upper Woburn Place, London WC1H 0QP. Tel: 01-387 1277

Tops Holidays, Hope-under-Dinsmore, Leominster HR6 0PW. Tel: 0568 611412

Triskell Tours, 35 Langland Drive, Northway, Sedgley. Tel: 090 73 78255

The Wayfarers, 22 Maltravers Street, Arundel, West Sussex BN18 9BU. Tel: 0903 882925

Waymark Holidays, 295 Lillie Road, London SW6 7LL. Tel: 01-385 5015

Wessex Cycling Holidays, 23 Elwell Street, Upwey, Weymouth, Dorset DT3 5QF. Tel: 0305 813965

Wilderness Expedition & Survival Training (WEST), Arrina, Shieldaig, Strathcarron, Ross-shire IV54 8XU, Scotland. Tel: 05205 213

Wildfowl Trust, Slimbridge, Gloucester GL2 7BT. Tel: 045 389333

Working Weekends on Organic Farms (WWOOF), 19 Bradford Road, Lewes, Sussex BN7 1RB.

Yorkshire Dales National Park, Colvend, Hebden Road, Grassington, Skipton, North Yorks BD23 5LB. Tel: 0756 752748

Youth Hostels Association, Trevelyan House, 8 St Stephen's Hill, St Albans, Herts AL1 2DY. Tel: 0727 55215

Zoo Check, Cherry Tree Cottage, Coldharbour, Nr Dorking, Surrey RH12 1HG. Tel: 0306 712091

Note to page 272. The tour operators who have helped WWF with loggerhead turtle conservation are: **Air Link Holidays**, **Amathus Holidays**, **Aspro Holidays**, **Grecian Holidays**, **Greek Islands Club**, **Horizon**, **Intersun Holidays**, **Portland Holidays**, **Sun Med Holidays**, **Thomson Holidays** and **Timsway Holidays**.

THE GIFT SHOP

Dreaming of a Green Christmas

The Eco-Fax: a gift for Green Yuppies

Environment-friendly fashion and jewellery

Leafing through the green catalogues

Child's play: toys and games

Don't look a gift-horse in the mouth, we are told from childhood. But there are many gifts which you as a Green Consumer might prefer not to be given — and equally would not buy for your friends. The previous chapters have highlighted many environmentally unacceptable products and many others which would make very successful and suitable gifts. Key issues covered in this chapter include over-packaging, endangered species and animal welfare.

You will find ideas for 'green' gifts throughout this book. If you are looking for a gift for a gardener, for example, check through *The Garden Centre*. If you want to surprise someone with a holiday, turn to *The Travel Agent*. If you are giving wine or champagne, check through the organic brands in *The Supermarket*.

Many products for the gift market are enormously over-packaged, either to tempt consumers into buying something they would not ordinarily buy — or into paying a price which they would normally think excessive. But there are many alternatives. We conclude that you can enjoy yourself hugely — and give others a great deal of pleasure — without damaging the environment in the process.

First, we give you some ideas for gifts that are widely available; and then we choose some ideas from the 'green' catalogues produced by environmental organizations. Shopping through these catalogues can give a double bonus — you can buy a green gift *and* know you're benefiting a worthwhile organization.

Remember, though, that not every item they offer is environmentally acceptable. Indeed, it is only a matter of time before the first Green Consumer Catalogue hits the shelves.

Anglers

Anglers are often in the forefront of the campaign to clean up our rivers and lakes. But they have also been under attack because of their use of lead fishing weights — discarded lead weights are poisoning swans and other water fowl.

A number of alternatives are available, including weights made from tungsten polymer, tin-rubber polymer, zinc and zinc polymer. Non-lead weights are generally more expensive, but worth it in environmental terms.

Suppliers include: **Angler's Snapshot** (the brand name is the same); **R.J. Lewis**, brand names *Plastex* and *Splitworm*; **Saturn Shot Supplies**, brand name *Saturn Shot*; **Thamesly Fishing Tackle**, brand name *Thamesly*; **Whimet**, brand name *Sandvik Safeweight*.

Aquaria

Before you give tropical fish, remember that around two-thirds of imported tropical fish are dead within a year of purchase. If you buy, make sure that the fish have been bred here, reducing the demand for fish caught in the wild. When furnishing your aquaria, avoid corals and exotic shells which will almost certainly have been removed from coral reefs or other threatened habitats.

Books

Build up your Green Bookshelf — or help someone else build up theirs — with books from the Friends of the Earth, Greenpeace, the National Centre for Organic Gardening, National Trust, RSPB, Traidcraft or WWF catalogues. **Hatchards** and **Claude Gill** bookshops can provide an initial reading list, prepared for Green Consumer Week 1988.

Calculators

Purists may object that mental arithmetic is the greenest option, but at least solar calculators dispense with the need to buy, replace and throw away batteries (see page 45 – 8) — and they also help to highlight the longer term potential of renewable energy. They are widely available through high street retailers. See also under Catalogues.

Clothing

In the fashion field, Katharine Hamnett had perhaps the greatest impact with her 'Stop Acid Rain' T-shirts. Indeed, T-shirts remain an excellent way of making a bare breast of your feelings — as our Catalogues section makes clear.

Wherever possible, pick natural materials (like cotton, linen and wool) rather than synthetic materials (nylon, polyester or rayon) which depend on such non-renewable resources as petroleum. But don't imagine that natural materials are automatically environment-friendly. Cotton, that most natural of materials, demands high inputs of fertilizers and pesticides. Grown in the wrong way, it can exhaust the soil.

Since no one yet offers organically grown cotton, you can't choose between environmentally acceptable and unacceptable cotton. For the moment, stick with cotton, but join campaigning organizations to ensure that the pressure is kept up on the cotton-growing industry to switch to more environment-friendly methods.

Avoid furs, even though they are 'natural'. See Furs.

Confectionery

Watch out for over-packaging, particularly of Easter eggs and other similar confections. The **Ferrero Rocher** chocolate box is a prime example. Each chocolate is wrapped in foil and a cup, with the two layers separated by a plastic tray. The outer container is also made of heavy plastic. You can buy some chocolates, like truffles, loose. Also look out for on-pack promotions, like the **Cadbury**'s *Wildlife Bars* which help to raise money for WWF.

Filofax

Given that you don't have to throw away your business diary every year, a Filofax seems a good idea. An essential for the Green Yuppie is *Eco-Fax* paper, available from Friends of the Earth (see under Stationery in the Catalogues section).

Food and drink

See Wines and Champagne, Chocolates, and Catalogues sections.

Furs

In countries like West Germany, where the fur trade claims that the average woman has 1.5 fur coats, fur may still be high on the list of desirable gifts — but things are changing rapidly in Britain and in a number of other English-speaking countries.

The Duke and Duchess of York, you may remember, were presented with fur coats during their wedding anniversary tour of Canada. It was a sign of the times that they ran into a storm of protest. The Duke subsequently returned the £19,000 full-length ranched mink coat he had already ordered as an anniversary present for his wife.

Lobbying: One of the most effective anti-fur organizations has been Lynx, founded a few years back by a Greenpeace splinter group. As the result of their lobbying, and the impact of their advertising campaigns, there has been a genuine fall in the demand for furs. **Debenhams**, for example, have closed down all their fur concessions.

Labelling: The British government planned to legislate for the labelling of furs taken from animals which are typically caught in vicious steel-jawed leg traps. These include the bobcat, coyote, cross fox, grey fox, red fox, white fox, lynx and wolf. Hundreds of thousands of such furs are imported into Britain every year. The labelling plans were abandoned following intense diplomatic pressure from Canada, which was worried by the threat to Eskimo trappers' livelihood.

Farmed furs: A very high proportion of furs now come from farmed animals, but remember that mink farms have caused widespread damage to wildlife. Escaped mink have wrought havoc with birds and other wildlife, displacing otters from many of their old haunts.

Fake furs: Some shops have responded by stocking convincing fake furs and products which mimic animal skins or bird feathers. You can find simulated beaver, mink, leopard or tiger-skin coats at **Selfridges**, for instance, where a fake tiger-skin coat will cost you over £200. For around the same price you can buy a dark leopard fake fur at **Harrods**. Alternative materials include cashmere, camel hair and velvet.

Jewellery

While it may be obvious that we should avoid any jewellery made wholly or in part from endangered species, other forms of jewellery may also carry an invisible environmental 'price-tag'.

Pearls, whether harvested from the wild or cultured, are unlikely to have caused major environmental problems, but precious metals are another matter entirely. Take gold. Apart from the appalling safety record of the gold mining industry in South Africa, where much of the world's gold is produced, there are a number of major pollution problems. A great deal of cyanide is used in gold processing, for example, and this can cause widespread water pollution problems. Cyanide is particularly toxic to fish. Later, when the sulphides are burned off, sulphur dioxide is produced, which can cause acid rain, killing trees and aquatic life.

The production of diamonds and other gemstones has often been associated with such environmental problems as deforestation (whether to clear the land for the mine and associated buildings, or to provide pit props and fuel), soil erosion, siltation problems in rivers, water pollution, air pollution and excessive water use. In some areas, like the Okavango Delta in Botswana, a planned diamond mine is threatening to disrupt the sensitive water regime of this wildlife-rich region completely.

Magazines

Why not give a subscription to a magazine like *BBC Wildlife*, *Country Living*, *Environment Now*, or *World*?

Memberships

If you are stuck with the clichéd problem of finding something to give the Green Consumer who seems to have everything, how about giving a year's membership of a suitable environmental organization? Check pages 326 – 31 to find out who does what. For young people, the RSPB and WWF both offer special memberships.

Some of these organizations have also come up with a novel twist: they offer you a stake in a threatened ecosystem to help save it from destruction. Friends of the Earth suggested one interesting solution in their 1987 Christmas catalogue, encouraging members to buy one-metre-square plots of threatened woodland overlooking the River Avon for £12 apiece! The money will help preserve the site, while the complicated ownership will foil future attempts to buy the plot for inappropriate uses.

More exotically — and more expensively — you could have a newly discovered tropical forest species named after you or a loved one for £3,000. Details of how to ensure a form of immortality — but possibly a rather truncated one, depending on how long your particular species survives — can be had from the Fauna and Flora Preservation Society (8 – 12 Camden High Street, London NW1 0JH).

Pets

Don't buy a dog or cat unless you are prepared to look after it. A thousand stray dogs are destroyed in Britain every day. Remember, too, that domestic cats are estimated to kill about 100 million birds and small mammals every year.

Among the more exotic pets, avoid tortoises: a two-year study by the RSPCA showed that 80 per cent of tortoises imported to Britain die while being shipped or during their first 12 months here. Be wary of tropical fish: ask whether they have been bred in this country (see Aquaria).

If you are looking for an alternative pet, try a stick insect. You will need a cage, some insects and the book *Keeping Stick Insects* by Dorothy Green, all available from **Small-Life Supplies**.

Toys

You can help shape a child's feelings for the natural world by buying suitable toys and games. Pick natural materials, like wood, rather than synthetics like plastic. Wherever possible, pick toys made from woods like oak or beech, rather than woods likely to have come from tropical forests (see pages 41 – 3). Avoid battery-powered toys. And choose toys that will last, rather than falling apart after a week or two. See also Games and Toys in the Catalogues section.

Trees

Barring hurricanes, few gifts last as long as a tree. Ask for native species at your local garden centre (see pages 97 – 8). The RSPB catalogue offers five rooted saplings of English Alder, Wild Cherry and Silver Birch suitable for establishing a bird-rich 'mini copse'. Disease-resistant elms are available through the Conservation Foundation. Another option is to subscribe to the Woodland Trust, which now owns more than 200 woodlands.

Videos

With over a third of homes now possessing a video recorder, it is worth looking through the video racks for wildlife or environmental films. There are titles to suit all tastes and most pockets. **Woolworths** offer the *National Geographic* Video Library. Other titles are available from organizations such as the National Trust, the RSPB and WWF.

Wines and champagnes

Organic wines and champagnes can be an excellent gift. Not only are some vintages superb, but your gift can provide a useful talking point to engage the interest of potential Green

Consumers. Check through the brands mentioned in *The Supermarket*. Another possibility is to get a copy of the National Centre for Organic Gardening's catalogue, which includes a range of organic wines. See under Catalogues.

Wrapping paper

You can now get some very elegant recycled wrapping paper. High Street outlets include Oxfam shops. Otherwise, check under Catalogues.

The Armchair Green Consumer: Buying through the Catalogues

One of the easiest ways to shop is with a catalogue, and the armchair Green Consumer is increasingly spoiled for choice. Campaigning organizations have found catalogues an effective way of raising income to support their programmes and projects.

Some, like those offered by Friends of the Earth and Greenpeace, are screened for environmental acceptability. Others, like those produced by the RSPB ('Every item you buy helps Britain's wild birds!' says its catalogue) and WWF, cover a much wider spread of products.

Often the gifts will have a theme relevant to the organization, but they might not all be acceptable to the Green Consumer. The RSPCA has a catalogue which raises money for the protection of animals against cruelty, but at the time of writing it does not yet feature the sort of cruelty-free products mentioned in *The Chemist*. Other catalogues also contain anomalies: the 1987 WWF catalogue, for example, offered a shaving kit for travellers built around disposable razors (for the issues, see page 253). This product had been dropped by 1988.

Note: The fact that a product is listed below does not necessarily imply that it is environmentally acceptable. Where we know of problems, we have mentioned them. But at least a fairly substantial proportion of the purchase price will go direct to the organization of your choice.

Acid Drops

The Acid Drops kit enables children to test rain to see how acid it is. The kit has been used in a nationwide survey organized by WATCH, the junior wing of the Royal Society for Nature Conservation. The WATCH survey indicated that clean rain was 'the exception rather than the rule'. Available from **Roopers Ltd**, PO Box 82, Tunbridge Wells, Kent, TN3 8BZ.

Aprons

Both the RSPB and WWF have aprons. Pick cotton aprons rather than plastic ones (see Clothing).

Badges

If you like to wear your principles on your sleeve, a range of colourful, topical badges are available from BUAV, Compassion in World Farming, Friends of the Earth, Greenpeace, the National Centre for Organic Gardening, the RSPB, the RSPCA, the World Society for the Protection of Animals, the Vegan Society, the Vegetarian Society, and WWF.

Basketwork products

Help Third World villagers make more money from their crafts. Cut out the middlemen by buying from ethical traders like Oxfam or Traidcraft.

Bath towels

Available from Traidcraft, who sell towels made by handloom weavers in Tamil Nadu, and WWF, who offer the Jungle Towel and Coral Reef Towel, for use either in the bath or on the beach. If a Penguin Beach Towel appeals, try the RSPB.

Binoculars

One of the best selections of binoculars, not surprisingly, is available from the RSPB. They offer the *Avocet* 8 x 42, *Compact 7 x 24*, *Goldcrest* 8 x 21, *Spottingscope*, and for beginners the *Observer* 8 x 40. Greenpeace sell **Tasco** 8 x 21 compact and 7 x 50 binoculars. WWF offer compact **Eonar** 8 x 21 roof prism binoculars.

Bird baths, feeders and tables

The RSPB is the supplier of choice here. They sell a wide range of bird tables, from terracotta *Tit Bells* to more luxuriously appointed roofed bird tables like the *Bird Haven*. For a low-tech alternative, try Traidcraft's *Coconut Bird Feeder*, made from a coconut shell, wood tray and coir string. But remember, never feed salted nuts to birds. Recent reports of bird deaths show that high-salt foods can be deadly for them.

Books

Several of the green catalogues feature suitable books, including those offered by Friends of the Earth, Greenpeace, the RSPB and WWF.

Calculators

The WWF calculator is solar powered, dispensing with batteries.

Calendars

A wide range of calendars, including a number of Advent calendars, are available from Friends of the Earth, Lynx, the National Trust, the RSPB and WWF.

Car accessories

Don't expect Friends of the Earth or Greenpeace to sell you trinkets for your car, but if you are looking for a gift for a car owner, check through the RSPB and WWF catalogues for accessories. WWF, for example, offers products like a stowaway snow shovel, back seat cover and a frost shield.

Cards   See Stationery.

Carrier bags

Take a bag with you when you go shopping, and you will save on the endless plastic bags offered by supermarkets and other stores. If you choose from bags offered by BUAV, the National Trust, RSPB or WWF, you can carry your shopping and spread the word at the same time.

Car stickers

Another way to spread the word. Rear window stickers can help recruit those behind you in the traffic jam! Available from BUAV, CLEAR, Friends of the Earth, Greenpeace, the RSPB and WWF.

Clothing

A number of organizations offer designer T-shirts and sweatshirts, including Friends of the Earth, Greenpeace, Lynx and WWF. Sample messages: 'Buy Products That Don't Cost the Earth' (SustainAbility); 'Help The Earth Fight Back' (Friends of the Earth); 'Born To Be Wild' (Greenpeace); and 'It Takes Up To 40 Dumb Animals To Make A Fur Coat. But Only One To Wear It' (Lynx).

Think green if you are buying a sweatshirt or T-shirt, child's pull-on hat (Greenpeace), jogging suit (Greenpeace, RSPB), pullover (National Trust, RSPB), smock (RSPB), nightclothes (use a T-shirt), ties (National Trust, RSPB), scarves (Greenpeace, Traidcraft), a waxed cotton country jacket (RSPB), nightshirt and slippers (WWF) or boxer shorts (WWF).

Confectionery

Try handmade chocolates from the National Trust and WWF.

Cosmetics

If you haven't got a local **Body Shop**, Friends of the Earth and Greenpeace offer a range of Body Shop cosmetics. The RSPB offers the **English Country Collection** of toiletries, produced without cruelty to animals. The National Trust also sells a range of cruelty-free cosmetics. Oxfam's catalogue features **Faith in Nature** products. One of the most exciting recent catalogues, which shows that cruelty-free products are anything but boring, is that produced by **Cosmetics To Go** (see page 264).

Diaries

A wide range of diaries are available from BUAV, Friends of the Earth, Greenpeace, the RSPB and WWF. Perhaps the most interesting is the Friends of the Earth *Green Diary*, which includes information on environmental issues.

Drawing pads, exercise books, scrapbooks

Recycled paper products are available from Greenpeace and Traidcraft.

Food

From Christmas cakes (National Trust, RSPB, WWF) to 'After Eight' Peace Cards, cool carrier and terracotta storage sets (all offered by WWF) you can order a considerable range of food related products through the green catalogues. Traidcraft's catalogue offers tea and coffee.

Games

You can buy well-known games like chess (Traidcraft), jigsaws (Greenpeace, RSPB and WWF) or a games compendium (RSPB) from green suppliers. Alternatively, you can buy a small number of green games. Examples include *Animal Soundtracks*, in which 4–8 year olds match sounds they hear on a tape cassette to photographs on a lotto board (RSPB), the *Bird Table Game*, which includes over 140 question cards to test your knowledge on 50 garden birds (RSPB) and the *Noah's Ark* board game (WWF). Friends of the Earth offer a *Rainforest* card game.

Gardening for birds

If you have a garden, consider planting berry-bearing or nectar-producing shrubs. The RSPB offers a collection of four shrubs: *Pyracantha*, *Cytisus Kewensis*, *Lavandula Munstead Variety* and *Cotoneaster dammeri*.

Gift vouchers

Offered by Greenpeace, the National Centre for Organic Gardening and the RSPB, and should be offered by more green retailers. It may be a lazy way to give, but it can persuade the intended recipient to look through a green catalogue — and pick up some useful ideas at the same time.

Hammocks

Traidcraft offer a hammock made from braided jute made by Bangladeshi women.

Jewellery

The best alternative catalogue for jewellery is Traidcraft's. The design is very much Third World. Oxfam also offers Third World jewellery, including earrings. Alternatively, try a handmade rainbow bracelet — made in Mexico with abalone and turquoise inlay — from Greenpeace.

Moth herbs

There is no need to use synthetic chemical moth balls. Switch to moth herbs like those offered by the National Centre for Organic Gardening, Country Herbs and the RSPB.

Mugs

For messages to sip at, try BUAV ('Rats Have Rights'), Friends of the Earth ('Pigs Can Fly, the Earth is Flat, Nuclear Power is Safe') and Greenpeace ('Pure Rivers, Clean Seas'). Other, more muted mugs, come from the RSPB, the Vegetarian Society and WWF.

Paper-making kit

Make your own recycled paper with a kit from Friends of the Earth.

Penknives

Swiss penknives are available from Greenpeace (in green) and the RSPB, which offers the standard red Swiss Army 'Walker' knife.

Pens

Use a fountain pen rather than endless ballpoints, the ultimate in throwaway 'convenience'. You can buy both, however, from BUAV (Sheaffer Rollball pen), Greenpeace (Sheaffer ballpoint), the RSPB (Parker pen) and WWF (Sheaffer Rollball pen or WWF Parker ballpoint).

Posters and Prints

Organizations like BUAV, Friends of the Earth, Greenpeace, Lynx, the Nature Conservancy Council, the RSPB and WWF offer a range of striking posters and prints on environmental themes. Generally, these are very good value for money.

Records, cassettes and compact discs

Keep an eye out for benefit concert and compilation albums from Band Aid, Greenpeace and other campaigning organizations. WWF offer 'Whales Alive', music and whale songs on record, cassette and CD.

Seeds

Friends of the Earth offer a three pack gift of seeds, including sunflowers, pumpkins and mustard. See *The Garden Centre*.

Stationery

If you can't find recycled paper products in your high street, ask local retailers to stock them. On the catalogue front, the greener the organization, the more likely it is to supply recycled paper products. Friends of the Earth and Greenpeace have been particularly strong in this department.

One product of the times offered by Friends of the Earth is *Eco-Fax* paper for your Filofax. Each pack contains 100 sheets of recycled paper in four different colours. WWF offers a 'personal organizer' with the panda motif.

Saving paper by recycling envelopes can look a bit grubby. Smarten up with re-use labels from BUAV, Friends of the Earth or Greenpeace. There is also a growing array of recycled paper products, including loo paper made from high-grade waste paper (Greenpeace, Traidcraft). Friends of the Earth offer a wide range of recycled paper products and provide a listing of other suppliers.

Buy your greetings cards from a green supplier such as Conservation Books, Friends of the Earth, Greenpeace, Lynx, Oxfam, the RSPB or WWF. Ask for cards printed on recycled paper. Postcards are available from almost all green groups and suppliers. A fair number are printed on recycled paper.

Tea towels

Available from Friends of the Earth, the National Centre for Organic Gardening, the National Trust, RSPB, Traidcraft and WWF.

Toys

For inspiration, check through the Greenpeace, RSPB, Traidcraft and WWF catalogues. The range is small, but growing. Possibilities include a seal glove puppet (*not* made from seal fur!) from

Greenpeace or a *Rain or Shine Weather Kit* from Friends of the Earth and WWF.

Umbrellas

Make a point as you shelter under a 1.35 m (53 inch) Greenpeace ('Stop Acid Rain') brolly.

Walking, hiking and back-packing equipment

See the RSPB catalogue.

Watches

The Unisex WWF Fashion Watch has a quartz movement and sports the panda logo.

Wines

See *The Supermarket* for information on organic wines and champagnes. The National Centre for Organic Gardening's catalogue offers a range of organic wines and wholefoods. The Centre's range runs from the Guy Bossard Blanc de Blancs to a Reichsteiner medium-dry grown in England. One unusual gift idea for well-heeled wine-drinkers: order a 12-bottle Organic Taster's Case of eleven organic wines. WWF also offers Ronald Searle's amusing book *Something in the Cellar*.

The Endangered Gift

Avoid products made from animal or plant species protected by CITES, the Convention on International Trade in Endangered Species.

Top of the CITES list are animals imminently threatened with extinction, including: all apes, lemurs, the giant panda, many South American monkeys, the great whales, cheetahs, leopards, tigers, all elephants, all rhinoceroses, many birds of prey, cranes, exotic pheasants and parrots, all sea turtles, some crocodiles and lizards, giant salamanders, and some mussels, orchids and cacti.

You should also avoid products which come from all other primates, cats, otters, whales, dolphins and porpoises, birds of prey, tortoises and crocodiles, as well as the African elephant, fur seals, the black stork, birds of paradise, the coelacanth, some snails, birdwing butterflies, black corals and orchids.

Some highly unlikely products are implicated in species extinction. For example, anyone who has bought aphrodisiacs, daggers or other products made from rhino horn has helped speed the disappearance of an extraordinary animal. During the last 20 years, more than 85 per cent of the world's rhinoceroses have been killed. The economic incentives are almost over-whelming: in South-East Asia, the Chinese pay over £10,000 per kg for rhino horn, believing that it brings sexual rejuvenation.

If you are travelling abroad and want to know what animal or plant products you can bring back, check with the **Department of the Environment's International Trade in Endangered Species Branch** or the **Department of Agriculture for Northern Ireland's Wildlife Licensing Section**.

Dreaming of a Green Christmas

If you are dreaming of a Green — but fairly conventional — Christmas this year, the first step is to select your *Advent calendars and Christmas cards* from among the growing range offered by groups like Friends of the Earth, Greenpeace, the RSPB and the WWF. We are not aware of any similar products suitable for Buddhist, Hindu, Jewish or Muslim festivals — so if you come across any, let us know. Check that your cards are printed on recycled paper. You can also buy *wrapping paper* based on recycled fibre from Greenpeace, Oxfam, Traidcraft and WWF. Alternatively, non-recycled wrapping paper is offered by groups like the RSPB (a nice range of bird-based designs) and WWF; this, at least, contributes to their campaigning coffers.

Christmas trees are a tricky issue. If you want a tree, it is probably better to have a real one than a plastic one — otherwise children may grow up thinking that when the forests are gone we can replace them with plastic ones. But, if you possibly can, buy a tree with roots, which you can use year after year. When it grows too big for indoor use, it can be replanted.

WWF also offers cakes, decorations, sandalwood-scented candles and crackers. Though crackers, in fact, are an extreme case of over-packaging! Available from the RSPB are Robin, Owl and Animates crackers. Animates crackers, also offered by Greenpeace, contain porcelain miniatures of endangered species. WWF offers 'Snow Baby' crackers containing porcelain miniatures of baby Arctic animals.

Finally, if you must add that final Yuletide flourish of artificial snow, Friends of the Earth recommend *Mr Snow* by **Haventrail**. This pine-scented product may come in an aerosol, but it is ozone friendly.

USEFUL ADDRESSES

Angler's Snapshot, Ross Keightley, 162 Old Lodge Lane, Purley, Surrey

Department of Agriculture for Northern Ireland's Wildlife Licensing Section, Dundonald House, Upper Newtonards Road, Belfast BT4 3SB. Tel: 0232 650111, ext 642

Department of the Environment's International Trade in Endangered Species Branch, Tollgate House, Houghton Street, Bristol BS2 9DJ. Tel: 0272 218202

R. J. Lewis, Barmby Avenue, Fulford, York YO1 4HX

Roopers Ltd, PO Box 82, Tunbridge Wells, Kent, TN3 8BZ

Saturn Shot Supplies, Unit 1, Bunting Road, Moreton Hall Industrial Estate, Bury St Edmunds, Suffolk. Tel: 0284 706 512

Small-Life Supplies, 9 Upton Avenue, Cheadle Hulme, Cheshire SK8 7HX. Tel: 061 485 2289

Thamesly Fishing Tackle, 278 Kingsland Road, Hackney, London E8. Tel: 01-249 1954

Traidcraft, Kingsway, Gateshead, Tyne and Wear NE11 0NE. Tel: 091 491 0591

Whimet, PO Box 102, Torrington Avenue, Coventry CV4 9AD. Tel: 0203 465 931

LOOK FOR THE GREEN LABEL

Writing *The Green Consumer Guide* has been both exciting and — at times — frustrating. The idea of shopping for a better environment has taken root in an extraordinarily short space of time. This has meant that we are now much closer to our targets than we were even a year ago. But the sheer pace of change has made the task of keeping abreast of the very latest developments infinitely more challenging.

Yet keep abreast we must. The emergence of the Green Consumer is now a Europe-wide phenomenon, which could have a profound impact on many areas of business, investment and employment. Although Britain has so far trailed other European countries, including The Netherlands, Switzerland and West Germany, there are encouraging signs that we may be catching up — particularly in terms of the advice available to the consumer.

More than anything else, the Green Consumer needs information on the most important issues and on the environmental performance of products. The first edition of *The Green Consumer Guide* is an important step in this direction, but the real journey has only just begun.

In West Germany, for example, they already have a Green equivalent of *Which?*. Moreover, the West German government has a nationwide scheme designed to identify and promote environment-friendly products. Britain should follow suit. Our own Better Environment Awards for Industry (BEAFI) scheme, run by the Royal Society of Arts and supported by key national organizations, helped catalyse a prestigious European awards scheme. But the BEAFI scheme, which already has a Green Products category, would need to expand considerably to rival the German scheme.

Labelling is another important gap in Britain's approach to date. The 'ozone-friendly' labels for aerosols and Friends of the Earth's *Good Wood Guide* labels, for rainforest-friendly hardwoods, show the way forward. But, as the confusion currently prevailing in the organic food sector shows, the ordinary consumer doesn't want to be overwhelmed by dozens of different labelling schemes. We need to move towards a single, high-profile Green Consumer label.

Looking back, the discovery of the Antarctic ozone hole has been the biggest single spur to the Green Consumer movement in Britain. It brought home to ordinary consumers the idea that their fingers are 'on the button', in the sense that certain products we use every day threaten, quite literally, to cost the Earth.

We began work well over a year before the ozone hole leaped into the headlines. Even so, the initial response to the news that *The Green Consumer Guide* was in preparation was so positive that the idea of an even more ambitious initiative began to surface. After discussions with leading environmental lobbying organizations like Friends of the Earth and the World Wide Fund for Nature, we decided to work towards Britain's first Green Consumer Week — in September 1988.

The Green Consumer coalition soon expanded to include a number of other campaigning organizations, from the Soil Association to the RSPCA. Equally important, we found we were able to pull in a range of partners from the business world. The Body Shop and Hatchards groups, for example, turned over their shop-fronts throughout the country for the Week, ensuring that the Green Consumer had a real presence in the High Street. Other partners included Brand New, part of the Michael Peters Group, the Merlin Ecology Fund, Safeway Food Stores, Tesco and the Design Council.

By informing consumers of the wider impacts of the choices they make every day at the cash-till, we hope to achieve a number of things. For example, we aim:

- to show you that, however serious the particular problem, there is something positive you can do immediately — whatever the Government of the day may (or may not) be doing

- to push farmers, manufacturers and retailers towards producing and buying green products on a much larger scale, helping to increase their availability and to cut their price

- to encourage companies (including supermarkets) to operate as Green Consumers, helping to increase the pressure on suppliers to develop and offer environment-friendly products

- to persuade designers that they should consider the environmental performance of the products they work on, from 'cradle to grave', from initial concept right through to final disposal or recycling

- to convince advertising, marketing and PR people that Green Consumers represent a significant new market sector which their clients should increasingly cater for. If advertisers can be converted to the cause, the basic message could reach parts of our consumer society it might otherwise never touch.

It is important to recognize that the power of the Green Consumer depends on the effectiveness and impact of many other people, including campaigners, lobbyists, journalists, politicians, lawyers, researchers, scientists and educators. The skills of all these people will be needed to ensure that the solutions to today's problems do not become tomorrow's problems.

Consider just one final example. The Green Consumer will generally avoid plastics where they are used for single-trip containers or other short-lived products. If, however, we immediately banned the use of any plastic in packaging, we would be faced with a doubling of the volume of domestic refuse — and a four-fold increase in its weight.

The task of designing, producing and selling genuinely environment-friendly products (and there will be environment-friendly plastics) that are also commercially viable and socially acceptable is one of the most exciting challenges we face. It will keep growing numbers of us busy well into the twenty-first century.

Even so, we should not under-estimate the power that each of us has today to start changing the world by operating as Green Consumers. Money talks — and there is growing evidence that major companies are waking up to the commercial potential of Europe's new green markets.

In short, your vote at the cash-desk has more impact than ever before. Use it.

The Consumer's Guide to Environmental Organizations

British Trust for Conservation Volunteers (BTCV)

36 St Mary's Street, Wallingford, Oxon OX10 0EU. Tel: 0491 39766

Main Aim: To involve people in practical conservation activity.

Issues: Urban clean up. Countryside conservation.

Number of Members: 9,000

Membership Fee: £10

What you Get: *The Conserver Magazine*. Summer and winter programme of projects. Annual report. Quarterly newsletter. Holidays offered. Local group activities every weekend.

Sales: Sell publications through a catalogue. Also offer 'Natural Break' holidays.

Green Consumerism: No specific ventures yet.

Council for the Protection of Rural England (CPRE)

4 Hobart Place, London SW1W 0HY. Tel: 01-235 9481

Main Aim: Campaigns for the countryside through well-informed research and briefing of national and local government and of the media.

Issues: Agriculture and land use. Reafforestation and woodlands. Planning. Transport — road networks and heavy lorries. Mineral working.

Number of Members: 32,000

Membership Fee: £8

What you Get: *Countryside Campaigner* (3 times a year). Yearbook. Affiliation to local branch. Local events.

Sales: No catalogues.

Green Consumerism: No specific ventures yet.

Friends of the Earth (FoE)

26-28 Underwood Street, London N1 7JU. Tel: 01-490 1555

Main Aim: Protection of the environment and promotion of sustainable alternatives.

Issues: Air, sea, river and land pollution. Ozone depletion, acid rain, carbon dioxide build-up. Tropical deforestation and soil erosion. Biotechnology. Energy related issues — nuclear, alternative and renewable energy. Pesticides and agriculture. Recycling.

Number of Members: 30,000 (220 local groups with a further membership of 8,000)

Membership Fee: £12 (£10 direct debit)

What you Get: Quarterly newsletter — *Friends of the Earth Supporters' News*. Details of local groups. Local group newsletter with details of local events and environmental issues. Earth Action youth group.

Sales: Catalogue offers a growing range of products.

Green Consumerism: Very successful in this area. Have advised boycotting: whale products, aerosols containing CFCs, tropical hardwoods from badly managed forests, non-returnable bottles, leaded petrol, food additives, and non-organically grown produce.

Recommend: recycled products, Body Shop products, bicycles and public transport, organic and low-additive foods, unleaded petrol, alternatives to tropical hardwoods, home insulation, draught-proofing and double-glazing and catalytic converters for cars. They can see potential for the Green Consumer to have a growing impact in a number of other areas, including: design; health; leisure activities; building materials; DIY and energy systems.

Greenpeace UK

30-31 Islington Green, London N1 8XE. Tel: 01-354 5100

Main Aim: Campaigns against abuse of the natural world through lobbying and non-violent direct action protests, which are backed by scientific research.

Issues: Toxic waste disposal in rivers, seas and atmosphere. Radioactivity. Endangered species.

Number of Members: 100,000 (UK) (250 local groups)

Membership Fee: £10

What you Get: Quarterly newspaper — *Greenpeace News*. Special mailing on issues. Events. Merchandizing catalogue.

Sales: Have a catalogue. Orders are handled by Traidcraft plc.

Green Consumerism: Have already run a few campaigns targeted at the

Green Consumer, including recommendations to boycott: whale products, kangaroo-hide running shoes and fish products from Iceland (to stop Icelandic whaling — see pages 190 – 1). They will be running a campaign for clean cars, recommending catalytic converters.

Marine Conservation Society

4 Gloucester Road, Ross-on-Wye, Herefordshire HR9 5BU. Tel: 0989 66017

Main Aim: Seeks to protect the marine environment and to promote its practical management by: lobbying and campaigning on marine issues; research on marine life and wardening of certain coastal sites.

Issues: Marine resource depletion. Fisheries conservation. Toxic waste disposal. Disposal of nuclear waste.

Number of Members: 2,000

Membership Fee: £8

What you Get: Quarterly magazine — *Marine Conservation*. Local groups which participate in research projects. Sales brochure.

Sales: Small merchandizing catalogue, mainly publications.

Green Consumerism: Have recommended that consumers avoid buying: marine curios, shells (including sea-urchin lights and air plants mounted on shells), oil from basking sharks (used in some products containing animal fats) and TBT paints on yachts or fish farm cages. They also research the quality of our beaches (see *The Travel Agent*, page 275).

National Society for Clean Air (NSCA)

136 North Street, Brighton BN1 1RG. Tel: 0273 26313

Main Aim: To seek the improvement of the environment by promoting clean air, noise reduction and other control measures, having regard to the implications for all aspects of the environment.

Issues: Ozone depletion, acid rain and the greenhouse effect. Transportation emissions and noise. Radiation.

Number of Members: 650 (includes industry and local authorities)

Membership Fee: £11

What you Get: Quarterly newsletter. NSCA Members Handbook. Access to library. Conferences and workshops.

Sales: Sell mostly publications.

Green Consumerism: Suggest that consumers avoid: asbestos and polluting fuels. Recommend: unleaded petrol, smokeless fuel and noise insulation. They are interested in developing the potential of the Green Consumer.

National Trust

36 Queen Anne's Gate, London SW1H 9AS. Tel: 01-222 9251

Main Aim: Protects places of historic interest or natural beauty, holding countryside and buildings in England, Wales and Northern Ireland for the benefit of the nation.

Issues: Conservation of buildings, landscapes and wildlife.

Number of Members: 1,543,000

Membership Fee: £16

What you Get: Magazine (3 times a year). Admission to all their properties. National Trust Handbook. Events and private viewings.

Sales: Shops at many of their sites.

Green Consumerism: They have not done much in this area, although they have stopped selling aerosols which contain CFCs.

Oxfam

272 Banbury Road, Oxford OX2 7DZ. Tel: 0865 56777

Main Aim: To relieve poverty, distress and suffering in every part of the world without regard to political and religious beliefs.

Issues: Deforestation and soil erosion. Pesticides and pollution. Relief aid.

Number of Members: No members

Membership Fee: Not applicable

What you Get: Not applicable

Sales: Oxfam have a large catalogue of products and publications. They also have Oxfam shops all over the country, all of which raise funds for the central organization.

Green Consumerism: Are concerned about unsafe pesticides and some cash crops, including beet sugar, because of the effects on Third World economies. They are interested in consumer power, although they have not yet made much progress in this area.

Royal Society for Nature Conservation (RSNC)

The Green, Nettleham, Lincoln LN2 2NR. Tel: 0522 752326

Main Aim: To act as a centre for developing national policies and services. It helps the nature conservation and wildlife trusts, and the urban wildlife groups, to be effective in promoting nature conservation and acquiring and managing nature reserves throughout the UK.

Issues: Acid rain. Deforestation. Water quality. Endangered wild flowers. Nuclear power.

Number of Members: Trusts only

Membership Fee: Not applicable

What you Get: Not applicable

Sales: Catalogue selling a range of products.

Green Consumerism: Interested in promoting organic foods and unleaded petrol, although as yet no specific ventures.

Royal Society for the Prevention of Cruelty to Animals (RSPCA)

The Causeway, Horsham, West Sussex RH12 1HG. Tel: 0403 64181

Main Aim: The prevention of cruelty and the promotion of kindness to animals.

Issues: Animal welfare

Number of Members: 23,000

Membership Fee: £8

What you Get: Postal vote for council. Quarterly magazine — *RSPCA Today*. Campaign literature.

Sales: Merchandizing catalogue. Have also aligned themselves with a petfood manufacturer, to raise funds. (Brand name *Duo*, manufactured by Luda.)

Green Consumerism: Suggest that consumers avoid: fur coats, some meat and all products involving cruelty to animals. They recommend cruelty-free products. They recognize that there is enormous potential in this area and have produced a brochure to explain the connections between what they do and a number of environmental issues.

Royal Society for the Protection of Birds (RSPB)

The Lodge, Sandy, Bedfordshire SG19 2DL. Tel: 0767 80551

Main Aim: The conservation and protection of wild birds and their habitats through campaigns, education and research.

Issues: Species extinction. Disappearing Britain. Modern intensive agricultural methods. Marine pollution. Land reclamation from wetlands, rivers and seas.

Number of Members: 423,000

Membership Fee: £12

What you Get: Quarterly magazine — *Birds*. Free admission to reserves. Local members' group.

Sales: Catalogue which includes binoculars and telescopes.

Green Consumerism: Alerted people to the fact that feeding salted nuts to birds can be deadly and campaigned against lead fishing weights when it was found that they were killing swans.

Soil Association

86 Colston Street, Bristol BS1 5BB. Tel: 0272 290661

Main Aim: To promote organic farming and gardening and to protect the environment.

Issues: Pesticide and fertilizer pollution. Countryside problems. Rural deprivation.

Number of Members: 4,500

Membership Fee: £10

What you Get: *Quarterly Review*; quarterly newsletter, *Soil Association News*; and magazine, *The Living Earth* (also quarterly). Advice on organic practices. Events.

Sales: Publications catalogue.

Green Consumerism: Actively promote organic practices and organic produce. They have the most widely recognized symbol to show that organic standards are being adhered to. Campaigned for real milk and recognize that there is considerable potential for Green Consumer activities.

Tidy Britain Group (*formerly* Keep Britain Tidy Group)

Bostel House, 37 West Street, Brighton BN1 2RE. Tel: 0273 23585

Main Aim: To protect and enhance the amenities of town and country in the United Kingdom, particularly by promoting prevention and control of litter and by encouraging environmental improvement schemes.

Issues: Litter and waste disposal.

Number of Members: Companies and organizations only

Membership Fee: Not applicable

What you Get: Not applicable

Sales: Plan to start merchandizing.

Green Consumerism: Already encourage sponsorship of litter bins and recycling. They will be doing research into packaging.

Town and Country Planning Association (TCPA)

17 Carlton House Terrace, London SW1Y 5AS. Tel: 01-930 8903

Main Aim: To campaign for a better environment by means of effective planning and community participation, with an emphasis on the needs of the disadvantaged.

Issues: Planning. Urban decline and regeneration. Energy issues. Transport issues. Revitalization of the countryside.

Number of Members: 1,350

Membership Fee: £24

What you Get: Monthly journal — *Town & Country Planning*. Discount on conferences. Discount on *Planning Bulletin*.

Sales: Publications only.

Green Consumerism: No specific ventures yet.

Transport 2000

Walkden House, 10 Melton Street, London NW1 2EJ. Tel: 01-388 8386

Main Aim: To lobby central and local government for more rational transport policies — in the interests of accident prevention, social justice, the protection of the environment and the conservation of land and energy.

Issues: Public versus private transport. Environmental impact of transport systems. Equity issues. Disappearing Britain. Energy conservation. Conservation of land.

Number of Members: Corporate membership

Membership Fee: Not applicable

What you Get: Not applicable

Sales: Mostly reports.

Green Consumerism: Lobby for public transport and therefore are against private road transport. Interested in the potential of the Green Consumer.

World Wide Fund for Nature (WWF; *formerly* World Wildlife Fund)

Panda House, Weyside Park, Godalming, Surrey GU7 1XR. Tel: 0483 426444

Main Aim: To achieve the conservation of natural resources in the UK and other parts of the world by education, public policy, site protection, species conservation and training.

Issues: Species extinction. Loss of habitat. Deforestation. Energy issues and acid rain. Air, sea and land pollution. Land use and rural economy in the UK.

Number of Members: 125,000

Membership Fee: £11

What you Get: Quarterly newsletter — *WWF News*. Annual catalogue. Events.

Sales: Merchandizing activities are a multi-million pound business which includes catalogues and on-pack promotions.

Green Consumerism: Recognize the enormous potential of the Green Consumer. Advise people to avoid holidays that endanger wildlife and encourage holiday-makers to let them know if they witness any particular problems whilst abroad eg abuse of chimpanzees in Southern Spain for tourist entertainment.

Index